7e 27

SIR FRANCIS BURDETT AND
HIS TIMES (1770—1844)

MACMILLAN AND CO., Limited
LONDON · BOMBAY · CALCUTTA · MADRAS
MELBOURNE

THE MACMILLAN COMPANY
NEW YORK · BOSTON · CHICAGO
DALLAS · ATLANTA · SAN FRANCISCO

THE MACMILLAN COMPANY
OF CANADA, LIMITED
TORONTO

SIR FRANCIS BURDETT.
Pencil-drawing by Sir T. Lawrence in the possession of the Lord North.
A photograph by J. R. Weaver.

SIR FRANCIS BURDETT AND HIS TIMES (1770–1844)

Including hitherto unpublished letters of Mrs. fitzherbert, George Prince of Wales, the Duke of York, the Duke of Clarence (William IV), Georgiana Duchess of Devonshire, the Duke of Wellington, Lord Chancellor Erskine, Lord Chancellor Brougham, Lord Grey (of the Reform Bill), Lord Anglesey, B. Disraeli (Lord Beaconsfield), Jeremy Bentham, Thomas Coutts, Harriot Duchess of St. Albans, Lord Holland, Lady Holland, J. C. Hobhouse (Lord Broughton), Lord Cochrane (10th Earl of Dundonald), the 4th Duke of Northumberland, Lord Langdale, Sir C. Manners Sutton (Lord Canterbury), Adelaide d'Orleans, Francis Place, Samuel Rogers, J. W. Croker, R. B. Haydon and others

BY

M. W. PATTERSON

Vice-President and Senior Tutor of Trinity College, Oxford

VOLUME I

MACMILLAN AND CO., LIMITED
ST. MARTIN'S STREET, LONDON
1931

COPYRIGHT

TO
MY WIFE
A GREAT-GRAND-DAUGHTER
OF SIR FRANCIS BURDETT

"I Think Sir Francis Burdett was the Greatest Gentleman I Ever Knew."—(*Disraeli*).

FOREWORD

SOME account must be given of the way in which the material for this biography was united. The "Coutts" papers were for the most part divided between the "Bank" (Coutts & Co.) and the late Baroness Burdett-Coutts. The "Burdett" papers were divided between the "Bank," the Baroness Burdett-Coutts, and Lord Latymer. Lady Burdett-Coutts at her death left all her papers to her husband, and he in his turn left them to his nephew, Mr. Seabury Ashmead-Bartlett (who, under his uncle's will, took the name of Burdett-Coutts). The great mass of the Burdett papers were those that formerly belonged to the Baroness Burdett-Coutts. When Mr. E. H. Coleridge wrote "The Life of Thomas Coutts" in 1919, he had not access to the papers formerly in the possession of the Baroness, and I have been able to supplement, and in some cases to correct his statements.

The Baroness did not wish the "Life" of her father to be written in her lifetime, but with the passing of her generation there is no further need for concealment. Sir Francis Burdett's "Life" ought to have been written long ago, and would have been written but for the scandal of his association with Lady Oxford.

Professor Halévy complains ("History of the English People," Vol. I, p. 519) that English biographies "as a rule have been commissioned by the family of their subject, and hence are full of deliberate omissions." There will be no such deliberate omissions in this biography.

I have to thank, in the first place, His Majesty the King for giving me leave to print letters written by or about members of the Royal Family.

I have to thank Lord Latymer, Messrs. Coutts & Co., and Mr. Seabury Burdett-Coutts for giving me access to the papers respectively under their control. There are many others whom I do not mention by name, but my thanks to them are no less sincere.

Among those whom I have to thank for giving me leave either to print letters of their ancestors or to reproduce pictures or photographs or documents are the present Sir Francis Burdett, the Lord North, the Duke of Wellington, the Duke of Northumberland, the Duke of Devonshire, the Earl Grey, the Earl of Ilchester, Lord Anglesey, Lord Abinger, and Sir C. Hobhouse.

I would specially like to mention with gratitude the advice and encouragement I received from the late Lord Oxford and Asquith. He took great interest in the progress of this biography. " I think a life of Sir F. Burdett will fill a gap in our chain of biographies. . . . I shall look forward with great interest to your book, and *inter alia* to the story of Lady Oxford," he wrote me in January 1925. (He had not yet become Earl of Oxford himself.) Had he lived, he would, I know, have written a foreword to this biography. But it was not to be. *Dis aliter visum.* I pay a grateful tribute to his memory.

Finally, I am under great obligations to my old friend Dr. Macan, sometime Master of University College, Oxford, for reading through the proofs and making suggestions, and to Mr. Stephen Gwynn for all the help he has given to make the book presentable for publication.

CONTENTS

xi

LIST OF ILLUSTRATIONS

xiii

SIR FRANCIS BURDETT AND HIS TIMES

CHAPTER I

THE BURDETT FAMILY

SIR FRANCIS BURDETT was the leading person in the movements that culminated in the events of which we are now
commemorating, or about to commemorate, the centenary
—Roman Catholic Emancipation and the Reform Bill.

He had pressed Roman Catholic Emancipation long
before it was taken up by the Duke of Wellington and Sir
Robert Peel. And through good report, through evil
report, he had been the protagonist of Reform. If Lord
Grey in point of time (1793) was before him, it must be
remembered that during the years 1810 to 1830 Lord Grey
and all the Whig Party were very lukewarm and indifferent
to Reform, while Sir Francis was consistently its advocate.

In a very real sense it is true to say that Burdett, not
merely in these questions, but in other matters as well, was
the educator of the English people. He was a whole
generation ahead of his contemporaries. Yet, so sound
and well-informed was his judgment, that though he passed
in his own day for an extremist, there is scarcely a single
political opinion which he advocated that is not to-day
accepted in the law of the land and in the belief of all British
parties.

He lived in a period when violent impulses and reactions
were given to all political life by the influence of the French
Revolution. He felt the impulses, like his contemporaries

and fellow-workers, but there were always restraining forces at work to counteract them; and the combination made him that valuable and very English product, a Reformer who knew how to accept a compromise. He was a very rich man, the holder of an old title, a passionate fox-hunter and sportsman, a great lover of society, the acquaintance, and often the intimate, of the most distinguished figures in the London of his day. Yet during the period of the Napoleonic wars and the struggle for Reform, he was a storm-centre of disturbance, the idol of mobs and the detestation of successive Governments. He was twice imprisoned on charges of sedition; but he did not desist from agitation till he considered that his main object was achieved. Then, however, he settled down quietly into a good Tory supporter of the Duke of Wellington.

No accusation of interested motives can be brought against either his advocacy of Radical opinion or his change to Conservatism. In almost fifty years of service in the House of Commons, where he was one of the most admired debaters, he neither sought nor took office; and three times he refused a peerage. He preferred to remain what he was, a freely chosen independent representative of the people, yet never a demagogue nor even a democrat. As a landed gentleman, with a long tradition behind him, he accepted leadership as part of his responsibility.

The Burdett pedigree, which lies in the Muniment Room at Foremarke, is a wonderful work, written on rolls of parchment, fortified by documents and coats-of-arms. It was originally drawn up by the College of Heralds in 1632, subsequent additions being made in 1797 and later.

The ancient home of the Burdetts was in Normandy, and the name in its earliest form is spelt either Burdet, Bordet, or Bourdet. It was probably not a " place " name, for no " de " is prefixed to it in Domesday Book; but the origin is quite uncertain.

In the year 1862 the Société d'Archéologie (of France) erected a plate in the church of Dives (not far from Deauville in Normandy) to commemorate the " companions of William the Conqueror," some four hundred and fifty in number, who sailed with him from that port on his English expedition. Amongst the names on the plate are those of Hugue Bourdet, Robert Bourdet, and Erneis de Buron. Thus, curiously enough, there are associated together in 1066 the names of Burdett and Byron—two families which have been connected in their later history.

In return for his services to the Conqueror, Hugo Burdet was given lands in Leicestershire, not as tenant-in-chief, but holding from the Countess Judith, niece of the Conqueror. In 1087 Burdet held land in Reresbi, Alebi, and Sixtenebi; but the greater part of his property was at Lowesby (Glowesbi), and it was here that the family established itself. Hugo Burdet became Lord of Lowesby. Later the Burdets acquired more and more property in all that part of the Midlands east of Tamworth where Warwickshire, Derbyshire and Leicestershire adjoin.

Some salient points in the curve of the family fortunes must be indicated.

In 1159 William Burdet, great-grandson to Hugo, the Conqueror's compeer, founded Ancote Priory in Warwickshire, to expiate his rash killing of his wife, whom a false steward had accused of infidelity during Burdet's absence in the Holy Land.

About 1312, five generations later, Sir Robert Burdet acquired through his marriage with Elizabeth, daughter and heiress of Sir Gerard de Camvill, the Manors of Seckingdon and of Arrow, both in Warwickshire.

Early in the fifteenth century Sir Nicholas Burdet, marrying Joanna, heiress of Henry Bruin, brought in the manor of Bramcote. Sir Nicholas was a soldier of high repute in the French wars under Henry V, and was made Chief Butler of Normandy and Governor of Evreux. He fell in the Battle of Pontoise in 1440. Sir Thomas Burdet, son to Sir Nicholas, was also a man of war, but becoming suspect to Edward IV through his attachment to the Duke of Clarence, was beheaded on an accusation of high treason. A lawsuit for the estates followed, and Arrow passed away from the Burdets to the Conways, one of whom had married the daughter of Sir Thomas's elder son.

In 1619 Thomas Burdet was created a Baronet by James I, with the title Sir Thomas Burdett of Bramcote. He married Jane Francys, who brought into the family Fore-marke, in Derbyshire, which since then has been the principal seat of the Burdett family. His son, Sir Francis, the second baronet, built and re-endowed the church of Foremarke, in which he and his wife are buried.

In 1716 died Sir Robert, the third baronet, who had sat in Parliament as member for Warwickshire and later for Lichfield. He survived his eldest son, and was succeeded in 1716 by his grandson, then an infant, also named Robert.

This Sir Robert, the fourth baronet, held the title for eighty years, and since he also survived both his sons, he was succeeded by his grandson, Francis Burdett, the subject of this memoir.

There is a tradition, to which Disraeli has given wide currency, that Sir Francis Burdett grew up in a household with Jacobite leanings. His grandfather, whom he knew well, had full experience of Charles Edward's rising in 1745, and the third baronet was a contemporary of James II and saw all the earlier period of Jacobitism.

The late H. V. Pycroft wrote to Sir Robert Burdett (the sixth baronet) :

9 Sept. 1879.

. . . My forefathers were possessed of Nether Hall, near Burton, once the seat of Lords of Montjoy & we have a curious tradition of the Pretender accompanied by Pole of Radborne & Burdett of Foremarke arriving on a visit by water from Twyford.

A Photograph of Foremarke.

By the kind permission of "Country Life."

There is also the story told in " Coke of Norfolk and his Friends " how T. W. Coke (Coke of Norfolk) in 1774, at the suggestion of his brother-in-law, James Dutton, for social reasons joined the Cocoa Tree Club. The Cocoa Tree was a high Tory Club, the headquarters of the Jacobite Party in Parliament. Young Coke knew nothing of its politics, and his father, Wenman Coke, in order to warn him of the folly of entering a club of whose political significance he was ignorant, secured for himself an invitation to the dinner that was to be given in honour of the new member. The chairman of the dinner was *Sir Robert Burdett*, and at the conclusion of the dinner Wenman Coke addressed Sir Robert and begged that his presence might make no difference to the first toast, " The Prince " (the Pretender), which he would drink in the customary manner. He then unbuttoned the knee of his breeches, knelt down upon his bare knee, and to the astonishment of his son, drank the toast in this posture and then quitted the room in silence.

Francis Burdett was born in 1770. Ten years before his birth the family home, Foremarke, had been rebuilt for his grandfather, Sir Robert, by the architect David Hiorns. It is a Palladian house, very typical of the eighteenth century, thus described by Woolfe and Gandon in "Vitruvius Britannicus " :

" The principal front is on the side of a hill, rising gradually from the River Trent, and commands a very extensive prospect of about 25 miles North, bounded by the Peak Hills. The South front looks upon Pasture ground, laid out in the style of a Park, by sunk Fences, with Plantations of Firs and Forest Trees disposed in such a manner as to resemble the work of Nature more than that of Art. The East Front commands about 20 miles towards Nottingham, with a perspective of the windings of the Trent terminated by the Castle. . . . The West front enjoys the rich valley leading up to Burton-upon-Trent about 8 miles in length, and incircled by the Staffordshire moorlands."

Francis Burdett was the child of Francis, Sir Robert's second son, the eldest son having died in infancy. His mother was Eleanor Jones, daughter of Sir William Jones, owner of Ramsbury Manor. Her sister and co-heiress married Sir William Langham, who took his wife's name, so that she became Lady Jones. He died before her without issue, and on her death the Ramsbury estate passed to her sister's, Mrs. Burdett's, son, who had by then become Sir Francis Burdett. Mrs. Burdett died on May 30, 1783.

Thus the future reformer descended from a companion of the Conqueror through a long line of prosperous and influential landowners. Between 1290 and 1695, Burdetts sat in at least twenty-three parliaments as members for the counties of Warwick or of Leicester. Sir Robert Burdett, the fourth baronet, represented Tamworth in Parliament for twenty years, so that Francis Burdett carried on the family tradition when he entered the House of Commons in 1796.

He continued another tradition when he married a lady of great fortune. Seckingdon, Bramcote and Foremarke had all come into the inheritance by marriage; Ramsbury was soon to come. Lastly an alliance with the leading banker of George III's reign cemented these territorial possessions.

Such were the somewhat unlikely antecedents of Horne Tooke's disciple, the future Reformer and champion of every popular cause.

Francis Burdett was the second son of his parents, but by the death of his elder brother in 1778 he became the heir. Two younger brothers and three sisters grew up, and one brother, William Jones Burdett, was always his close ally.

At eight years old Francis entered Westminster School.

The Dame's House in which he lived was that of " Mother Clapham," on the site of what is now Dean's Yard. In those days the " Town Boys " (all those who were not King's Scholars) were boarded in Dames' Houses, and it was not uncommon for the " Town Boys " to get up plays in their boarding-houses, intended to rival the annual Latin Play of the King's Scholars. In allusion to some such performance Mrs. Burdett wrote to her friend Mrs. Tracy on November 29, 1782 :

" Next Saturday a few of the schoolboys are to perform a play at Mrs. Clapham's, Frank among the number. At present he has but a short part in it. ' Tamerlane ' is the play; they have invited us. . . .

" My dear Frank improves beyond my expectations. Last Sunday I gave him Wilson's Sermons to read, and he desired after he had read one to read another, for he said they were not only good but entertaining. The remark gave me great pleasure. He will sit and converse with you as rationally as any man of thirty."

He was indeed sententious from a very early age.

We do not know much about Francis Burdett's schooling. But a Mr. Stevens, commissioned by Sir Robert to report on the progress of the younger brother, Jones Burdett, then aged seventeen, reported this :

" In the way he is going on it appears to me that he may rise gradually to the Top of Westminster School and at last know nothing."

It is not probable that Francis Burdett learned more at Westminster than did his younger brother. Bad as the knowledge of the classics is in many members of our Public Schools to-day, it is not so bad as it was at Westminster in 1789.

Burdett matriculated at Oxford from Christ Church on December 13, 1785, but, in accordance with a custom of

those days, continued his school life at Westminster,
reaching the Sixth Form in 1786, when he was expelled for
taking part in a rebellion against the Head Master, Dr.
Samuel Smith.[1] Thus he began early as a rebel against
authority. He was, no doubt, a ringleader among the
"contumacious" boys, for we are informed that Dr.
Smith went up-school armed with a thick stick, with which
he felled Burdett.

In 1786 he went up to Christ Church, but there is no
record of his career at the University. Only one of his
letters belonging to these years has been preserved. It
shows him in November 1787 already turning an attentive
ear to politics, at the age of seventeen. It is addressed to
his aunt, Lady Jones, who, being herself childless, became
after Mrs. Burdett's death in 1783 a sort of mother to her
nephews and nieces.

DEAR AUNT JONES,

I hope Uncle Jones's gout is better, & that this
sudden change of weather does not affect him. Supposing
him to be a politician I will now address him on that subject.
I mean by that to endeavour to entertain him on that head
by giving him the conversation & opinions of people here.
I suppose he has seen the King's Speech & the Address
etc. These are things of course. I shall therefore commence by telling him, Burke still pursues his plan of
Impeachment [2] with unbated [*sic*] vigour & has already
entered the lists to encounter the Minister, who as yet has
not thought it worth his while to answer his antagonist,
so that at present political affairs wear an unaccustomed
serenity of aspect, but however the augmentation of the
army, the necessity of the late armament [3] & the subsidiary

[1] Head master 1764 to 1788.

[2] The impeachment of Warren Hastings.

[3] Owing to the disturbances in Holland and the collision between
the Orange and the Democratic parties. Our relations with France
were consequently strained. See Stanhope's "Pitt," Vol. I. pp. 272, 279.

treaty with the Hessian Prince will open a wide feild for Parlimentary debate & contention : these are the topicks of conversation in London, about which various are the opinions, some wonder, some admire, some condemn. There is also another thing which engages at present the whole attention of the Learned world : it is a political preface written by Doc. Parr & published with Bellendenus's work.[1] I would recommend it to Uncle Jones's perusal, as I should imagine it would afford him great amusement, both on account of the pureness of the Latinity & the matter it contains. I have just finished it; the plan of it is (aluding to the three great Luminaries of former ages Cicero, Seneca, & the Elder Pliny) to paint out Fox, North, & Burke as the three Luminaries of the present age. It celibrates Fox for his active penetrating mind, North for his more solid judgement, & Burke as an Orator & Rhetorician; he then artfully introduces Sheridan (who is the hero of the piece) as possessing the united talents of all three; he then speaks of Pitt, but not in such terms; he says he is a good Orator, but rather [torn] the ear than convinces the understanding, & says he is a trict up Orator, or one made merely by art, & speaks meanly of his abilities as Minister & politician. Having given you a short sketch of this admirable work & an account of everything that passes here, I must take my leave of you, (I could write about this for a week). When I cast my eye back I find I have been writing to Uncle Jones in answer to Aunt Jones's letter, for Bellendenus has carried me beyond the limits of my paper : your letter I must reserve for another opportunity. . . .

yours affectionately,

Francis Burdett.

---

[1] In 1787 Dr. Parr brought out a new edition of the three books " De Statu " of William Bellenden, a learned Scot, Master of Requests to James I.

Francis Burdett left Oxford without taking a degree at the end of 1788 or the early part of 1789, and, according to the custom that prevailed among young men of quality, went on the " Continental tour." The person chosen as Cicerone to him on the Continent seems to have been M. le Chevalier, already famous as an archæological globe-trotter, who had gone to the East as private secretary to de Choiseul, French Ambassador at Constantinople, and had assisted him in exploration of the Troad. This, at any rate, is the statement made in a generally reliable pamphlet ("Memoirs of the Life of Sir Francis Burdett," 1810), which is borne out by allusions in the correspondence to a friendship that existed as early as 1791, and only ended with Chevalier's death in 1836. But in the letters before me that Burdett wrote when on tour, no reference is made to Le Chevalier, and from what we know independently of Le Chevalier's movements, he cannot have been with Burdett the whole of the time.

Here is the first of Burdett's letters from abroad :

Paris,
19 April, 1789.

DEAR AUNT JONES,

My brain being no longer in that chaotic state into which it was thrown from the confusion, which such a variety of new objects occasioned, I now with the greatest pleasure take up my pen to fulfil my engagement with you, & commence a correspondence, which I hope will be maintaned with as much regularity as the unsettled state of a traveller will permit.

We intend to leave Paris some time next week, a discription of which I shall not pretend to give you, as I find it impossible to give one which can at all convey to you an Idea of Paris, that must be reserved for some future opportunity or for some abler pen.

Such a mixture of Pomp & Beggary, filth & magnificence,

as may be truely said to beggar all discription. Suffice to say, that it is the most ill-contrived, ill built, dirty, stinking Town that can possibly be imagined; as for the inhabitants they are ten times more nasty than the inhabitants of Edinburgh. At the same time there are many Publick buildings, & many parts of the Town which are extremely magnificent. You find the same inconsistency pervade everything here, things the most incongruous, the most opposite in nature to one another, are here united.

We arrived here at a very unfortunate time, the Theatres being shut as is customary in Lent. There is to be a Tragidy to-morrow, at which performance we shall be present. The opera is, I understand, a very fine exhibition here, we intend seeing one before our departure. We have dined once with the Duke of Dorset,[1] who was vastly polite to us & has honoured us with another invitation.

I have just received letters from my Father & sister, which I have read with as much pleasure as a ship-wreck'd Mariner views a distant sail. Tell my Father & Sister this must be looked upon as an answer to their letters, as I have so many other correspondents.

We intend staying a day or two at Versailles, after which we shall pursue our rout into Switzerland, we shall make some stay at Strasbourg. Therefore your next letter you had better direct there. The direction will be thus,

A Monsieur F. BURDETT
Gentilhomme Anglais,
La Poste Restante
a Strasbourg
en Alsace.

My love to my Father & Brothers & Sisters, & except [*sic*] the same yourself, but do not forget Uncle, believe yours

most affectionately,

FRANCIS BURDETT.

[1] The Duke of Dorset was English Ambassador in France.

It is to be noticed that Burdett left Paris before the opening of the States-General on May 5, 1789, and did not witness its early scenes.

During the long summer of 1790, Burdett was at Florence, for we read in the " Taylor Papers " of " cricket matches on the Prato " in which he " took a very active part." In June he set out with a Captain Fitzgerald for Sicily, and described his experiences in a letter to his father (at Ealing), dated July 7. From Catania they made the ascent of Mount Etna, which was the chief object of the tour, and by which the young gentleman counted himself " richly repaid for all his trouble." The view of the whole island of Sicily, which " appears too small a base for the immense height of this volcano," fascinated him. " I believe I should have stayed there until now had not the guide reminded me it was necessary to descend if I meant to get to the bottom that night." From Catania they reached Syracuse, where they hired mules and crossed the island to Palermo, and found travel most uncomfortable owing to the lack of inns. A Capuchin convent sheltered them, but unattractively.

" I cannot give you an idea of the grotesque appearance these holy people made with their heads shaved & their long beards & their garment intended to represent that of the primitive Christians. They all supped in the same room, each having his small napking plate & jug of wine & water to himself. There were 14 of them : the Principal sat at the top of the hall in the middle of which hung a small lamp which cast a glimmering light around. We were seated on either side of the Principal who asked us many questions about England & whether the King of Naples was our King. I was much surprised at his ignorance but did not take the trouble to set him right. Having eat a small plate of fish, the youngest Capuchin took away our plate & brought us by way of desert a cloth full of raw beans which they eat with great avidity. After this repast we retired to our chamber where we laid ourselves on the floor preferring that to the filth of our bed. We rose early the next morning & pursued our route to Palermo not without having indemnified the Fathers for their hospitallity."

First and last, Burdett disliked all that he thought Popish, though he was a champion of Catholic Emancipation.

In the autumn, having completed his tour of Italy, he reached Vienna, after suffering much " from the immovable obstinacy of German Postillions." Here he was introduced to the Emperor, in company with a Sir John Macpherson : " The Emperor honoured us with a very marked and peculiar attention, talking to us near an hour uninterruptedly." There were many balls and assemblies at the houses of the different ambassadors, and the young man went three or four times a week to pay his respects to the old Prince Kaunitz, author of the Franco-Austrian alliance of 1756. Of his visit to Berlin which followed, we know from another source that he got into trouble with the authorities, but certainly for no political reasons; and by July 1791 he was back in London, after an absence of two years and a quarter, having come of age early in the year.

In the long letters written to his aunt, Lady Jones, during this period of travel, there is not a trace of any concern with what was happening in France. Yet it has been repeatedly stated that Burdett about this period was closely in touch with revolutionary France. For example, his friend Lord Langdale (Henry Bickersteth), in his " Memoirs," says :

"He made the grand tour in 1790 and had thus an opportunity of witnessing, if not the rise, at least a considerable portion of the early progress of the French Revolution. He returned to England in 1793."

The writer in the " Biographie Universelle " makes the

same mistake of dates, and goes so far as to say that Burdett
" passait sa vie dans les clubs et suivait assidument les
Séances de l'assemblée nationale." This latter statement
is a mere inference, and an incorrect inference.

Burdett went abroad, not in 1790, but in 1789, and, as
we have seen, left Paris for Switzerland ere ever the States-
General met on May 5. So he can hardly have witnessed
the early progress of the Revolution, much less can he have
attended the clubs or the meetings of the Constituent
Assembly in 1789, 1790, and 1791.

It is certain, as his letters show, that he returned to
England in July 1791 and remained in England for the rest
of that year. There is, however, a gap in the materials for
his " Life " for the whole of 1792 and the first half of 1793.
It is conceivable that he went abroad a second time, but
there is not a vestige of evidence to point that way. The
suggestion in these writers is that Burdett's Radicalism had
its source in his experiences in France at the time of the
Revolution. But this is, I think, a misreading of the
situation. The French Revolution no doubt gave to him,
as it gave to Wordsworth and others, an uplift of the spirit,
and quickened his natural passion for liberty. In 1791 he
wrote the following verses on the Revolution :

" En vain, braves françois, vos calumniateurs
Vous reprochent à l'envie, et augmentent vos erreurs.
La lecon que vous donnez si belle aujourdhui
Impose silence enfin à vos lâches ennemies,
Interdit, tout confus, ils n'ont jamais cru voir
La raison en France l'emporter sur la gloire,
Où la philosophie ne permet plus le Trône
D'un frivole éclat imposer aux hommes,
Et la belle justice, en s'élevant, apprendre
A ceux qui sont dignes sa douce voix d'entendre,
Les hommes sont égaux, ce n'est pas la naissance,
C'est la virtue, tout seule, qui fait la différence,
Elle ajoute ces parrolles si vraies et si beaux,
C'est le crime fait la honte, et non pas l'échaffaud,
Ainsi parle la raison, et le peuple l'entend,
Et d'un voix unanime crient, à bas les Tyrants.
Ne craignez donc rien quoique, généreux françois,

Il s'éleve contre vous tous les faux préjugés,
Que les Tyrants s'agitent et conspirent contre vous,
La victoire est la votre, la honte est à eux.
Tout le monde applaudit à votre effort sublime,
Et toutes les nations vous accordent leur estime.
Allez donc hardiment, continuez du courage,
De l'esprit humain le plus frappant ouvrage."

These are spirited lines, even though they are written in faulty French. But the French influence was in him the thinnest veneer. His Radicalism, when it came, was not a foreign product. It was as racy of the English soil as was the Radicalism of Cobbett, the only difference being that whereas Cobbett was sprung from lowly stock, Burdett was of blue blood, and had been brought up in the traditions of an English gentleman. There was in his Radicalism an appeal not to the " Rights of Man," but to Magna Charta and the ancient liberties of Englishmen before Whigs and Hanoverians, the monied and fund-holding interests, had ever been heard of.

The only thing that we do know about Francis Burdett's career in the years 1792 and 1793 is this : that on August 5, 1793, at St. Martin's-in-the-Fields, he married Sophia, youngest daughter of Thomas Coutts the banker. Since Francis Burdett in a sense married his wife's family, it is desirable to sketch the Coutts history, which shall be done in another chapter.

CHAPTER II

THE COUTTS FAMILY AND BURDETT'S MARRIAGE

The " Life of Thomas Coutts," by E. H. Coleridge, was published in 1920, but unfortunately many of the family papers were not available to Mr. Coleridge, and his account of Thomas Coutts, excellent though it is, requires some supplementing and correction.

Thomas Coutts, born September 18, 1735, was the fourth and youngest son of John Coutts, Lord Provost of Edinburgh, and of his wife Jean Stuart, eldest daughter of Sir John Stuart (second baronet) of Allanbank. Through his mother Thomas Coutts was of kin with the Cochranes, Earls of Dundonald.

He came to London in 1752. For a time he was in partnership with his brother James, but James retired in 1775, and Thomas was to all intents the creator of the bank now known as " Coutts & Co."

Though a shrewd man of business, he had in matters of the heart an incurably romantic vein. On May 18, 1763, he married Susannah (Betty) Starkie, the nursemaid of his brother's child. The marriage caused a temporary estrangement between the two banking partners, but the dissolution of partnership, when James Coutts retired in 1775, was due to peculiarities of character developed by the latter—developments that alarmed the clients of the bank.

From 1763 to 1775 Thomas Coutts and his wife lived at 80 St. Martin's Lane, and there his children were born— no fewer than *four* sons (all of whom died in infancy) and three daughters (the " three Graces," as they were nick-

THOMAS COUTTS.
From a miniature by Meyer in the possession of the Lord Latymer.

MRS. COUTTS (SUSANNAH STARKIE).
From a miniature by Meyer in the possession of the Lord Latymer.

named), who ultimately became Lady Guilford, Lady Bute and Lady Burdett.

There is no reason whatever to suppose that the marriage of Thomas Coutts with Betty Starkie was unhappy, or that she conspicuously failed to rise to her position as the wife of a wealthy banker. Sir Francis Burdett wrote to his wife on January 21, 1818 (and Sir Francis was a very fastidious man) :

" I loved your mother, and if ever one mortal was attracted warmly to another, I am persuaded she was to me—in spite of many errors and sometimes being dissatisfied with my conduct—and it will be my pride to boast she was not mistaken."

Betty Coutts was, no doubt, not an intellectual person. We read, for example, in the " Papers of Sir Herbert Taylor " (afterwards Secretary to William IV),[1] writing from Bologna, 1789 :

" Mr. Coutts and his wife and daughter passed through, but we did not make their acquaintance. We were afterwards amused with the accounts of Mrs. Coutts. One of the stories told of her was that being asked her opinion of the amphitheatre of Rome, she replied that when furnished and whitewashed it would be a *very* pretty building."

Tom Coutts was the ruling spirit in his household, but Mrs. Coutts, till she was overtaken by mental prostration in her later years, took a full place in the family life, and was adored by her children.

When a millionaire banker is married to a serving-maid, scurrilous stories are bound to pass into the currency of the town. The age was rather gross—the age of Gillray's caricatures. Mr. C. C. Pearce, in his " Jolly Duchess," retails many stories of this sort from a scurrilous paper

[1] " Taylor Papers," p. 8.

written twenty years after Betty Coutts' death. Thus he tells us that when Mr. Coutts appeared at Court the King asked him why he had not brought his daughters to the Drawing-Room. Mr. Coutts, with great humility, replied that in reality he did not know any lady with whom he dared to take the liberty of requesting her to introduce his daughters. "Why, you're Lord Bute's banker," said the King, " aren't you ?   Ask Lady Bute, ask Lady Bute."

This story is a silly lie, as will be apparent from letters which follow. There were many titled ladies, from Georgiana Duchess of Devonshire downwards, who would have been glad to oblige Coutts by the introduction of his daughters. And, as a matter of fact, they were presented not by Lady Bute, but by the Duchess of Buccleuch.

At the end of 1775 Thomas Coutts and his wife moved from St. Martin's Lane to the Banking House, 59 Strand, and it was there that his three daughters were brought up, Susan (born March 20, 1771), Frances (born January 9, 1773), and Sophia (born 1775). They were educated at a school kept by the Misses Stevenson in Bloomsbury, and in July 1787 the eldest and the youngest, Susan and Sophia, were sent to complete their education in Paris. Their sister Frances (Fanny), for reasons of health, remained at home.

The girls were put in the charge of a Madame Daubenton as chaperon. Susan naturally took the lead of her younger sister, and it was she who wrote most of the letters home. In one of them she describes graphically, if not always grammatically, a riot at the Italian Theatre in Paris.

Susan Coutts to Fanny Coutts.

Paris
(Dec. 1787)

My Dear Fanny,
      . . . We have this morning received our most *beautiful & elegant* present from my dear mama, & tell her

that we do not know what to say to equal her *goodness* in getting us them. . . . Orange is no longer the *tip top* fashion. *Pink & Black* is the great rage. They were here *bonnets* very much *disabille*, pink lining, black at top & the crown pink. Black ribbons tipped with a little pink fringe is the most newest fashion, then black, pink, or white feathers. *Coq* feathers, black & pink mixed, is very much the mode—those sort of bonnets are charming. We have had an orange bonnet which is very pretty—orange is not quite *ridiculous*. We have had our bonnets some time. I will *inform* you how they are made—orange all except the lining, which is white, & the ribbons are those black with orange spots that you sent us.

There has been at the Italian Theatre the greatest riot that ever was remembered here. Last Wednesday, 26th, there was a new piece given, entitled " Le Prisonnier Anglois," which was very bad stuff & they would not let it continue : all the house was of one mind, it was so extremely bad, the piece being not let to go on. One of the actors asked, what piece the public would have in its stead. Everybody cried out, " Des Etourdis ou le mort supposé" (which is, by the by, a most *delightful* comedy in 3 acts) : the actor *s'est retiré*, & everybody were waiting in expectation for this favorite & charming comedy (which had only been acted four or five times). The curtain drew up & one of the actors came on & said they were extremely sorry but one of the actors was not to be found who acted the principal character in the comedy desired, but hoped they would have " La Servante Maitresse " instead. The curtain dropped (you must know it is a very pretty piece, & Mlle Nevaud [? Renaud], the famous singer, which they make such a horrid fuss about, acts in that piece). Upon which they began to hiss & whistle in such a manner nothing was equal to it & they cried out nothing but " Des Etourdis." The curtain drew up in the middle of all this noise, & " La Servante Maitresse " begins. Mlle

Nevaud & Schenard [1] (an actor) comes on; they hiss her in the most furious manner, crying "Des Etourdis" etc. & Schenard begins to laugh (he is an actor who generally plays the fathers' parts) upon which all the *critics* in the pit cry out "Mettez vous à genous et demandez pardon pour avoir ris";—he wont, & they will not let them sing or speak or do anything till Schenard begs pardon, which he was resolved not to do, but an actress, Mme Gontier,[2] an *oldish* woman, just goes upon her knees & begs pardon for (him); no, "that would not do," they all cried out; "it was not her that had offended them" (it was very ridiculous enough of her to go upon her knees). This noise what with singing, laughing, talking lasted till ten o'clock without stops & everybody was going away, the Guards drove all the people out of the pit, but to no purpose, for they all mounted up to the boxes & the amphitheatre, to prevent the company from stirring out of their boxes & left the Guards to their meditations in the pit—continually roaring for Schenard to ask pardon & *afterwards* to have the comedy of the "Des Etourdis." The noise lasted till 12 o'clock when they all decamped, saying, "Adieu à demain." (I forgot to tell you that nothing is so common here as throwing apples or oranges on the stage, & that night there was a most enormous quantity thrown all about.)

Thursday the 28th they announced in the "Journal," "Des Etourdis." . . . The instant Schenard appeared the noise began again, insisting him to beg pardon, which he did, but they would have (him) to go upon his knees, which he would not do. They would not let the piece go on, till he did what they wanted; they whistled, sung, made a great circle & danced altogether in the pit : never was there ever known to have been such a riot. This noise went on till near half-past nine, & then they peacably let the spectacles begin & it ended at 12 o'clock.

---

[1] Simon Chenard, French actor, 1758 to ? 1831.
[2] Madame Gonthier, French actress, 1749 to 1829.

You must know that when they give here a new piece, all the actresses & actors are obliged all to be in the way, in case the piece should fail, that they may give the spectacle called for by the public, & the actor that acted the principal part in the Des Etourdis was not to be found. The poor actor was put in prison, was brought out the 28th to play, & then was sent back to prison & remained 2 days. There were likewise 2 or 3 persons in the pit who were taken to prison for their insolent & outrageous behaviour & they say they are to remain for a year. This enraged the public, & they all exclaimed that they would make no more noise if they would let the prisoners free, *which they would not do*. However, at length quite tired & spent with *roaring & squalling*, they let the spectacle peacably continue without any more noise, & Schenard begged pardon, but not on his knees.

By the end of 1787 Thomas Coutts had become seriously alarmed about the character of Madame Daubenton, to whom he had entrusted his daughters, but his anxiety was not as yet shared by the girls. He wrote to the Duchess of Devonshire, and received replies from the Duchess, and from John Crawfurd, who stood in some sort of confidential relationship to her.

Georgiana, Duchess of Devonshire, to Thomas Coutts.

(Dec. 1787)

Dear Sir,
       You do me perfect justice in believing that I am truly interested about yourself & Miss Coutts, & very much concerned at your uneasiness. . . . I am so well aware of the difficulty in finding a proper person, or in depending upon French recommendations that my opinion very strongly is that if you take them from Mme D. you should place them as pensioners (which indeed I always thought a preferable situation) at the convent of Penthemont. They would have the same masters as in a private

house : this mode of education has been followed not only for the Princesses of the Blood, & French ladies of Fashion, but indeed all through Europe.   The late Duke of Aremberg's Duchess & this Duchess were brought up at Penthemont; I believe Ly C. Tufton is just gone there : & Miss Poultney & Ly Belmour & Ly Sophia Hobart, Ld Buckinghamshire's daughters, spent two or three years there—Miss Coutts will go in with the advantage of your establishing them in the most liberal manner & with the recommendation of the D. & Dss of Polignac, Mme de Langeron & the Duke of Dorset, to whom I would write for this purpose. . . . Another temptation to this wd. be that it would avoid all éclat; as you could say that you had placed your daughters in the convent for great facility they would find in learning French with so many young people : & indeed I am certain that the advantage gained would be very great both to their speaking the language & forming their manner.

I am Dr Sir,

yrs etc.

G. Devonshire.

By midsummer 1788 the girls had themselves become convinced of the " shocking improprieties " of Madame Daubenton, and in July Thomas Coutts, taking with him his wife and Fanny, visited Paris, and thence, with his whole family, took two months' holiday on a tour through Switzerland, returning to Paris on Sept. 30, 1788; and there he remained with them till May 1789 (the opening of the Revolution).   Whatever his real motive was, the ostensible reason for his stay was to arrange for the settlement of his three daughters in some securer place than the house of Madame Daubenton.   He finally settled on the Convent of Penthémont,[1] to which he had been recommended by the Duchess of Devonshire.   In the interval the girls had a gay time, constantly going to the Opera and to the Italian

---

[1] " Four Fascinating French Women," by Mrs. Bearne, p. 150.

Theatre, taking lessons from the celebrated musician Piccinni, who was described by M. de la Borde,[1] a banker friend of Thomas Coutts, " *aussi pauvre d'argent qu'il est riche en génie musical*," and reading French history with the Abbé Beaurieu, " a very Parson Adams." The hospitable table of their parents was graced by the presence of many fashionable people, such as the Elchos and the British Ambassador, the Duke of Dorset. Balls were quite the rage, and the Coutts gave a ball at the Hôtel de l'Université : through the medium of the beautiful and accomplished Georgiana, Duchess of Devonshire, they were introduced into the highest circles of French Society. It will be remembered that Francis Burdett was in Paris that April, and it is possible that he there met his future bride, but no record of such meeting has been preserved.

At the end of April or the beginning of May Thomas Coutts terminated his stay at Paris. He had secured a noble French lady, the Comtesse d'Auteuil, as chaperon to his daughters at the Convent of Penthémont.

The Convent of Penthémont was, we are told, " one of the two most fashionable establishments of education in France," attended by " all the daughters of the greatest families. . . . It was extremely expensive. . . . The establishment was on a magnificent scale, the life sumptuous, and the extravagance in the dress of the pupils increased by the example of the fashionable women of the Court who were constantly to be seen there. The educational staff included not only a dancing-master, but also a *maître de ballet de l'Opéra ;* balls took place every week during the Carnival, friends and fiancés were admitted; indulgence and luxury, not serious study, prepared the young girls for the brilliant fortune in prospect for so many of them.

Thomas Coutts returned to London in May, but he only stayed there a short while. The progress of the Revolu-

---

[1] La Borde was banker to the French Court, but retired in 1770.

tion in Paris made him uneasy—for the Bastille had fallen on July 14—yet Charles Fox assured him there was no ground for anxiety.

Charles James Fox to T. Coutts.

Brighthelmstone,

17 Aug. 1789

DEAR SIR,

. . . I am convinced your daughters are as safe at Paris as they would be in London, but if either you or they think otherwise, I own I think no improvement from masters can be put in ballance with the uneasiness you must feel at being separated. . . .

yours ever,

C. J. FOX.

In October 1789 Coutts returned once more to Paris to carry off " the Graces " on a continental tour, this time to Italy. We have no detailed account of the travel, but we know that they were at Naples in February 1790 and in Rome as late as May 1790. Francis Burdett was at this time also on his tour in Italy, but there is no record of his having met them there.

Travelling back from Italy by way of the Tyrol, they were delayed first at Augsburg and then at Aix-la-Chapelle by illnesses of the two girls. At Aix-la-Chapelle Prince Ferdinand de Rohan, then acting Regent of Liège, overwhelmed them with attentions. At the beginning of 1791 they were for two months in Paris, and once again were treated as persons of the greatest consequence. Great bankers have special importance in times of European war.

It was not till the end of March 1791 that the whole family returned to the Strand, where a warm welcome awaited them from all their friends. In May the girls were presented at Court by the Duchess of Buccleuch and the King was affable.

Coutts writes to his friend Colonel Crawfurd :

" My daughters receiving visits from all the world and launching out into all companies has formed a new scene to Mrs. Coutts and me. They have been very flatteringly received at St. James."

The only person who kept his distance, to Coutts' great chagrin, was the Prime Minister, the younger Pitt. Writing to Pitt's mother, the Countess of Chatham, on July 25, Coutts says :

" Indeed I am sorry to say I have found a marked difference & coldness in him to me for a long time. . . . After my long absence I received very uncommon attention & kindness from many of the first persons & characters of the times, not only to myself but to my young family : nor can I trace the smallest neglect from any person besides, which perhaps makes it strike me the more."

Writing again to her a week later, and thanking her and the rest of her family for their kind attentions, he adds :

" I certainly do not expect Mr. Pitt to waste his time upon *me*. I only thought after so long an absence it was particular he should hardly even on seeing me by accident take any notice or make a single enquiry about me or my family ; and it struck me the more forcibly that really from His Majesty to my humble neighbours in the Strand, I met with nothing but the most flattering congratulations, and it cannot fail to be rather mortifying to find so distinguished an exception."

The banker was not long to be kept at arm's length by Mr. Pitt. And indeed in July 1791 the statesman had cares enough on his mind to preoccupy him. Coutts had chosen his moment of departure from Paris wisely.

For meanwhile the volcano of the French Revolution was pouring its fiery and destructive lava over France and neighbouring countries. Mirabeau, who might have guided the torrent of the Revolution into a well-ordered channel, had died on April 2, 1791, and with his death the Moderates had lost any control they might have had. The King had made his ill-starred attempt at flight; riot stalked through the fair fields of France; châteaux were burnt, abbeys sacked; priests and nobles had fled the country and had been proscribed as *émigrés ;* the Tuileries had been stormed; the King and Queen imprisoned; war declared by the Legislative Assembly on Austria and Prussia (April 1792). With the massacres of September an organised system of terror had been inaugurated by Danton, and the Revolution started to devour its own children. Belgium was overrun, the Scheldt declared an open river in defiance of treaties. In November and December Edicts of Fraternity were issued by the Convention offering assistance to all peoples which rose against their rulers. On January 21, 1793, Louis XVI was executed, and on February 1 France declared war on England and Holland.

Meanwhile " the Graces " partook sufficiently in the gaieties suitable to their age, and in 1792 were taken by the young Lady Chatham to St. James's on " the Birth-day," and made happy by her kind treatment of them. For exercise they were constantly on horseback. They were, according to their father, " very happy and without thoughts of matrimony." He wrote to the Duchess of Devonshire in June : " My daughters all like the country best, and I only wish there were gentlemen of the same taste who could discover how happy they might make them." There were, however, several visits—some of them prolonged—to Cowdray in Sussex, and it might already have been surmised that its owner, Lord Montague, was attracted by one or other of " the Graces."

He was, however, forestalled by Francis Burdett, who

seized the youngest, Sophia. There is no allusion to Burdett in the Coutts family papers of 1792 and the first part of 1793, so it is probable that the courtship was short.

We do, however, know that Burdett was known to Coutts as early as the spring of 1791; for the banker recommended the young traveller, then visiting Berlin, to the good graces of Frederick Duke of York. The Princes of the Blood Royal had no money secrets from Coutts, treated him as a confidential adviser in the most delicate (and even indelicate) matters, and rewarded him with all civilities. The letter from the Duke of York shall be given in full :

Berlin,

May 24, 1791.

DEAR SIR,

I take the opportunity of a messenger returning to England to-morrow morning to return you many thanks for your obliging letters and to assure you that I take care to see all the gentlemen you was so good as to recommend to me and to acquaint them with your recommendation of them; one of them Mr. Burdet, I am sorry to tell you has got himself into so very disagreeable a scrape here last night that the English Minister Mr. Ewart has found himself under the disagreeable necessity of desiring him and four other young English to leave the town as soon as possible, they were all led away by one young man, who ought to have known better, to commit such riots in the town as were quite abominable.

With regard to the plan you was so good as to propose to me to pay my debts, should my other two brothers agree to it, I shall not have the least objection, as I even think that it is better than the one which was intended before.

I am very glad to hear that the presentation of your daughters went off so well.

We have been received most astonishingly well here.

The reviews in this part of the Prussian Army concluded yesterday. To-morrow I go to those of Magdeburg from whence I have to return here and wait for the final answer from Russia. Should it be war we shall go to the army on the frontiers of Courland who will begin their operations as soon as our fleet can come to their assistance; should it be peace, I shall then make a short tour and return to England. . . . I cannot add more at present except to desire to be remembered to all friends. Believe me ever, yours most sincerely,

FREDERICK.

Coutts may even then have had his eye on the young heir to two great properties as a possible son-in-law. But it is unlikely that he could have guessed how strangely this well-endowed young English gentleman, with a baronetcy at least in the offing, would run up against the most cherished prejudices of the banker's royal patrons and other potentates.

At all events, the marriage took place at St. Martin's-in-the-Fields on August 5, 1793, and Thomas Coutts gave his daughter an immediate dowry of £25,000. The bride was a good-looking girl of eighteen, with raven-black hair; the bridegroom was a tall young man of twenty-three, with a prominent aquiline nose and clear-cut patrician features. His length of leg, when compared with the rest of his body, was remarkable.

A sheaf of letters has been preserved congratulating Sophia's parents on her wedding, among them one from the Dowager Countess of Chatham, and another from the Burdetts' friend and kinsman, Mr. Pyott, at Foremarke, which shows that Burdett's father was prevented by bad health from being present at the wedding.

This marriage was destined to last for more than fifty years, and was only to be dissolved by death. They died within a few days of each other in 1844, and were buried

LADY BURDETT.

From a miniature by Cosway in the possession of the Lord Latymer.

on the same day in the same grave. But the anticipation of Mr. Pyott, that " every human happiness will attend " the marriage, was not realised in its early stages.

It would seem to our modern notions that the marriage never got a fair chance. Burdett had no home of his own, and though he appears to have taken a house at Canterbury, the couple lived most of their time with the bride's parents. Mr. Coutts had inspired all his children with a surprising affection. They habitually began their letters to him, " My ever dearest love." Also the three sisters were evidently a most united band, and showed great disinclination to see it broken up.

Nevertheless, but for a tragic happening this must soon have come to pass; for one wedding was to lead to others. Susan, the eldest sister, soon became engaged to Lord Montague of Cowdray, and Fanny, the second, lost her heart to Burdett's younger brother, Charles Sedley Burdett. From September to October of this year the newly married pair joined the Coutts family on a tour, which was to end at Foremarke. But just as they moved to Buxton, terrible news came in : the two prospective bridegrooms, who were in Germany, had been drowned at the Falls of the Rhine.

According to the *Gentleman's Magazine*, " the unfortunate fate of the travellers was owing to a very rash attempt from which no remonstrance could divert them. His Lordship, accompanied by Mr. Burdett, was uncommonly anxious to pass the famous waterfalls of Schaffhausen, which had hitherto been unattempted by any visitor. The magistrates of the district, having heard of the resolution of the travellers, and knowing that inevitable destruction would be the consequence of such an attempt, had ordered guards to be placed for the purpose of preventing the execution of it. Having provided themselves with a small flat-bottomed punt, as they were about to step into it, Lord Montague's servant stopped short, and as it were instinctively seized his master by the collar, declaring that for the moment he should forget the respect of the servant in the duty of the man.   His Lordship, however, extricated himself at the expense of part of his collar and neckcloth, and pushed off immediately with his companion.   They got down the first Fall in safety, and began to shout and wave their handkerchiefs in token of success.   They then pushed down the second Fall, by far more dangerous than the first, from which time they have not since been seen or heard of."

After news of the tragedy had come in, Coutts and his party prolonged their stay at Buxton till the New Year, and towards the end of January 1794 made the long-deferred visit to Foremarke.   But here again misfortune overtook them.   Sir Robert Burdett and his son Francis were both confined to bed by illness, and on February 3 Francis Burdett the elder died, leaving the young Francis heir to his grandfather's baronetcy.   The party left Fore-marke on February 6, taking with them Francis' brother, William Jones Burdett, in order to set him down at Oriel College, Oxford.

In March they returned to London and took up their residence at 1, Stratton Street, where Sophia Burdett's first child, also called Sophia, was born in June.

Stratton Street remained the Burdetts' headquarters, but they were often away from London.   In July they went for a short time to Canterbury, but rejoined the Coutts family at King's Gate, Lord Holland's house in the Isle of Thanet, which Coutts had rented.   Among others the Duke of Clarence honoured the family with a visit here.

At the close of 1794 the Burdetts were at Canterbury and the Coutts in London.   In January 1795 Thomas Coutts, who " liked the bustle of the world," bought outright the freehold of 1, Stratton Street, and from that date—with one short interval—it remained his chief residence till his death in 1822.

Meanwhile the glamour of the Burdett marriage had worn off. Burdett cannot have been an easy person to live with. Even before he had cast a roving eye on other ladies, he had withdrawn himself to a large extent from his wife's society, " poring " over books almost the livelong day.

His own account was that after returning from his travels abroad he had discovered how " ignorant " he was; he disliked the general run of Society, with its futile talk, and thought that some two or three years' study was necessary if he was ever to be of any use to his fellow-men. But Sophia had always lived a sociable life at home, and needed its support no less than that of ordinary food.

There are also some suggestions in the letters that Burdett's relations had treated the members of the Coutts family as not quite their social equals. Time and again husband and wife seemed on the point of separating, but there were reconciliations.

It would be tedious to reproduce the letters which passed between Burdett and his father-in-law on this subject. But they contain a few characteristic sentences. On January 2, 1795, Burdett writes :

" I could not help smiling at the article of ' poring,' it appear'd so odd, that I whose bum underwent Martyrdom at School for eight years of my life, who notwithstanding its daily sufferings could never be forced to five minutes application, should now be thought to have too much."

Again, on January 5 :

" I will say but one word more on the article of poring ; having lost twenty of the best years of my life, I find it necessary (for it is not by choice) to sacrifice many an hour, which I would gladly pass in the society of Sophia, and Freinds like yourself if I had them, to make up for the loss of that time which, tho' it cannot be regained, may make it less to be regretted, and I look upon the next two or three years of my life as all that remains to me to acquire whatever can render me useful to my Fellow Men or estimable in the eyes of those who know me, and above all in my own; I am therefore tenacious of every moment."

It is perhaps worth noting also how he defended himself from the charge of slighting his wife's family.

" I really was not able last Winter to go into company at all, I tried it once or twice at Brooks's and other meetings of young men my former companions at Westminster, Oxford, etc., and I confess I felt a little shy about asking them to the House on account of your Daughters, for the World is so full of ill nature : I fear'd anything which might have the appearance of design, and probably like men who try to avoid one thing I run into another extreme."

This plea lost whatever validity it may have possessed after 1796, when Susan Coutts married Lord Guilford, son of Lord North, George III's Prime Minister.

But the complaints of Burdett's neglect continued, and were increasingly concerned with his attention to other ladies; and a letter of his, written five years after his marriage, is virtually a confession of infidelity.

Sir F. Burdett to T. Coutts (at Bath).

Stratton St.
28 Jan. 1798.

MY DEAR SIR,
        I will not delay an instant answering your kind & sensible letter & will treat you with the same candour you have treated me. I am as much as you can possibly be convinced of the truth of your Ideas respecting Sophia : had that not been the case, long e'er this we should have parted. I never could have suffered all I have on Her

account, but that I was satisfied (however unfortunate for myself) that it arose from the best of hearts. I could not therefore resolve to increase Her load of grief in order to releive myself. She was to be pitied not blamed. The truth (in my opinion) is, marriage is ill calculated to realise the fleeting dream of happiness, much less those Ideas which youthful imagination creates : it is I think the worst bond & has with great truth been call'd the grave of love. I have never witness'd one which I could think deserved to be coveted. Indeed (you will think me wild) I am convinced all the present Ties of Society are calculated to obstruct human happiness. They are in opposition to every law of Human Nature : if anyone is inclined to doubt of the truth of this, let Him look at the result of them, is it happiness ? To return to Sophia & myself, there is a certain something in our characters which does not assimilate, & yet if I was to be ask'd to name a woman under the wide canopy of Heaven who I believed to be endowed with the purest & greatest virtues, I should boldly say it was Sophia; but certain it is from some unaccountable principle in human nature, that virtue neither creates love nor procures happiness. Shakspear traces it by one stroke of his Pencil, when he makes the Prince confess,[1] He could have better spar'd a better man. It is very wimsical that what you say—which seems to be stamp'd with the mark of truth—that is, to have such a being as you describe Sophia attached to a Man is the greatest possible happiness, should however be contradicted by my own experience. Had she been as bad as She is good, it never would have cost me a thought. I allow your parallel as to Her character : She is worthy of a Brutus, but alas (& I will speak of myself with the same candour I have spoken hitherto) the materials that compose my Frame are of a very different texture to those which formed that great man. I can boast none of that firm inflexible resolution which places Nature's great Favorites

[1] " Henry IV," Act v, sc. 4.

even above Her own laws : with feverish veins & an
unruly imagination I am ever led astray from that sober
path, which leads to the temple of Virtue, to wander in the
mazes of a Labyrinth after a Phantom of happiness, which
tho' ever seemingly near, is never to be attained, but which
still intices to persue by rearing the mask of present pleasure.
The best part of my character is a strong feeling of indignation at injustice & oppression & a lively sympathy with the
sufferings of my fellows.   I scarcely know what I have
written, but I have put down at the instant such feelings
as your letter gave rise to, & with the same confidence with
which it was written : one thing I will say, that as far as I
am able I will make Sophia happy.   Believe me, yours
very sincerely,

F. BURDETT.

A cartoon of Gillray's, published on August 1, 1798,
shows that by that time Burdett's liaison with Lady Oxford,
of which more must be said later, was already the talk of
the town.   But it is necessary first to trace the process by
which the town became so greatly concerned with Burdett
and his doings.

Yet, before closing this chapter, it is proper to say that
if Burdett's letters convict him not only of inconstancy in
marriage, but of disagreeable priggishness, they show also
that he submitted without resentment to his father-in-law's
admonitions.   This is to the credit of both men, perhaps
chiefly of the elder.   Thomas Coutts evidently had an
irresistible good-nature.

It should be observed also that when Burdett accused
himself of ignorance he is not to be taken too literally, for
his letters show considerable reading as well as a very
competent knowledge of French, to which he appears to
have added Italian.   He must have been a reader always,
for his letters and speeches abound in quotations of English
poetry, ranging from Shakespeare to Armstrong's " Art

of Preserving Health," and of the Latin classics, including
Persius, who is not very generally known.

These literary ornaments to his style might perhaps have
been omitted without loss; but his speeches prove constantly that he had equipped himself most seriously by the
study of law and of history for the work which was to be
his—that of a representative of the English people.

CHAPTER III

As early as 1795, Coutts had bethought him of a plan to cure that morose sulkiness which was then Sophia Burdett's chief complaint against her young husband—for, it must be remembered, Burdett, though so sententious in utterance, was only twenty-five.

Coutts proposed to get his son-in-law into Parliament, and the *modus operandi* deserves to be preserved in a picture of the times.

In February 1795 the banker wrote to a representative of the Duke of Devonshire :

" Mr. Burdett grandson of Sir Robert Burdett will possess a considerable land Estate part of which he is already in possession of by the death of his Father & second Brother & the rest comes to him at the demise of his Grandfather & of his Aunt Lady Jones. He seems to have no desire for public life, on the contrary is fond of retirement & study, but it strikes me that it would be for his advantage to be at least in one Parliament. And in this view I have secured him a seat (in case he should choose it) when the General Election comes round. He is a young man of considerable talent & of the most honourable principles. I had the pleasure of introducing him to Lord George Cavendish, who I had the honour to be well acquainted with—also last summer to Lord John who then did me the honour to dine with me in Stratton Street.

" He has not been yet in London this winter, but I should be happy (when there is an opportunity) to present him to the Duke of Devonshire.

"To what follows I neither expect nor wish for an answer at present, & my sole intention being to lay before His Grace what occurs to my mind *as from myself entirely*—having never spoken a word on the subject to Mr Burdett or any of his family. In case the Duke of Devonshire should wish to bring in an independent gentleman of Mr Burdett's description (in the event of Lord John wishing to quit it) as a locum tenens in the minority of His Grace's own immediate representatives—perhaps Mr Burdett might not prove unacceptable to the Duke or to the County. I know he has a particular attachment to the family of Cavendish & he is a man of such nice honour, that if the measure should in other respects at any time prove convenient, I am confident their interest would be very safe & never be sullied or diminished by adopting it. And if Mr Burdett should agree to go into Parliament—which I am by no means sure that he will—I think such a seat would be more congenial with his feelings than any that I shall have in my power to propose."

Burdett, however, showed no eagerness, and wrote to Coutts on April 30, 1795 :

"You know I am not at all anxious for a seat in Parliament, therefore I would not put myself to the slightest inconvenience about it, and certainly would not borrow money to effect it. If I have it by me, as I value it less than almost anything else, I would give it for that purpose."

Evidently Coutts, as banker, convinced the young man that he had this unvalued possession standing available.

Meantime domestic bickerings went on. "It is impossible for one person to keep constantly amused an invalid scarcely amusable," Burdett wrote, suggesting that Sophia would be happier with her sisters. At the end of the year Coutts was writing a violent remonstrance, and Burdett defending himself against the charge of excessive attention to certain ladies. In these unhappy circumstances Sophia's son, Robert Burdett, was born on April 26, 1796.—About the same time her husband was entering the House of Commons.

The negotiation with the Cavendish family having led to nothing, Coutts resorted to the purchase of Boroughbridge in Yorkshire, one of the Duke of Newcastle's seats. The third Duke had died in 1795, heavily in debt, and the fourth Duke was a minor, eleven years old, so that the affair lay with the trustees, Messrs. Knight and Mason. Four thousand pounds was the price agreed, Sir John Scott, the Attorney-General, afterwards Lord Eldon, holding the other seat.

When the matter was broached to Burdett, he wrote :

F. Burdett to T. Coutts.

Cheltenham.

DEAR SIR,

I have no objection to accepting the offer of the Duke of Newcastle's Borough, if I have got the money which is more than I know. I forget how much it was you mentioned to me, but that's of no consequence if I have it. Yours,

F. BURDETT.

The bargain took this precise form :

Memorandum.   3rd May, 1796.

" That it is agreed between the Trustees of the lately deceased Thomas Duke of Newcastle & Mr Thomas Coutts —that on Francis Burdett Esq. being returned a member to serve in the ensuing Parliament & having sat fifteen days without any Petition or objection having been preferred against him, The said Mr Coutts shall pay the sum of Four Thousand Pounds by applying the same towards discharging the Debt due to him by the said lately deceased Duke—

which £4000 is to be in full & to include all charges &
expences whatsoever; & if such Parliament shall be dissolved before its having sat for the period of six years, The
Trustees promise & undertake to bring the said Mr Burdett
in again to Parliament to sit for such time as (together with
the time past) shall complete the period of six years in all,
& no longer—At the end of which period Mr Coutts under-
takes that Mr Burdett shall pledge his honour to vacate
his seat if he should be called on so to do by The Trustees.

"It is also agreed between the said Trustees & Mr
Coutts that during the period of six years above mentioned
if Mr Burdett's seat at any time should be vacated by his
acceptance of any Office or otherwise, He shall be reelected,
He Mr Burdett in that case paying any sum not exceeding
Three Hundred Pounds that the Trustees may state to have
been expended on the occasion.

J. G. KNIGHT.
G. W. MASON."

Thus, though he spent a large part of his active life in
denouncing the rotten-borough system, it was as a member
for a rotten borough that Burdett entered Parliament.

But he had bought his seat in what was virtually the open
market; he owed allegiance to no man, and though he had
shown no eagerness to enter public life, from his first entry
on it he took his own line, with energy and the utmost
courage.

Within a year of his becoming member for Boroughbridge, the death of his grandfather brought him the rank
of baronet and succession to a great estate.   He was in a
position to be fearlessly independent, and he used it—
developing also in the exercise of his parliamentary rights
a notable gift of pungent speech.   At times he was over-
vehement in expression, but the circumstances in which he
spoke gave excuse, if not justification.   He had a right to
say of himself, in the letter of self-excuse addressed to his

father-in-law, bearing date January 28, 1798, the bulk of which has been already quoted :

" The best part of my character is a strong feeling of indignation at injustice and oppression, and a lively sympathy with the sufferings of my fellows."

But it is necessary to review at some length the events and emotions of the period in which this aristocratic tribune of the people began his stormy career.

Burdett, as we have seen, was brought into Parliament by the agency of Thomas Coutts, his father-in-law. Coutts was also father-in-law to Lord Guilford, who had deserted the Tory politics of his father. Guilford had been the go-between in forming the famous (or infamous) Fox–North Coalition of 1783, and on its dissolution had adhered to the politics of Fox, and was now one of the Opposition leaders in the House of Lords. Though not keen on Parliamentary Reform, he was bitterly opposed to the policy of the French War and the reactionary measures it involved at home.

Lord Holland, in his " Memoirs of the Whig Party," says of Lord Guilford :—

" He was of an indolent, careless disposition, easily satisfied with his company, averse to, if not incapable of, any extraordinary exertion of mind, or any great and powerful emotion. Yet he had many of the qualities requisite to form a leading publick man—high honour, great frankness, a sound understanding, considerable talents for publick speaking, and a temper more conciliatory than any man, Mr. Fox excepted, among the leaders of Opposition. Mr. Fox thought him superior to his father in sterling abilities, in cultivation of mind, and decision of character. Even in wit and humour, though confessedly inferior to Lord North, he was by no means deficient. He had at an early period of life vehemently opposed Parliamentary Reform; and though he might acquiesce in it, he said that he could not take it up with all the zeal of a convert."

If Lord Guilford was opposed to the policy of the French War, so also was Thomas Coutts, though he was no politician, but merely a banker with his finger on the financial pulse of the nation.

On December 1, 1792, he wrote to Colonel Crawfurd :

" As to Foreign affairs there would be nothing so good as to acknowledge the French Republic. . . . By treaty with them more may be done to keep peace & quiet at home & elsewhere than by a Prussian Army & an English squadron."

Again in January 1794 to Caleb Whitefoord :

" With respect to French opinions—' the war made against their growth' seems to me to be exactly the way to encourage instead of destroying them. There is no instance of opposition by force of arms subduing opinions. . . . And if we had prevented the invasion of France, I firmly believe many of the enormities committed would have been prevented—nay such was *even last Year* their dread of the English name that we might have kept them within their bounds."

Again on September 2, 1796, to Whitefoord :

" From the very beginning I was so far from thinking the war just or necessary that I always have thought it would lead to very fatal consequences."

About Reform he wrote to Colonel Crawfurd on December 22, 1792 :

" As to reform of Parliament or of Laws, they should always be reforming & repairing. The Constitution with all its excellencies is not perfect & is subject to dilapidations.

" But let such things be gone into temperately & at proper time. The truth is a good wise Minister should look before & do things before they are asked by the people."

And on January 1794 to Caleb Whitefoord :

" Men are too much enlightened nowadays to be driven. . . . It should be the business of a great Minister to foresee the storm, & by wise & gradual measures prevent the mischief, retrenching useless sinecures etc."

And as to Pitt's finance, he wrote to Whitefoord, on September 21, 1796 :

" The Foleys or any other mad extravagant heirs of fortune never in their minority borrowed money on such ruinous terms after a night spent at the gaming table."

The men-folk at 1 Stratton Street must therefore have been in agreement on matters of public policy. Coutts, Guilford and Burdett were all opposed to the French war and Pitt's repressive action at home.

At the time when Burdett entered Parliament public attention was monopolised by two prime interests : the French war and the condition-of-England question at home.

It is no part of my task to sketch, however briefly, the course of the French Revolution. The Girondins had unbounded faith in formulæ. Fanatics, convinced that they were " called " to regenerate the whole world, they had proclaimed war on Austria and Prussia in 1792 as a means of bringing about the Universal Millennium. But their dreamy philosophism soon gave way to the hard realism of the Jacobins. The Convention, in defiance of treaties, proclaimed the Scheldt an open river, and issued the Edicts of Fraternity, instigating foreign peoples to rise against their rulers. Would it have been possible for

England to avoid engaging in the war? A generation that has seen millions of lives laid down and millions of money spent to vindicate the sanctity of treaties and to restore the integrity of Belgium will hardly think it possible. The whole history of England from 1700 had shown that the one point in the European system on which England was most sensitive was the integrity of Belgium. She can never suffer a strong Power to hold the Belgian coast-line or point a cannon at London from Antwerp.

If Coutts thought the war an avoidable mistake, that was, in general, the opinion of the followers of Fox. They had gloried in the early successes of a " people rightly struggling to be free." Like the youth of Wordsworth, Southey and Coleridge, they had been fascinated by the glorious promises of the age.

> " Bliss was it in that dawn to be alive,
>   And to be young was very Heaven."

The view of the Foxite party that war was avoidable is well expressed by Lord Holland : [1]

" An influence in France, founded on national amity & a good-will towards her new institutions, might at one time have been easily obtained. Such an influence might have modified the principles & softened the excesses of the French Revolution. It would have secured a general peace & prevented the necessity of formidable armies in France, which alone furnished the means & perhaps created the inclination for conquest. They in a short time threatened every country in Europe with destruction. We adopted a cold distant & inexplicable line of policy. The consequences were the reverse of what an opposite system would have produced."

That is one of the great might-have-beens of history. The war was probably unavoidable, in any case, but the frigid

[1] " Memoirs of Whig Party," p. 29.

pedantry of Grenville and the unsympathetic posture of Pitt made it certain.

By 1796 the war had not been a success. England had not yet won a decisive battle—for that name can hardly be applied to the glorious 4th of June (1794). But she had used her sea-power to capture the Cape and Ceylon (from the Dutch) and various West India islands. On land, the coalition of England, Austria and Prussia had proved a disastrous failure owing to the diversity of the allied aims. Austria and Prussia were far more interested in the partition of Poland than in the conquest of France, and the sub- sidies granted by England were used for the former rather than for the latter purpose. England had cut an inglorious figure in the fiasco of the Toulon occupation (1793). The result was that by 1795 Belgium had been annexed by France, Holland had been converted into a Batavian Re- public dependent upon her, Prussia had been bribed into an inglorious peace. Bonaparte by the Italian campaign of 1796, which led to the prostration of Austria in the Treaty of Campo Formio, had emerged as a military genius of the first order. Verily the younger Pitt, unlike his father, was no born organiser of victory.

And what was the condition of England at home ? The Revolution of 1689 had made the Crown responsible to Parliament, especially the House of Commons. But the House of Commons was responsible to no one. Publica- tion of debates was illegal, and no division lists were given to the world. The obvious game for the Crown to play was to get control of the House of Commons. Prerogative was replaced by influence. In order to check this game, the Act of Settlement (1701), which gave the Crown to the Hanoverian line, enacted that " no person who has an office or place of profit under the King, or receives a pension from the Crown, shall be capable of serving as a Member of the House of Commons," but before the Hanoverians succeeded, this clause was repealed, and much intricate legislation issued in the result that most offices and all pensions were compatible with seats in the House of Commons (though the holders of many political offices had to vacate their seats on appointment and offer themselves to their constituents for re-election).

With the advent of the Hanoverians, the Crown became an asset of the Whig Party (for all Tories were regarded by the first two Georges as Jacobites). The Whigs saw their opportunity. With Walpole as their leader, they were the great organisers of corruption as the general system of government. It was not simply that they gave sinecures and cash payments to those who voted for them in the House of Commons. The whole system of representation played into their hands.

Constituencies were of two kinds : County and Borough. The county constituencies were the most independent part of the electorate. Each county was represented by two members, but the vote was confined by the great disfranchising statute of the Middle Ages (1430) to *free*holders of land worth at least forty shillings per annum. Hence the voters in a county election were (*a*) the squires, (*b*) the landed magnate, if there was one, (*c*) the yeomen freeholders. The franchise in the counties was uniform. No leaseholder had a vote.

The borough franchise, unlike that of the county, varied indefinitely from place to place. There were some " open " constituencies (like Westminster), where the voters were the mass of the inhabitants, but in most cases the vote was confined to members of a corrupt corporation. It is doubtful whether any Parliamentary borough had been created since 1485 with an honest purpose. Hence the existence of what were called " rotten " or " pocket " boroughs, many of which were in the hands of the great Whig lords, but the greatest holder of " pocket " boroughs was the Crown.

George III had also seen his opportunity. Why should

he not use the system devised by the Whig oligarchs, not in their, but in his own interest ? He broke the power of the Whig oligarchs by turning against them the system they themselves had devised. His aim was personal rule, not through prerogative, but through corrupt influence over the House of Commons. That was the basis of the power of his Tory Minister, Lord North. That, too, was the basis of the power of the younger Pitt. It is ridiculous to regard the younger Pitt as the " Apostle of purity," except in the sense that he was personally incorrupt. He had risen to power by a Court intrigue, and his whole system of government was based on corruption— sinecures, offices, pensions, peerages, rotten boroughs, etc. But it is obvious that under such a system the House of Commons had lost its *raison d'être*—which is to control the executive.

Two further causes made the claim of the House of Commons to represent the people of England at this time an idle mockery. First, after 1760, the small freehold farmers were rapidly disappearing. This calamity was due to a number of causes. The adaptation of improved methods to farming and the practice of enclosures favoured farming on a large scale. The large landowner could, while the small farmer could not, afford the necessary outlay of capital. Every wealthy man also was eager to buy land, for it was the source of political and social power. Home industry (weaving), by which the family of the small freeholder kept the household going, was increasingly replaced by the factory system. The result was that with the disappearance of the freehold yeomen the county constituency became more and more confined to a smaller body—the squires.

Secondly, the Industrial Revolution led to the rise of large manufacturing towns, especially in the North of England, where coal and iron lay side by side. Hence the growth of a vast population entirely outside the old electorate.

By 1796 the House of Commons as a representative body

had become an utter fraud. It merely represented an agricultural interest in a country which was rapidly ceasing to
be agricultural. The great majority of the members of the
House of Commons were the nominees of some 154 persons.
Reform *must* have come before 1800 by the logic of events,
had it not been for the French Revolution, which threw
all the upper classes into panic, and made them think any
change the beginning of revolution.

The Reform Movement had its genesis in the events of
the Middlesex election (1768), when Colonel Luttrell, who
had received a minority of votes in the contest with John
Wilkes, was declared by a corrupt House of Commons the
duly elected member for Middlesex. This scandal, with the
revolt of the American Colonies, whose slogan was " No
taxation without representation," brought the question of
representation to the front. The Society of the Supporters
of the Bill of Rights, founded in 1769 by Wilkes and others,
had as its avowed aim the proper representation of the
people in Parliament. But Wilkes was an unprincipled
character, and Horne (Tooke) led a secession from the
society, on the ground that the aims of the society were
being diverted from the political cause to the personal
interests of Wilkes (the payment of his debts, etc.). Horne,
followed by a large minority, seceded, and founded a "Constitutional Society," but it did not thrive.

The movement of the Yorkshire freeholders in favour of
Reform was supported by the younger Pitt and aristocratic
Whigs, who, in annoyance that the " system " devised by
themselves was being used by the King in his own interest,
with disastrous results both at home and abroad, patronised
the movement. But on Pitt's accession to power the
" Reformer " became very tame as " Minister," and after
putting forward a paltry scheme for gradually buying up
rotten boroughs (1785), characteristically gave up all attempt
at Reform, discovering beauties in a system which secured
him a large majority.

The philosophic dissenters next took the matter in hand (Price and Priestley). It was chiefly because they despaired of acquiring religious freedom for Nonconformists, except through a Reformed Parliament, that they advocated Reform. But the French Revolution broke out, and the ideas of the philosophic Nonconformists were not popular in the year that saw the birth of Burke's " Reflections on the French Revolution " (1790). In Birmingham a " Church and King " mob wrecked the residence and destroyed the scientific instruments of Priestley. Many houses of Non-conformists were destroyed in the riots.

The year 1792 witnessed the rise of a new phenomenon. Hitherto the Reform movement had been directed from above. But the working men themselves now took a hand in the matter. For in this year Thomas Hardy, a London shoemaker, founded the "Corresponding Society," of which the avowed aims were Universal Suffrage and Annual Parliaments. The Society took as its gospel Tom Paine's " Rights of Man " (of which the first Part was published in February 1791, the second Part in February 1792). This work declared that all political power emanated from the " people," and advocated the abolition of the monarchy and the House of Lords. The Corresponding Society circulated it among the lower classes.

But it was not only the working men who were active in the cause. In April 1792 Charles Grey (afterwards Lord Grey of the Reform Bill) founded an Association of Whig gentry known as the " Friends of the People " to promote Parliamentary Reform, and though Fox was never a member of the Association, he lent it his support. And this Association was the chief solvent in the disruption of the Whig Party. The Conservative wing of the Whigs (Portland, Windham, etc.) transferred their support to Pitt, while the " New Whigs," led by Fox and Grey, remained in opposition.

There was still another society in existence in London for

the promotion of Reform. It was known as the " Society for Constitutional Information." Horne (Tooke) joined it in 1780, and it took a lease of renewed life after 1791, and seems to have occupied a middle position between the other two. Romney, the painter (some time in the late 'nineties), also joined it, and several prominent Frenchmen, such as Roland and Barrère, were at one time or another admitted as members. Burdett, also in the late 'nineties, joined it as a member of Parliament.

As against these Reform societies a counter-movement of the anti-Reformers was organised by Reeve's " Association for the Preservation of Liberty and Property against Republicans and Levellers " (November 1792). It looked as though England, no less than France, was to be governed by clubs.

After the September massacres (1792) the tide of popular feeling in England set strongly against the Reformers, who were generally ostracised. The Reform societies in November of that year foolishly sent a deputation headed by Joel Barlow[1] and John Frost to congratulate the Convention on its successes. The Edicts of Fraternity and the execution of Louis XVI (January 1793) added volume to the tide of reaction, and such a wave of anti-Jacobin frenzy swept over the country that nothing could have prevented war. The war was actually declared by France on February 1, 1793. It is to be noted that after the outbreak of war, even the " Corresponding Society " (for some years at least) had no further communication with the French Government.

Undeterred by these malign events, Charles Grey on May 6, 1793, brought forward his motion in the House of Commons that Parliamentary Reform should be taken into consideration. The proposal was rejected by 282 votes to 41.

Pitt then adopted a policy of severe repression by pro-

[1] Joel Barlow. See p. 124.

secutions in the Courts of Law. His action cannot be justified by the calmer judgment of posterity, and the kindliest interpretation of his character can only be that he, like others, was swept off his feet by the maelstrom of anti-revolution passion. For the mass of the English people were intensely loyal, those who aimed at revolution being a feeble and contemptible minority. The best antidote to disaffection would have lain, as Fox and Grey maintained, in a course of moderate Reform, not in sweeping away, one after the other, all the safeguards of personal liberty. The Great War of 1914 to 1918 has shown that it is quite possible, while waging war abroad, to carry out reforms at home. But it was not to be. Muir and Palmer in 1793 were tried with revolting cruelty in Scotland by the Lord Justice Clerk, Braxfield,[1] for advocating Parliamentary Reform and were transported to Botany Bay.

In 1794 the Habeas Corpus Act was suspended, so that Government could detain in prison without trial any suspected person. Thomas Hardy, the founder of the Corresponding Society, Horne Tooke and others were put on their trial for high treason (October). The doctrine of " constructive "[2] treason was pressed by Sir John Scott, the Attorney-General. " The conspiracy to assemble a Convention was a conspiracy to make the King govern with a new kind of Legislature—other than Parliament." By his coronation oath the King could not consent to this; therefore he must resist and such resistance must endanger his life, and therefore Hardy, Tooke, etc., had " compassed the death of the King."

The case of Hardy was taken first, and the eyes of all England were upon it. The Whig leaders such as Grey were of opinion that if Hardy was convicted their own lives

---

[1] Weir of Hermiston in Stevenson's novel.

[2] i.e. " construing " the Treason Act of 1352 so as to bring under it offences which did not come under its letter—in other words, straining it.

would not be safe. A wholesale proscription and judicial murder of political opponents—such as had disgraced the reign of Charles II—was, luckily for Pitt's reputation, prevented by Hardy's acquittal. The acquittal was a triumph for his Counsel, Erskine, who had to prove that the Convention was not an attempt to supersede Parliament *vi et armis*, but was merely an attempt to bring public opinion to bear on the action of Parliament. Tooke's trial had its humorous side. Tooke had sat with Pitt as a delegate in a " Convention " for Reform in 1782, and he now subpœnaed Pitt himself as a witness. The Government had seized a letter from Jeremiah Joyce, a friend and co-prisoner of Tooke, who had been tutor to Earl Stanhope's sons. The letter ran :

DEAR CITIZEN,

This morning at 6 o'clock citizen Hardy was taken away by order from the Secretary of State's office; they seized everything they could lay hands on. Query, is it possible to get ready by Thursday ?

yours, J. JOYCE.

This letter had been interpreted by the authorities to refer to a rising; but Tooke explained in court that it referred merely to a list of all the " places " held by the Grenvilles which was to be used to throw odium on Pitt and his relatives, friends and dependents.

Tooke was acquitted, and after one more failure the Government dropped the other prosecutions.

On October 27, 1795, a monster meeting was held in Copenhagen Fields under the ægis of the "Corresponding Society" denouncing the war and calling for Reform. Two days later the coach of the King, on his going to open Parliament, was hustled by a mob clamouring for peace and bread, and one of the carriage windows was smashed by a stone.

Taking advantage of this episode, Pitt hurried two Bills through Parliament.   Of these the Seditious Meetings Bill (to be in force for three years) enacted that no meeting of more than fifty persons should be held without the consent and presence of the magistrates, who, if they thought good, were authorised to disperse the meeting.

The Treasonable Practices Bill made it treason even to write or speak against the Constitution.   As Fox indignantly pointed out, " if he criticised a system which allotted two members to Old Sarum and none to Manchester, he might under the Bill be sent to Botany Bay."   These Acts led to a large decline in the numbers and activity of the Corresponding Society.   But the year 1795 closed in gloom. The harvest was bad and unemployment was everywhere increasing.

Such was the condition of England when Burdett entered the new Parliament of 1796.   As a young man he had shown his sympathy with the French Revolution by the verses he had written in 1791; and there is extant an early letter written by him to Coutts containing a rhapsody on Fox. Unfortunately there is no clue as to the place from which, or the exact time at which, it was written.   Its date may have been any time between 1793 and 1796.

F. Burdett to T. Coutts.   [Undated.]

" . . . Charles Fox's letter is the most interesting thing to me at the present moment; it is but this minute arrived, I was oblig'd to send to London on purpose for it & I believe it is the only one in the County; I dare not show it, for all my Freinds here are so extremely zealous that the very name of Charles Fox, that wonder of the age, whose mind is so superior to the times in which he lives, whose abilities & integrity will adorn the page of History when his opponents shall have sunk into everlasting oblivion, that great Man whom neither the threatening brow of power nor the mistaken zeal of his fellow-citizens could ever shake from his firm purpose, but halt, I perceive I am going to make a great oration, which is not my intention—however some warmth on the part of an honest & great man is surely excusable, especially at this time when no man seems to know who to trust; however, such as he is, he is the detestation of all the people I meet with, his very name is esteem'd sacrilege by the pious, who look upon him as past reclamation : in short ignorance & prejudice are his enimies, no wonder he has so few freinds."

In Parliament from 1796 to 1802, Burdett took his own line. He did not attach himself to the Whig Party, nor put himself under the leadership of Fox, for two very good reasons. First, the years 1797 to 1801 were marked by the secession of Fox and the Whig Party from Parliament; and secondly, Burdett was never a Whig, but in part a Tory, in part a Radical. No one will ever understand Burdett's career unless he grasps that fact. What he was opposed to was the " system " (of corruption), whether worked by Tories or Whigs. He stood outside the ordinary party allegiances, and at this time was far more Radical than the aristocratic Whigs. In the 1796 Parliament he was an uncompromising opponent of the " system " as worked by Pitt. The " secession " of the Whig leaders made it easy for him to come to the front. When the regular Opposition leaders retired from their task, this young free lance had the field to himself. He roundly denounced the war as an attempt to crush "Liberty" abroad and stifle "Freedom " at home. In this unjust estimate Burdett mistook effects for motives. The idea that Pitt entered on the war with the aid of despots to crush liberty abroad is no more true than Talleyrand's contention in 1814 that the aim of the war had been to restore " Legitimism," though it is true that the result was to restore many legitimate sovereigns and to repress Liberalism for a generation on the Continent. In

fighting French aggression Pitt had to use the instruments
ready to his hand—the despots of Russia, Austria, Prussia,
just as in 1914 England, in resisting Prussian aggression,
had to use the Tsardom. Similarly, it was not Pitt's
deliberate purpose to destroy liberty at home. " He goes
furthest who knows not where he is going." He felt
himself driven to repression by what he conceived the facts
of the situation. But this only means that he was a man of
ordinary judgment without any demonic flash of genius.

If the condition of England in 1796 was bad, that of
Ireland was far worse. That unhappy country was
centuries behind England in civilisation and was rent asunder
by every kind of division, religious, racial, social. By the
repeal of Poynings' and other Acts, a quasi-independence
had been given to the Irish Parliament in 1782. But from
no point of view was the settlement a success. The
Parliament represented a small dominant Protestant caste
and that alone. In 1793 to prevent the spread of French
sympathies, votes were given on a wide franchise to Roman
Catholics. But no Roman Catholic could sit in Parliament.
The Parliamentary system was even more corrupt than in
England. The Irish executive was not responsible to the
Irish Parliament, but was appointed from England, and the
Royal assent was only given to Irish Bills under the Great
Seal of England on the advice of the English Ministers.
The dominant Protestant Church was detested by the
peasants from whom it exacted tithes.

The first of the Irish to feel the influence of the French
Revolution were the Protestant nonconformists of Ulster,
who, with the Catholics, were equally opposed to the claims
of the Established Church. In 1791 Wolfe Tone, a free-
thinker of Dublin, founded the United Irishmen. His
scheme was to inaugurate a National Union of nonconformists and Catholics against the dominant caste and
Church. Agrarian evils gave impetus to the movement.
The avowed aim of the United Irishmen was to secure

Parliamentary Reform, the abolition of tithe, and the removal of agrarian grievances. But the peasantry were mostly Roman Catholic, the landlords were mostly Protestant. So the line of cleavage tended to become religious, Protestant *v.* Catholic. Matters drifted into civil war. The dominant Protestants organised themselves into " Orange " Lodges, while the Catholics organised themselves as " Defenders." When the United Irishmen saw that they could not secure their aims by their own power, they resorted to treasonable practices and despatched secret envoys to the French Directory. Of these the most notable were Wolfe Tone, Lord Edward Fitzgerald (a son of the Duke of Leinster and nephew of the Duke of Richmond), and Arthur O'Connor, whose elder brother Roger was a close friend of Burdett.

The French expedition, sent under La Hoche at the end of 1796, owing to a storm failed to effect a landing in Bantry Bay, but the situation was very critical at the time of the mutinies in the Fleet (May 1797). Luckily the mutinies were quelled in time, and a second French expedition was frustrated by Duncan's victory over the Dutch fleet at Camperdown.

Meanwhile the Corresponding Society had been quickened into new life, and negotiations proceeded between its members and the United Irishmen with a view to securing help from the French Directory.

On February 28, 1798, an Irish priest, O'Coigley, Arthur O'Connor, nephew of Lord Longueville, and Binns, a member of the Corresponding Society, were arrested at Margate in the act of embarking for France, and were put on their trial for high treason at the Maidstone Assizes, May 21 and 22. O'Coigley was found guilty and hanged on June 7. Arthur O'Connor and the other prisoners were acquitted, but Arthur O'Connor was immediately rearrested in Court on a new warrant from the Government. His acquittal was largely due to the fact that the

Whig leaders (Fox, Sheridan, Erskine, the Duke of Norfolk, etc.) went down to Maidstone and at the trial testified to his good character. This is Lord Holland's account:

" What passed at Maidstone exposed the Opposition to much calumny. Arthur O'Connor had without scruple summoned all his acquaintances in that party to speak to his character. From pardonable motives of humanity & friendship, they endeavoured to give the most favourable colour they could to his views & opinions about England, & they thereby exposed themselves to the imputation of being implicated in the plot, or at least accessory to the designs which he soon afterwards confessed."

It is noticeable that Burdett was not one of those called to testify on O'Connor's behalf. Perhaps with the reputation he had by that time acquired, it would have done the accused more harm than good. But O'Connor, during the week that he had spent in London before going down to Margate, had lived (with the exception of the last night) in Stratton Street, and Burdett took an active interest in his support, as can be seen from the following letter:

Sir F. Burdett to (Duke of Portland).[1]

Stratton Street
April 14, 1798.

My Lord,
     Having applied to the Privy Council for leave to see Mr O'Connor in order to procure him all those means of defence which justice requires, & which the Laws of the country intend & afford, & having been referred to the Secretary of State's Office, & from thence by Mr Wickham under Secretary of State to the Court, & having made the same application to Judge Buller, who declined doing anything in the business, as he said he had no power to give

---

[1] The Duke of Portland was Secretary of State.

any such permission, but that he conceived it lay in the breast of the Privy Council & that at all events the Secretary of State was the proper person to apply to, as he would lay it before the Privy Council in case himself should not have the power to grant the request. Under these circumstances I now apply myself to you for permission to see Mr O'Connor, being convinced that unless he is permitted to communicate with somebody in whom he can reasonably place confidence, it will be impossible for him to procure proper means for his defence, & his Tryal will be little more than a mere mockery; altho' this request appears so reasonable & such a request as cannot with any regard to Justice & Humanity be refused, & altho' it is neither fair nor fit that the Prosecutor shall be put in possession of the defence or means of defence of the Person accused, yet if the permission to see Mr O'Connor can be granted to me upon no other condition than that a Person appointed by the Prosecutor shall be present & a witness to all that passes between Mr O'Connor & myself, I ask to be permitted to see him under that condition.

I am, my Lord,
your most obedient servant,
FRANCIS BURDETT.

That Burdett's connection with O'Connor was notorious at this time is shown by Gillray's famous caricature (August 1798) of " The New Morality," in which Burdett is represented holding a placard with the inscription :

> " Glorious Acquittal
> Arthur O'Connor.
> Dedicated to Lady Oxford."

Meanwhile the flames of open rebellion had blazed forth in Ireland. Government, not having sufficient regular troops, largely employed the Orange yeomanry, and indescribable atrocities were committed on both sides.

Pitt had become convinced that a Parliamentary Union of Great Britain and Ireland was necessary ; and so he pushed on the Act of Union (1800), which was only carried in the Irish Parliament by wholesale bribery.

In the Parliament of 1796 to 1802 Burdett's maiden speech was delivered on the motion of Fox for conciliating Ireland (March 23, 1797). He attacked " the oppression of an enslaved and impoverished people by a profligate Government." He proclaimed his affection for Arthur O'Connor, then in prison on a charge of treason. " Good God, that treason to Ireland and the name of O'Connor should be preposterously linked together, as he is capable of everything that is great generous and noble for his country's good." He rejoiced *à la* Chatham at Irish resistance, and demanded the impeachment of Ministers. In 1798 he again spoke on behalf of the O'Connors, who were under arrest once more.

If Burdett was not one of those called to witness to O'Connor's character at the Maidstone Assize, May 21 and 22, he was present and took part in the extraordinary riot that marked the end of the trial. Though all the accused were acquitted except O'Coigley, the judge directed that the accused should not be discharged. It was well known that Bow Street runners were present with a warrant for the arrest of O'Connor on a new charge. When the Bow Street runners moved forward, there was a concerted attempt to prevent the re-arrest. O'Connor had lightly jumped over the bar of the dock, and tried to escape by the door on the left leading to the Narrow Street of Maidstone. There was a scene of indescribable confusion,[1] many of the lights—it was an early hour of the morning— having been extinguished, but finally O'Connor was captured by the runners and brought back. Lord Thanet and a lawyer, R. C. Ferguson, were afterwards indicted as ringleaders in the attempted rescue. They were tried in

[1] For plan of court see Erskine's speeches.

the King's Bench on April 25, 1797, and convicted. Our knowledge of the part played by Burdett in the *mêlée* is derived chiefly from the evidence given by Sheridan in this latter trial. At the beginning of the riot Burdett was sitting with Sheridan in the box reserved for witnesses. When O'Connor had been frustrated in his attempt to escape, and was being brought back again, Burdett turned to Sheridan and said in a panic, " They will kill O'Connor," and thereupon he took a leap right over the heads of Counsel for the Crown on to the table in the middle of the Court. Sheridan in his evidence declared, " I saw very distinctly Mr. Ferguson stop Sir Francis and use some action saying, ' You had better keep away.' " Government had good ground to prosecute Burdett as a ringleader in the riot. Had it not been for the action of Ferguson, he might very easily have found himself in the dock with Ferguson himself and Lord Thanet. It is stated by Lady Holland in her journal that it was only owing to Coutts' influence with the King that Burdett was not included in the prosecution.

On May 26, 1797, Burdett supported Grey's famous motion for Reform. " Had there been a fair representation of the people," he said, " neither the war nor oppression at home would have been possible. The ancient Constitution has been undermined. . . . All our evils can be traced to CORRUPTION. . . . If monarchy cannot exist without Corruption, it must go. I prefer hard liberty to servile pomp."

On June 5, 1797, Burdett opposed the Bill for preventing intercourse with the mutinous ships, on the ground that such a step would only exasperate the sailors.

On January 3, 1798, and on November 11, 1800, he exposed the evils of excessive taxation. His chief ground of objection was that the money so raised was spent on " the prosecution of this disgraceful war and this infamous system of Corruption. Pitt has squandered the wealth and shed the blood and annihilated the liberties of the English people." He pointed out that taxation of the rich inevitably caused unemployment among the poor. " I would as soon put faith in an architect, who talked of laying an immense weight on the head of a column without increasing the pressure at the base, as in a financier who talked of depriving the rich of their wealth without injuring the poor."

On November 11, 1800, he pressed home the charge that scarcity and high prices were due to the millions squandered on the war and wholesale corruption. " In consequence of the great amount that has to be paid away in taxes, the cultivator has to raise the price of his produce, the place-man is forced to pay ten for what he before paid five, his salary is in consequence raised etc. . . . In short, after taking all the reductions from a man's income, very little remained applicable to a man's private use."

On June 13, 1798, Sir John Scott, the Attorney-General (his colleague in the representation of Boroughbridge), had brought in a Newspaper Regulation Bill. Its object was to fix responsibility on the *real* owners of newspapers. Burdett spoke for the freedom of the Press. " The Press like the air is a chartered libertine. . . . It behoves us to keep the Press free, to watch it with all the anxiety which a lover bestows upon his mistress—to be fearful lest the breath of Heaven should visit her face too rudely—to be a little blind to her faults and exceedingly kind to her virtues,[1] but at all events not to suffer the slightest attack upon her person."

Speaking on the Address relative to a Union with Ireland in April 1799, Burdett in bitter language denounced Pitt's scheme. " The word ' Union ' was applicable to the most opposite things; it might mean a union accomplished by a conviction in the minds of the Irish people of its advantages;

---

[1] Matthew Prior, " An English Padlock,"

" Be to her virtues very kind,
Be to her faults a little blind."

or it might mean a union effected by a mere hollow vote of a corrupt Parliament, seconded by military power. . . ." He thought Pitt " totally incapable of conciliating the people of Ireland. . . . a man who has insulted them beyond the power of forgiveness and injured them beyond the power of reparation."

There was one other person of whom Burdett fell especially foul in this Parliament, and that was Pitt's friend and supporter, Wilberforce, the enthusiast for the abolition of slavery. Wilberforce belonged to the familiar type of wealthy Evangelicals who try to combine the best of both worlds, living in extreme comfort at home : ostentatiously uniting with it religion and piety and withal very narrow-minded, the supporters of " accepted usages " and the " social order." Wilberforce had a blind eye to most evils other than slavery. Sensitive to the sufferings of slaves, he was not sensitive to the sufferings of Englishmen at home. The miseries endured by those incarcerated in English prisons left him cold. Burdett was inclined to mock at his " religion " and " piety." In his speech on the Habeas Corpus Suspension Bill (December 18, 1800) he said : " There were certain gentlemen in that House who took every occasion to make loud and strong professions of vital Christianity and Religion. If these gentlemen really believed what they professed ; if they sincerely believed in the interposition of Divine Providence to punish nations for the delinquency of their conduct, he would call their attention to the tremendous curse pronounced by the sub-limest of the prophetical writers against the Babylonian tyrant, because he had reduced cities to ashes—because he had deluged the earth with blood—but, what was more heinous than all the rest, because *he opened not the door of the prison-house.*"

On November 26, 1800, there was a scene in the House, when Wilberforce taunted Grey with " a strange uncouth and unnatural union with persons . . . disaffected to the

Government " (meaning Burdett). Grey stigmatised this statement as a " calumny," and demanded an explanation. Wilberforce shuffled, and Sheridan replied defending Burdett for what he had said. " He was at a loss to discover how Wilberforce, possessing as he did, for he said so himself, a vast deal of candour and charity and religion, could make charges which he could not prove and say that a man was improperly connected with others without stating who those others were."

Burdett said he looked on Wilberforce's calumny with sovereign contempt and reiterated his views. Tierney and Grey again asked Wilberforce for a direct answer as to whom he meant. Wilberforce once more shuffled, and Tierney invited the House to take action. But eventually, after some heated words, he withdrew his motion.

There were two other questions in this Parliament on which Burdett expressed his views. He opposed Lord Auckland's Bill to make adultery a misdemeanour and to prevent the marriage of guilty parties in a divorce suit. The Bill was not carried.

Another Bill concerned his friend, Horne Tooke. Humorously enough, Horne Tooke had been returned to Parliament by the influence of Lord Camelford for the rotten borough of Old Sarum, but his eligibility as a parson was challenged by Lord Temple. The matter was finally compromised, Horne Tooke being allowed to retain his seat, but parsons being declared ineligible for the future. Burdett defended the right of his friend, and incidentally the right of other parsons. " It was admitted that a clergyman could get rid of Orders by behaving himself improperly. Was then the only objection against the eligibility of a clergyman to sit in Parliament to consist in his not having rendered himself criminal ? "

On February 3, 1801, Pitt announced his intention to resign. He had not given a positive pledge to the Irish Catholics that Catholic Emancipation would accompany the Union, but he had certainly led them to believe that this would be the case. Finding himself "up against" the King's conscience, George III being convinced that assent to such a measure would be a violation of his Coronation oath, Pitt resigned (March 14, 1801), and Addington, the Speaker, at Pitt's suggestion, became Prime Minister. Pitt's enemies asserted that since peace was absolutely necessary, and he could not bring himself to "eat the dirt," he put Addington in, intending when the dirt had been eaten to resume office.   Certain it is that shortly afterwards —the reason assigned was the precarious sanity of George III—he gave the King a pledge that he would never again stir the question of Catholic Emancipation during the King's life.

Burdett was no more favourable to the new Ministry than to the old.   The Parliament of 1796 (now afforced by the presence of a hundred Irish members) was drawing to a close.   The Peace of Amiens had been signed (March 27, 1802), and Burdett, in a set speech of some duration (April 12, 1802), moved for an inquiry into the conduct of Pitt's administration.

"The time has at length arrived—when we may be permitted to make up our accounts of blood and treasure." He declared that the war had been provoked by Pitt and the "Crowned Plunderers, Austria and Prussia." The avowed aims of the war were the recovery of Belgium and the deliverance of Holland, though by many of Pitt's party it was swollen into a war for Religion, Social Order, and Civil Society, by which they meant Despotism. . . . But now Ministers say they have made a safe and honourable Peace.   How can a Peace be safe or honourable by which every object of the War has been abandoned? . . . But say for the sake of argument, this is an honourable peace.   If it is, why did we ever go to war at all?   Such a Peace could have been attained at any point.   Pitt is now content to receive from 'the child & champion of Jacobinism' as indemnity for the past and security for the future, Ceylon and Trinidad ! ! ! Every prognostication of Pitt had been falsified. He said that the war would be short; that France would be ruined by the issue of Assignats. He relied on the Emperor Paul—his Magnus Apollo—God's own soldier, yet for a barren rock in the Mediterranean he too fell off. . . . Every object for which the war was fought has been yielded by the Peace. But if the war has been uniformly unsuccessful abroad, Pitt has been uniformly successful at home in destroying Liberty. He has destroyed everything valuable in the Constitution. King, Parliament, the Prince of Wales, the Bank, the City, the Laws, everyone has suffered. ' My sounding steps,' he thought, ' will not be heard amongst the din of war.' It has been against the liberties and properties, the laws and Constitution, manners, customs and character of Englishmen that Ministers have fought." This was followed by a terrible indictment of the Irish Government, in which he accused its members of having " flogged, tortured, and massacred" the people of Ireland. " Can we allow all this to be washed in Lethe and forgotten ? "

He ended with words of true statesmanship. " If you wish for energy and exertion, you must not be out of love with democracy. If you want virtue you must give it motives. If you want patriotism, you must afford a *patria* by a fair government embracing and taking in the people, by restoring to the people their rights and giving them a fair representation in this House."

Burdett had the vision, which the great Prussian statesman Stein had in 1807, when he transformed Prussia and gave its people something, *i.e.* a *patria*—worth fighting for.

Earl Temple, in reply, characterised Burdett's speech as " the most extravagant ever uttered within these walls, much better fitted for a tavern audience than the House of Commons."

But even if Burdett's language had been sometimes

extravagant, his view of the situation was substantially correct. How could the Peace of Amiens be regarded as safe and honourable? Where was Pitt's boasted aim of security, when the Low Countries (the cause of the war) were left in French hands, and the cannon was pointed at London from across the narrow seas ?

Apart from these more general issues there was one question in particular that Burdett made his own in this Parliament, thereby arousing the bitter antagonism of Government, and that was the condition of prisoners in Cold Bath Fields Prison. It was largely on this question that he fought his election for Middlesex in 1802, which must be described in another chapter.

CHAPTER IV

IF mutiny can ever be justified, that of the Fleet at Portsmouth in 1797 had many justifications. The pay and pensions of the sailors remained at the rate at which they had been fixed in the reign of Charles II, but there had been an all-round rise in prices, and the pay was therefore inadequate. The distribution of prize-money was also unfair, and the sailors complained of light weight in the supply of provisions and of the harsh behaviour shown towards them by certain officers. The mutiny, which broke out on April 15, was conducted with the utmost respect to authority, and on Government promising a pardon and increase of pay, the sailors returned to their duty on April 22. But owing to Pitt's delay in securing the immediate sanction of Parliament to the increased pay, there was a recrudescence of the mutiny on May 7. Trusting, however, to Lord Howe's assurance that Government would keep its promise, the sailors finally submitted on May 14. But on May 22 a more alarming mutiny broke out in the fleet at the Nore, and the mutineers were joined by a squadron of ships that had deserted Admiral Duncan's fleet blockading the Texel. It was more revolutionary in character than that at Portsmouth, and would have led to the subversion of all discipline. The mutineers closed the mouth of the Thames and seized ships laden with stores making for London. They ultimately quarrelled among themselves, and one by one the ships returned to their allegiance, the ringleaders being executed and many others imprisoned by sentence of court martial. Some thirty-

three of the mutineers were sent to the Cold Bath Fields
Prison in Clerkenwell.

This House of Correction had been built by the magistrates of Middlesex under the authority of an Act of Parliament and had been opened in 1794.

It is stated that certain of the prisoners had obtained some
paper, but as they had no other writing materials, they had
to use skewers as pens and tobacco juice or blood as ink
in order to inform their friends of their condition. Sir
Francis Burdett was present at a dinner-party at which
several of these letters were produced by a gentleman who
was collecting money for the dependents of the imprisoned
men. Burdett, always sensitive to physical cruelty, determined to visit the prison to ascertain the facts for himself.
He paid three such visits—the first on November 28, 1798,
in company with Mr. Courtney, M.P., and Colonel Bosville;
the second at the beginning of December, and the third
on December 29, 1798, in each case accompanied by
another gentleman. On no occasion did he go alone. He
lost no time in bringing before Parliament the state of
things he had discovered.[1]

Apart from the case of the mutineers, on various
occasions when the suspension of the Habeas Corpus Act
was discussed Burdett had concerned himself with the
treatment of persons detained on mere suspicion. On
December 21, 1798, he cited the case of " the Manchester
men, dragged from their families and homes on April 10
on mere suspicion, exposed to the derision of crowds,
loaded with irons and taken to Town, where they were
lodged in Cold Bath Fields. From the effects of travelling
in this state, their legs were very much swelled, and the
knocking off the irons was a very painful operation. After

[1] Prof. Coupland, "Life of Wilberforce," p. 432, is wrong in
stating that it was Sheridan and the Whigs who pressed for an inquiry
into the prison. For one thing most of the Whigs had seceded from
Parliament. It was Burdett who headed and maintained the attack;
Courtney was his assistant, and Sheridan gave some help.

an examination by the Privy Council they were put into separate cells and for eight weeks were starved on bread and water."

Wilberforce distinguished himself on this occasion by saying he had been to the prison, and everything was all right.

There was one man detained on mere suspicion whose case was specially debated in December 1798 in the House of Commons. That man was Colonel Despard. In our estimate of his treatment at this time we must ignore the fact that subsequently in 1802 Colonel Despard entered into a mad plot and was executed for high treason. He was in 1802

> " A man
> Whom the vile blows and buffets of the world
> Have so incensed that he is reckless what
> He does to spite the world."

But in 1798 Despard had a thirty years' record of honourable service in the army behind him. On March 12 he was arrested on suspicion of treasonable practices and confined a close prisoner for ten days, but was then released. On April 22 he was rearrested on a warrant from the Secretary of State (the Duke of Portland) and was committed to Cold Bath Fields Prison. For seven months he was confined to a damp cell, seven feet square, without either fire, candle, chair, table, knife, fork, or glazed window and without any book to read. Till July or August he never was allowed to see his wife except through an iron gate. After November 1, he was allowed to see her in the porter's lodge, but in the presence of turnkeys and others, and it was only after November 25, when his legs, according to his wife, were ulcerated with frost, that, on the intervention of the Hon. Valentine Lawless and Mr. Reeves, a magistrate, he was removed to a room that had a fire.

On December 21 his case was brought before the House

of Commons by Mr. Courtney. "... Among the prisoners at Cold Bath Fields I saw a gentleman, with whom I was acquainted above thirty years ago; an officer distinguished in the Service and amiable in his character and manners—I mean Colonel Despard. He was confined till November 25 in a solitary cell, where even his wife was not allowed to visit him. . . . These cells are so cold that at this season of the year it is scarcely possible to exist in them. The cold may in some degree be tempered by closing the wooden shutters : but if the unhappy prisoner wishes to be cheered by the air and the light of Heaven, he must admit the rain and chilling blasts of winter at the same time. . . . It is scarcely necessary to inform the House that the prison of which I have been speaking is that which is commonly called the Bastile. Do gentlemen doubt it ? I can assure them it is known by that name. When I took a coach in Oxford Road, I desired the coachman to drive me to the Bastile. 'Very well, sir,' was the answer. Being curious to know whether he really understood, I said, 'You know it, then.' 'Oh, yes, I know it : everybody knows the Bastile in COLD BATH FIELDS.' . . ."

Mr. Courtney was supported by Burdett in his declaration of sympathy against this oppression.

When Burdett went for a fourth time with Lord Hervey to visit the prison on January 2, 1799, he was refused admission. The Duke of Portland, then Secretary of State, had written the following letter to Lord Titchfield, Lord Lieutenant of Middlesex, and *mutatis mutandis* to the Sheriffs of London and Middlesex.

"Information given upon oath before a Magistrate by the Keeper of H.M.'s Prison in the Cold Bath Fields having been transmitted to me : from which as well as from verbal Representation that has been made to me on the same subject, it appears that Sir Francis Burdett, Baronet, having obtained admission into that prison had conducted himself when there in a manner that tended to affect the Discipline & good Government of the Prison & to give countenance & encouragement to prisoners confined therein under the sentence of the Law for the most heinous offence : I send your Lordship a copy of the Information above-mentioned, as well as a copy of the Letter I have written on this occasion, to signify His Majesty's Commands to the Gaoler, that *he on no account permit Sir Francis Burdett to visit the Prison* or to have access to any of the prisoners in his custody : & I am to signify to your Lordship the King's pleasure, that you recommend to the Magistrates for the County at their ensuing Quarter Sessions to make due enquiry into all the circumstances of this case."

Portland also wrote to the Governors of Newgate, Cold Bath Fields, and Tothill Fields prisons, ordering that Burdett should not have access to any of the prisoners.

In compliance with Portland's orders, the Middlesex magistrates in Quarter Sessions held an inquiry in January 1799. It is to be noted that the magistrates, as well as Aris, the Governor of Cold Bath Fields, were implicated in Burdett's indictment; for one of his charges was that the magistrates in their supervision had been grossly negligent. The results of their inquiry—with the depositions of Aris and other officials of the prison, together with the letters of the Secretary of State—were printed as a Parliamentary Paper and presented to the House of Commons on March 5, 1799. It was an *ex parte* statement. There can be little doubt that the aim of the Government was to bring Burdett within the meshes of the law, or at the least to represent him as the friend of mutineers and traitors. The Governor, the doctor, the clerk of the prison all asserted—obviously it was agreed among them—that the visits of Sir Francis had excited a turbulent spirit among the mutineers and others.

I have before me two hundred and ten folio pages of

SIR F. BURDETT VISITING COLD BATH FIELDS PRISON.
Caricature by Gillray.

letters and affidavits made by prisoners and others in the Cold Bath Fields Prison. It was the confident expectation of Aris that Sir Francis Burdett would be " caught out." He told Rance, a turnkey, on December 31 that he would have kicked Sir Francis out of the prison had he known what he now knew. He refused to let the mutineers have the tobacco left for them by Sir Francis. Both Aris and Ford the magistrate, it is alleged, wanted some of the mutineers to swear they knew Sir Francis at the time of the mutiny. The sailors were stripped to the skin to find evidence of their correspondence with Burdett. Aris is said to have told a prisoner named Oldfield that he was suspected of corresponding with Burdett, " who was no better than he should be. Burdett would not come there any more till he came a prisoner, which would be soon, for he was a damned rascal." Aris clearly knew that he had the support of Government behind him.

Burdett was not daunted. In December 1798 he had given notice of his intention to bring forward a motion concerning Cold Bath Fields Prison. But the Government anticipated him, for W. Dundas, a kinsman of a Secretary of State, made a motion on the day before that chosen by Burdett; and a Select Committee, presided over by Dundas, was appointed to investigate. Its report, presented to Parliament on April 19, 1799, was a general whitewashing of the prison. " The cells are dry and airy . . . the health of the prisoners has been generally good." Colonel Despard's grievances were minimised. The visiting magistrates were commended for their " laudable vigilance." But there was one reservation amid the general praise :

" Your Committee have however to remark that the printed regulations for the management of the prison have not been hung up in a conspicuous part of the prison, as is required by the statutes relating thereto; and that the journals of the prison, as directed by the regulations, have not been fully and regularly kept."

This report also was really an *ex parte* statement made by creatures of Government. How little attention was paid by Aris to their points of criticism will be seen a year later.

Burdett, in discussion upon the Report, complained of the manœuvre by which he had been forestalled :

" Sir, why all this anxiety to take out of my hands and to stifle any real enquiry into the practices of this prison ? How happens it that, as soon as I gave notice of a motion upon the subject, I am instantly held up to the world as an object of odium, stigmatised by a Secretary of State, my conduct condemned unheard, and without any examination even of those members of this House who accompanied me in my visit to the prison, and, by what legal authority I am still to learn, excluded from visiting any prison in England ? How comes it to pass that three hon. members who never before appear to have thought of an enquiry become all at once so very solicitous and hasty to move for a Committee of Enquiry ? Themselves perhaps can explain it. But I can explain the motive of the Minister and Secretary of State for wishing to prevent any real enquiry. Because a fouler premeditated system of iniquity never existed in any nation upon earth : and such, I trust, with the assistance of this House, I shall make it appear to the confusion even of those faces which are not accustomed to blush. The base and impotent attempt to criminate me I shall for the present pass over, contenting myself with barely stating that I visited the prison three times and should have visited it a fourth time in the usual and customary way by a written order from one of the Magistrates : that I never visited it alone : and that several gentlemen, some of them members of this House, can inform the House what my conduct was. Sir, I declare upon my honour that I never saw the face of any man in that prison, except Col. Despard, until the day I first visited the prison."

He went on to examine these "very extraordinary papers."

"*Aris* the Jailer acknowledges upon oath that he visits his prison with a stick in his hand: that he strikes his prisoners with stick and fist. He who has an absolute power over them to render their existence as miserable as he pleases cannot forbear personal violence with his own hands. He also swears that the prisoners have a plan to murder his son who locks them up and the doctor who so tenderly takes care of their health.

"*The Doctor* too swears that he believes they have a plan to do him mischief and that he does not dare to visit his patients 'without assistance, which he always takes with him.' What a tale is this to be told, by themselves too!"

"Sir, this is too important a subject to be shuffled over with so light an enquiry. I produce to you a monster, the infamy of whose existence will not rest with its original authors and systematical contrivers, but will extend to every Englishman, who shall not exert every effort in his power to put a stop to its continuance. This enormous collection of cells or stys (for they are fitter for beasts than men) contains within its walls, not only convicts of every description—convicts for different felonies—convicts by martial law for Mutiny—convicts for illegal lottery insurance—convicts for gaming—for obstructing custom-house officers and excisemen—for Libels; but it also contains debtors, vagrants, and paupers: to which are added persons detained for examination and reexamination, and persons in custody for trial; but stranger still, persons taken up on bare suspicion by the Secretary of State, some of whom have been kept there 12 months and may be kept there as many years, perhaps till death releases them, in a state of torture hitherto unknown in this country, without any crime, without any charge, without any trial, without any possible remedy: and not only persons suspected (or pretended to be suspected) in the Metropolis, but from every part of the realm—from Lancashire : perhaps shortly from Scotland and Ireland. All these persons of such different descriptions are intrusted to the care of the same man called a Governor, who lays all under contribution. Every article is turned to profit—the food, the fuel, the mattrasses, the beds, the apartments, the kitchen, even the hospital are all sources of profit to the Governor. From those prisoners who have anything he receives a weekly payment, and even those who have nothing serve the purposes of his avarice : for the example of the cruelties exercised upon them is motive sufficient to extort the last farthing from him who has one. He receives what he calls *TIP* from his prisoners, and presents from their friends for admission—he even borrows hundreds of pounds from his prisoners; for some of these sums he has been afterwards arrested; and I think even now (with my curtailed means of information) I should have no difficulty to prove that he has borrowed from his prisoners nearly £1000, how much more I know not. And what, Sir, if it shall be found that he even sells their bodies : and has therefore an interest to make them undergo such treatment as to render their condition insupportable and induce them to become soldiers and sailors—sure never to be in a worse condition.

" I am not now, Sir, barely stating what a man in such circumstances may be expected to do. I speak of what I aver he has done. I call for an enquiry into the horrid facts, and I offer proofs. I say that his means of extortion are, for his prisoners, dark cells, close confinement without exercise, without sufficient food, without warmth, without light, without cleanliness, without proper opportunities for their natural occasions, without intelligence given or received, debarred from books, pen, ink, paper,—their friends excluded. I say he keeps them hungry, cold, motionless, and heavily ironed. I say they receive from his hands and from his turnkeys blows and death by torture. . . .

" The wretched sufferers who survive have exhausted every other means of relief; they have petitioned the Admiralty, they have petitioned repeatedly the Secretary of State, they have petitioned the Magistrates, they have looked in vain to the piety of the Chaplain, and to the humanity of the Surgeon for compassion. They have in vain expected justice at least from the Coroner. Complaint in the Bastile is High Treason against the Governor, and as such it has been treated. Where an *intention* to complain has been even suspected, it has been cruelly punished with torture. Some have died under the punishment : some perhaps are now dying : and therefore I demand a speedy but not a short nor superficial enquiry."

Sir Francis moved that the Report should be re-committed, and was warmly supported by Sheridan; but his motion was rejected by 147 votes to 6. The verdict of posterity will be with the 6.

All these charges brought by Burdett against Aris and the prison officials are to be found in the two hundred and ten folio MSS. pages of letters and affidavits of prisoners, which Burdett bound. into a volume still extant. It would be absurd to accept all their assertions as *proven*—it is difficult to believe, for example, that a number of the sailors were thrown into irons *simply* for giving three cheers in honour of the Duke of Clarence's birthday—and it is to be remembered that the tradition of English prison administration was altogether evil.[1] It had always been the custom to give better accommodation to prisoners who could pay. And Aris was working a system thoroughly bad in itself. But there were ample grounds for instituting a thorough inquiry. Apart from the charge of corruption, the greatest

[1] Lecky, " History of England," Vol. VII, p. 331, " England ranked in most matters relating to the treatment of criminals shamefully below the average of the continent."

evil was the utter failure to classify the prisoners and differentiate the treatment accordingly. The convicted felon was often better treated than the man accused of no crime whatever. One of the prisoners who wrote to Burdett on December 19, 1798, took a sound line : " As to the merits of a defence set up in reply to the prisoners' complaints—that this is not a place of convenience & comfort—we proceed upon the ground that, *if it ought not to be a place of ease & comfort to felons, it ought to be nothing more than a place of security for Debtors, Paupers, Vagrants & every other description of persons whom the Law has not pronounced guilty*."

A further series of outrages enabled Burdett to press the case home against Aris for his cruelty and against the Middlesex magistrates for their criminal negligence. On July 22, 1800, he moved once more in the House of Commons for an inquiry into the management of the prison.

" It was stated," he said, " in the Report of the Grand Jury (of Middlesex) that the prisoners had not bedding enough for the summer season : what then must be the wretchedness of their situation in winter, shut up in a damp cell without even a fireplace ? . . . The case of Mary Rich was too shocking to be described. She was not even a person accused, much less convicted of any crime. She had been detained in the prison merely to give witness against a man who had tried to rape her, but owing to the unparalleled barbarity of her keepers she had become unable to do so. The manner in which these proceedings were justified added to their enormity. She lay naked, because her only rug had been taken to cover a woman in labour : she was stated to be a worthless girl, and to have said to a nurse, that she never would have complained, if the gentleman had given her the money he had promised. But was this nurse to be believed, who was one of the double-allowance prisoners, whom the Governor used well, that he might maltreat the rest with impunity ? . . . The justices concluded their report by saying that upon the whole Mary Rich appeared to them to have been properly treated. Did not this circumstance afford a damning proof of the negligence and insensibility of the magistrates? A scene of iniquity hardly to be paralleled was declared by 12 magistrates to be innocent and not to attach the smallest blame to the author. They had examined Mr. Aris; but was he the proper person to examine concerning his own atrocities, or the felony committed by his son? Why did they not examine the person from whom the silk handkerchief was stolen by the latter and those who were eager to give evidence of similar abuses? However, since they were of opinion that there was nothing wrong in the case of Mary Rich, it was probable they would declare the conduct of the Governor and his son to be immaculate."

Burdett having moved : " That an humble petition be presented to his Majesty praying that his Majesty would be pleased to give directions to cause an enquiry into the state and management of the prison in Cold Bath Fields," the motion was carried. This was a triumph for the mover; and so were the findings of the Commission appointed. As a whole, these gave a triumphant vindication of Burdett's attack on the administration of the prison. Among other things the Commissioners reported :

That no provision had been made for warming the rooms or cells in cold and damp weather as directed by the Act of 1799.

That the regulations for the management of the prison had not been submitted to the judges of Assize as directed by Act of Parliament nor were they hung up in any part of the prison. That as prisoners could avoid the prison dress, if provided with clothes by friends, the intentions of the Legislature that prisoners should wear a uniform to humiliate the wearer, and make escape difficult, were wholly frustrated (" we cannot but observe in these powers to dispense a motive to corrupt and a temptation to be corrupted "). That the journals and accounts of the prison had been very irregularly and incorrectly kept.

That the better rooms in the prison were assigned to prisoners who could afford to bribe the Governor who had " been sometimes tempted beyond what he had had the fortitude to resist."

That there had been overcrowding in the prison, and in many cases two people had lived and slept probably without separate bedding in a space adapted only for one—that persons not yet convicted, but detained on suspicion were improperly treated—that there was no proper classification of prisoners. (" In the present state of this prison we do not hesitate to pronounce it an improper place of confinement for those several descriptions of unconvicted prisoners : nor indeed, until its discipline, regulations, and arrangements shall have undergone considerable alterations, can we consider it as much less improper for persons convicted of misdemeanors.") That the food given to those detained on suspicion was inadequate and inferior to that given to convicted prisoners. They blamed the irregular facility with which the punishment of refractory behaviour had been inflicted. As to Aris, they reported that many charges of peculation and of accepting bribes had been brought against him which ought to be investigated by a court of law competent to take evidence on oath.

When Burdett's career is surveyed it should not be forgotten that the first conspicuous action of this rich young man in Parliament was to secure elementary concessions to justice and humanity for the oppressed.

A Photograph of Ramsbury.
By the kind permission of " Country Life."

CHAPTER V

SOCIAL SURROUNDINGS AND LADY OXFORD

It has been already noted that by the death of Sir Robert Burdett, the fourth baronet, on February 15, 1797, Francis Burdett succeeded to his grandfather's baronetcy and to the Burdett estates in Derbyshire and elsewhere. His mother's sister, Lady Jones, died in the spring of 1800, and on her decease he inherited the whole of the Ramsbury estate. Under the terms of her will he was compelled to take the name of Jones, and for a few months in 1800 he was known as Sir Francis Burdett Jones, but he quickly reverted to the style of Sir Francis Burdett. In 1801 he must—quite apart from his wife's fortune—have been a wealthy landed proprietor, owning two noble family seats—Foremarke and Ramsbury.

The existing house at Ramsbury is a perfect and unspoiled specimen of a late seventeenth-century building, and the large gateway is of the same date. The house has been generally assigned to John Webb, pupil and kinsman of Inigo Jones, as architect, but Mr. Tipping [1] has given reasons for believing that the work is somewhat later, and belongs to the generation in which Wren and Grinling Gibbons were supreme. The house is beautifully situated in a well-timbered park, with gardens which run along the banks of the Kennet, artificially widened and spanned by a bridge. The grounds rise from the river to woodlands which on the south march with Savernake Forest. Some

---

[1] See *Country Life* of October 2, 1920. For the history and illustration of Ramsbury, see *Country Life*, August 10, 1907, and October 2, 1920. I am indebted to *Country Life* for leave to reproduce the photograph of Ramsbury.

79

of the timber was cut down by Sir Francis Burdett to help in the payment of his expenses for the Middlesex election (1802–1804), but there is to-day no lack of stately trees. In the interior there is carving by Grinling Gibbons. There are Adam mantelpieces, and Lady Jones is said to have added much of the Chippendale furniture. The stables in the Park, as at Foremarke, are a characteristic feature and illustrate the tastes of seventeenth- and eighteenth-century squires.

When in London, Burdett lived with his father-in-law at 1, Stratton Street, and here he must have been brought into contact, direct or indirect, with those who lived in the highest social circles.

The Prince of Wales would come " to make his bow " at dinner. The Duchess of York would invite the party to Oatlands. The Duke of Clarence and the Duke of Kent (when he was at home) were on intimate terms with Thomas Coutts. Mrs. fitzherbert, the injured " wife " of the Prince of Wales, wrote confidential letters about her troubles and called at Stratton Street. So did Augusta, the morganatic wife of the Duke of Sussex. Here are some hitherto unpublished letters :

Prince of Wales to Mrs. Coutts.

[Undated.]

DEAR MRS. COUTTS,

I find much to my regret that I shall not have it in my power to make my Bow to you & your aimiable family at dinner this day; all I hope & trust to is that you will allow me when I return to Town to avail myself another day of the pleasure of waiting upon you. May I beg of you to present my best compliments to Mr Coutts. I have the honour to subscribe myself,

dear Madam,
very sincerely yours,
GEORGE P

Carlton House.

Frederica [1] *Duchess of York to T. Coutts.*

8 March, 1793.
Oatlands.

I return you many thanks, Sir, for your letter & kind enquiries; my health is much better than I could have expected & the hopes I entertain of the Duke's speedy return (which I hope will not prove fallacious) contribute much towards its not being so; I beg you will believe that I am very sensible of your attention & good wishes towards the Duke & myself. . . .

I hope that when the season is further advanced, Mrs Coutts & your daughters will do me the pleasure of coming here some day to dinner. I shall be happy to see them, & I think they will be pleased with this place, which in summer is really worthy of notice.

I am Sir with great esteem,

your affectionate servant,

FREDERICA.

D. of Clarence to Thomas Coutts.

14 Nov. 1794

DEAR SIR,

I must acknowledge the receipt of yours of 9th instant. My only motive for not having informed you of the particulars of the sale of Petersham is my ignorance. I know the terms are advantageous to myself, & I will make Robinson give you an account of the proceeding. I cannot upbraid your daughters preferring the country to

[1] Frederica was the daughter of Frederic William II. of Prussia, and married the Duke of York in 1791. Her chief amusement lay in pet dogs. She died in 1820, and is buried in Weybridge Church (cf. "Croker Memoirs," Vol. I, p. 122). "The Duchess of York's life is an odd one—she seldom has a female companion. She is read to all night, and falls asleep towards morning, and rises about three; feeds her dozens of dogs, and her flocks of birds, etc., comes down two minutes before dinner, and so round again." Cf. also "Greville Memoirs," Vol. I, p. 5.

Town, for I am entirely of their opinion, & as Mrs Jordan is gone with child more than 6 months, she is sometimes fatigued & consequently cannot play so often.

As I ever respected the abilities of Lord Landsdowne, I am happy to hear such an account from you of him : the others [1] are very violent indeed.   Relative to your sugges-tion to me, my dear friend, respecting the Prince's house-hold, I cannot but think that as you are in the habit of writing to the Prince yourself, & as I cannot do you the justice you can yourself, you had better write to the Prince & explain your motives & reasons.   I am sure he will not take it ill.   My best wishes and compliments attend Mrs Coutts & your fair daughters, & ever believe me to be, dear Sir,

yours sincerely,

WILLIAM.

D. of Clarence to T. Coutts.

Bushey House [2]

18 Oct. 1797

DEAR SIR,

I am to acknowledge the receipt of yours of 15th inst. & in answer to which I must observe that nothing can give me greater pleasure than being considered from Birth, Education, & Character a genuine Englishman of the old stamp.   I therefore rejoice from the bottom of my heart at the glorious success of Admiral Duncan.[3]   I wish this propitious event may render the Directory inclined to treat upon fair & honourable terms, I am confident the French will be fully employed by the Emperor tho at all times I laugh at the idea of invasion.   I feel exceedingly your kind wishes, & the interest your family take in my

---

[1] *i.e.* the Whig leaders, Fox, etc.

[2] On the death of Lord North (Prime Minister, 1770–1783) the Duke of Clarence had bought Bushey Park.

[3] The Dutch fleet was crushed at Camperdown, October 11, 1797.

welfare. I lament the state of health of Lord Guilford, who, I believe to be an aimiable & good man.

Mrs Jordan is getting both fame & money; to her I owe very much, & lately she has insisted on my accepting four & twenty hundred pounds, which I am to repay, as I think proper. I am concerned to hear the Dutchess of York is so delicate : if the Duke will take care of himself, he may still recover.

My best wishes & compliments attend Mrs Coutts & your worthy family & believe me to be, dear SIR

yours sincerely.
WILLIAM.

D. of Clarence to T. Coutts

Bushey House
9 Dec. 1797

DEAR SIR,

I must acknowledge the receipt of yours of 5th instant, in answer to which I cannot help observing I think your observations relative to the taxes & the return of peace highly judicious; in my private opinion, the French not being able to do anything against this country will be obliged to make peace upon our own terms. As for Ireland, believe me, force only will do, & force will bring that deluded country to reason, provided the French do not effect a landing, of which I do not see the least danger if we are vigilant.

Mrs Jordan's indisposition has been miscarriage. She is now better & will, I hope, follow your advice, which is the advice of prudence & discretion; she desires her best compliments.

My good wishes attend Mrs & Miss Coutts & particularly at this season of festivity. As for you my good friend, I trust I need not say much, as by this time you are acquainted with my sincere regard & esteem.

In the meantime, adieu, & ever believe me, dear Sir,

yours sincerely,
WILLIAM.

Thomas Coutts was in correspondence not only with the royal princes, but also with their morganatic wives. The first of these was Mrs. fitzherbert.

Maria Anne Smythe, born in 1756, married first, in 1775, Edward Weld of Lulworth Castle and secondly, in 1778, T. fitzherbert, who died 1781. She had no child by either marriage. Rumours were current in 1785 that the Prince of Wales intended to marry her. But there were two fatal objections to the proposed union : (1) By the Act of Settlement (1701) the Prince would forfeit the Crown if he married a Roman Catholic; (2) by the Royal Marriage Act (1772) he could not marry till he was twenty-five, without the King's consent.

Fox in a letter dated December 10, 1785, pointed out to the Prince the perils in which he would involve himself by such a marriage. The Prince, in a disingenuous reply, led Fox to believe that no such marriage was contemplated; yet four days later, on December 15, 1785, Mrs. fitzherbert in her own house was privately married to the Prince by the Rev. Robert Burt (rewarded with the Vicarage of Twickenham). The witnesses to the ceremony were her brother, John Smythe, and her uncle, a Mr. Errington. The papers proving the fact were at a later date (1833) deposited in Coutts' Bank, and only opened in the reign of Edward VII. They were transferred to the archives at Windsor Castle in 1905. Fox, on the strength of the Prince's letter, had on April 30, 1787, in the House of Commons absolutely contradicted the truth of the report of the marriage " in point of fact as well as law," saying that he had " direct authority " for the denial. A few days later he learned the truth. Mrs. fitzherbert was naturally furious at this attack on her honour, and she never forgave Fox. The Prince was in a dilemma. He sent for Charles Grey, confessed to the marriage ceremony, and asked him to say something in the House of Commons which " for the satisfaction of Mrs. fitzherbert might take off the effect of Fox's declaration."

MRS. FITZHERBERT.
From the unfinished painting by Thomas Gainsborough. By kind permission of Mrs. Alfred Noyes.

Grey refused, and the Prince fell back on Sheridan. But on February 7, 1789, both Grey and Sheridan categorically denied in the House of Commons the truth of the rumour that the Prince had gone through a form of marriage with Mrs. fitzherbert. Fox was absent from illness, but Grey committed him in his absence to the truth of his former statement.

The Prince at the time of the marriage ceremony had promised Mrs. fitzherbert £10,000 a year, but he was only able to give her £3,000 a year. On April 8, 1795, he married Caroline of Brunswick. From 1800 to 1810 he renewed his relations with Mrs. fitzherbert, who canonically was his true wife. Mrs. fitzherbert, who behaved admirably, was always treated with respect by the Royal Family. William IV wanted to make her a Duchess.

Here is a latter from her written shortly before the Prince of Wales' official marriage to Caroline of Brunswick.

Mrs fitzherbert to T. Coutts.

Grafton Street
16 Dec. (1794)

MY DEAR SIR,

I am afraid you will think me very negligent in having been so long thanking you for yr very kind letter, but the hurry & bustle I have been in, in being obliged to change my house has given me such employment that I have not had a moment to myself. I have been in Grafton Street about a week, & like the house I have got very much altho it has put me to many inconveniencies, as I was not only obliged to buy the Lease but the furniture, & as cash is by no means plentyfull with me. However I have managed it for the present by paying five hundred pounds down, & the rest I have given a bond for payable in three months which I wish I may be able to pay, for I am sure you will feel shock'd as well as myself when I tell you that no one step has been taken to secure me even the very small allowance I am now in possession of, nor does he I believe think it necessary I should have an existence; from feeling I had a right to have some provision made I took the advice of some of my friends & wrote him a letter upon the subject, thinking it would be proper to settle this matter before the Princess of Brunswick came to England as after that period it might have appeared indelicate my working on any subject. It is now ten days since my letter has been received, & I have had no other answer than a verbal one to say *he shall not answer it*. He must be very ill-advised to behave in this manner considering everything that has passed & instead of irritating me & adding insult to injury he ought if it was only for his own credit endeavour to conduct himself better. I feel I am getting angry, & therefore I will drop this odious subject. It is only to you my good friend I speak so plainly, for I assure you however poignant my own feelings are upon this subject as well as every other that concerns him, I am perfectly silent, & tho it is a hard task I think I shall feel more comfortable hereafter. At least I shall have the approbation of my own conscience & heart in knowing however provoked I have never said or done anything to injure or hurt him. I wish to god you were coming to Town, it would be a great satisfaction to me to see you, & I think you cannot stay much longer where you are. Pray let me hear from you soon & tell me when I may expect you.

I hope Mrs Coutts has got the better of her cold & that the rest of your fireside are quite well. Pray remember me most affectionately to them all & excuse me having bored you with this tiresome scrawl, but I know your good heart feels for me. I know I am safe in communicating my distresses to you. In my next I will be more entertaining, but I am very nervous today & good for nothing, therefore the sooner I release you the better. Pray let me have a line from you & believe me always my Dr Mr Coutts,

yrs very sincerely & faithfully,

M. f.

George IV had the effrontery in 1825 to deny to Croker that he had ever married Mrs. fitzherbert. The evidence on the matter is overwhelming and the whole of his conduct can only be stigmatised in language which respect for the Crown forbids me to use.[1]

Mrs. fitzherbert's letters to Coutts sufficiently characterise her royal lover :

Mrs fitzherbert to T. Coutts.

36 Pultney Street
Bath.
[? 1796 ? 1797.]

My Dear Sir,

A thousand million of thanks for two very kind letters I have received from you. The last you were so kind as to write I got only yesterday & was very sorry I was not in Town when you were so good as to call in Grafton Street. I arrived here last Wednesday. I had intended being here some time ago but was prevented on account of company here, who as I was not particularly anxious to meet made me defer my journey, till I knew the coast was clear. The Duke & Duchess of York leave this place to-morrow, they are very popular here & very much liked. I own honestly to you I am not sorry they are taking their departure, for I never wish to see or meet any of the family, & shall feel much more at my ease, tho they dont annoy me, as I came here purposely to see my mother who is in a very indifferent state of health, & I dedicate the whole of my time to her. She desires I would remember her most kindly to you & Mrs Coutts.

Pray tell Mrs Coutts from me I hope she is now quite well & satisfied having all her daughters with her & she dont want me to scold her & preach to her. I quite envy the happiness of your fireside. Pray give a thousand loves to them all from me. I hope to see Dr Lady Guilford when

[1] See " Mrs. fitzherbert," by Wilkins; Trevelyan's " Lord Grey of the Reform Bill," p. 18 ff.

I return to Town, for we have never met since she was
married,[1] which I have often regretted.

A thousand gratefull thanks attend you My Dr Sir for
your kind anxiety about me. I will do what you desire
about signing their absurd paper whenever I get it. This is
the first time that I have not been punctually paid, & God
knows when they will think proper to let me have any
money. One grievance never comes alone, for another
person who has always been the most punctual person in
paying me money that is due to me has had two or three
paralitick strokes & is incapable now of transacting Business, & I cannot get a farthing, & if the others dont pay
me soon you will hear of me being arrested & sent to a
prison. If that should be the case pray have a little compassion & come & see me.

Believe me my Dr Sir

your most obliged & affectionate

M. fitzherbert.

A later glimpse of this lady appears in the correspondence.
On January 6, 1831, Sir Francis Burdett wrote to his
daughter Sophia, Mrs. Trevanion, from Brighton :

" I miss you much here & Trevanion too, your absence
quite breaks up our party. We were at the Pavilion the
night before last, the King & Queen very kind, the apartments splendid, & Mrs fitzherbert looking handsomer than
anyone. The Queen was very particularly attentive to
her. Indeed she merits it, in every point of view."

This is the more notable because Queen Adelaide was a
pattern of propriety and perhaps had even more than
Victoria to do with establishing the " Victorian " standards
of social censure.

Mrs. fitzherbert died at Brighton in 1837.

Next comes Lady Augusta Murray, the second daughter

---

[1] Lady Guilford was married February 28, 1796.

of the fourth Earl of Dunmore; she was married to the Duke of Sussex at Rome on April 4, 1793, by an Anglican clergyman named Gunn, and the marriage ceremony was repeated on December 5, 1793, at St. George's, Hanover Square. A son was born on January 13, 1794, but the marriage was disallowed by George III in August 1794 as contrary to the Royal Marriage Act of 1772. In January 1804 a Bill was filed in the Court of Chancery by Lady Augusta against the Duke of Sussex and T. Coutts, asking that Coutts might be restrained by an injunction of the Court from paying the Duke of Sussex a sum of £4000 per annum, part of an annual pension of £12,000 settled upon the Duke; which sum of £4000 had been settled by deed upon Lady Augusta for the education and maintenance of the children she had by H.R.H. There were difficulties raised by the Court. But on March 19, 1806, Farington writes : " The Duke of Sussex is on the point of making an arrangement with Lady Augusta Murray." A smaller settlement was made on Augusta. " He takes the son and proposes to place him at Winchester School, but the daughter, which he does not believe to be his, he leaves with Lady Augusta."

In 1806 Lady Augusta by royal licence assumed the name of d'Ameland. The children took the name of d'Este. The son, Sir Augustus Frederick d'Este, filed a Bill in Chancery in 1831 to prove his rights as a Royal Prince, and the marriage of his father with Lady Augusta valid. He put in all his father's love-letters to his mother, and contended that the Royal Marriage Act did not apply to marriages contracted outside English jurisdiction.

On the death of the Duke of Sussex in 1843, his claim to succeed to the Dukedom was disallowed by the House of Lords. He died unmarried in 1848.

Of Lady Augusta, Farington (" Diary," Vol. II, p. 274) in 1804 says : " She has a very singular-shaped face. The lower part from the nose, falling as if shaved off—her sister still more plain. I thought them coarse, and confident-looking women. She has entered herself in the subscription-book at Ramsgate ' *Duchess of Sussex.*' We saw her son, a fine boy of eleven or twelve years of age seemingly, and very like the Royal Family. He is said to be called the ' Prince.' "

Lady Augusta was painted by Romney.

The Duke of Sussex subsequently married Lady Cecilia Underwood, daughter of Lord Arran, and widow of Sir George Buggin, afterwards created Duchess of Inverness by Queen Victoria.

Lady Augusta (d' Ameland) to T. Coutts.

June 30, 1796.

My dear Sir,

You are so good that I know you will forgive me for troubling you, & I will not apologise for doing it, but immediately tell you my present distresses. My situation far from being meliorated is every day growing worse. I have not seen one single Guinea since I last spoke to you; according to your advice I wrote to Mr Pitt & received no answer. I expect every day to be taken to prison; this morning I received the enclosed letter from my landlord. Pray do me the favour of showing it to Mr Long, & pray ask him what I am to do, & when I may hope to receive money. Do have the goodness to tell him, that I shall esteem it a very particular favor to know whether Mr Pitt will take into consideration the content of my letter & whether I may hope for the *speedy & effectual* relief promised me by the Chancellor. My dear Sir, you have acted towards me with the kindness of a father, therefore wonder not at my depending on your goodness not only to pardon this, but to exert yourself in my favor : & pray believe me with the sincerest esteem your much obliged

obedient servant

Augusta.

Do pray see Mr Long, shew him my letter, & tell me what hopes I may entertain, for really I am beyond conception miserable.

Another letter from the same lady of a much later date may be appended here :

Lady Augusta d'Ameland to T. Coutts.

Arklow Place
Cumberland Gate
Sept. 16, 1816.

MY DEAR MR COUTTS,
     I signed on Saturday with very great pleasure & gratitude the Deeds on which your goodness has so aimiably lent me the £800.   I assure you, my dear Mr Coutts I very sensibly feel your kindness, & thank you for this last proof of friendly regard with heart-felt gratitude.   It now seems difficult to understand how I can, while basking in the sunshine of such recent generosity, wish to extend its effects further, & ask a new & almost greater favor.   But I will tell you how this happens.   Tho' I know how to appreciate all you have done for me, yet I can wish you to do more because I would then be solely dependent upon you—a man who acts as Father, Friend, or Brother is a safe reliance.

In your last letter you asked me what had become of the Title Deeds belonging to the purchase of my house in Arklow Place.   It then first occurred to me, that Mr Cooper had given them to a man whose name I dont even know, as his security for the loan of £2000, a man of whom I know nothing, & to whom I pay besides £200 a year.   Were I to die before this £2000 were paid, my son might be cheated out of the property, nor could I tell him where to apply.

I mentioned this to Mr Dickie the other day, & asked him if he thought you would be angry were I to state to you that I wished very much all these papers were safely lodged in your possession; he said, Certainly, such a thing was very

desireable & advised me to write to yourself, my wishes &
my motives.

Now really, my dear Mr Coutts, it is very possible these
Title Deeds may not be safe in the hands of their present
possessor; besides my House cost me more than £8000—
I have been offered twelve for it—& this man, (who I
believe is an Attorney) may put difficulties in the way of
returning the Deeds, should I die while he continues to
hold them.   It is these considerations that supersede my
feelings of seeming ingratitude, while I ask more of him
who has already done so much; but, my dear Mr Coutts
refuse me, if you disapprove of my adding this request to
the others.   It cannot alter the sentiments with which I
acknowledge your past kindness, nor the affectionate love
with which I am your much obliged & grateful

etc. etc.
AUGUSTA.

There were all kinds of other visitors at Stratton Street :
for example, the famous Georgiana Duchess of Devonshire,
who lived till 1806.   Among the intellectual friends of
Coutts were John Home, the author of " The Tragedy of
Douglas," his old school-friend Caleb Whitefoord, wit and
art-collector, and Henry Fuseli, the Swiss painter (R.A.
1790), who seems to have spent a large part of his time at
Stratton Street and to have sold to Coutts many of his weird
pictures.

On September 17, 1800, Frances (Fanny) Coutts, the
second daughter of T. Coutts, married John Stuart, first
Marquess of Bute.   It was in many ways a singular match,
as the Marquess was fifty-six years of age, a widower and
already the father of seven sons and two daughters, while
Fanny Coutts was only twenty-five.   But seemingly it was a
love-match.   Coutts wrote his account of it to La Comtesse
d'Albestroff, once the mistress of Charles Edward the
Young Pretender.   She was a pensionary of Coutts.

30 Dec. 1800.

London.

If you have not heard of it before, you will be surprised, I believe, to hear of my daughter Fanny having been married the 17th of Sept. to the Marquis of Bute. The match has been her own choice & fancy, entirely, & she continues to believe it will secure her happiness. If so I ought to be content, though I confess his age (56) appeared to me a great objection : & the marriage was by no means my choice or Mrs Coutts'. His Lordship is a well-bred & accomplished man, with good talents & many good & aimiable qualities. He has also remarkable good health & looks younger than any of his brothers—even than the youngest, who was lately made Archbishop of Armagh, Metropolitan of Ireland. . . .

John Stuart was the eldest son of George III's Prime Minister (1761–1763). Born in 1744, he had married as his first wife (November 12, 1766) Charlotte Jane, eventually sole heiress of Herbert, Viscount Windsor and Baron Mountjoy. Horace Walpole writes, " Lord Mountstuart is married to a rich ugly Miss Windsor. . . . Lord Beauchamp is going to marry the 2nd Miss Windsor. It is odd that these two ugly girls through such great fortunes should get the two best figures in England " (December 1761).

It was through his first wife that Stuart inherited the great Cardiff property from the Earls of Pembroke. He accumulated great numbers of titles. From 1766 to 1776 he was Tory member for the family seat, Bossiney. On May 26, 1776, having acquired the Cardiff estates, he was created Baron Cardiff. He then entered the diplomatic service. He was envoy at Turin 1779–1783, and he supported the Fox–North Coalition of 1783 ; he was Ambassador to Spain (March to December 1783), and again at a critical period as Earl of Bute in 1795–1796 (his father having died in 1792).

In 1794 he had also succeeded his mother as Baron Mount Stuart and on March 21, 1796, he was created Viscount Mountjoy, Earl of Windsor, and Marquess of Bute.

These were not his only titles to fame, for he was made F.S.A. (1776), F.R.S. (1799) and a Trustee of the British Museum (1800). From 1794 till his death in 1814 he was Lord Lieutenant of County Bute.

To marry a man of so many titles and such great possessions was—as the world judges—a great achievement for Fanny Coutts. But nothing will get over the fact that he was a queer man. Nothing could be stranger than the letter he wrote to T. Coutts on February 4, 1800, within a week of his first wife's death, from Luton Park.

The letter begins by reference to certain confidential letters left by his wife to a certain Mr. Deare, one of which, by a breach of confidence, Mr. Deare had read to certain of the partners of T. Coutts & Co., while a second, addressed to the Bishop,[1] was opened by Lord Bute himself.

"I did not chuse the Bishop to see a letter though addressed to him without my first perusing it. . . .

"The world is to suppose matters very extraordinary where a wife is afraid to leave her last wishes in her own portfolio but has recourse to a stranger, & a stranger she abhorred. What will the Bishop say? I must by force put this letter into his hands, which I do not at all like. For my own sake & defence also it becomes expedient to confide the others to a friend. It would be natural to have recourse to relations. Mr Mackenzie,[2] but he is too old to be trusted. And as to brothers & sisters, My Friend, My Friend, they do not love me. Because a person is my near relation, it does not follow he should be my Friend.

[1] The Bishop is Lord Bute's younger brother, the Bishop of St. David's : made Archbishop of Armagh in December 1800.
[2] Mr. Mackenzie was Lord Bute's uncle, brother of the Prime Minister. On succeeding to property he had taken the name of Mackenzie. He died a very old man in 1800.

If he is, no tie to be sure is stronger. No. I will not open my mouth to my relations. I will talk to my real friend : in other words, My Dear Coutts, I will talk to you. . . .

"Here I must appear before you in a new character, a moral & a religious man, I believe you have hitherto formed little idea how much I am both. That two men, & one a clergyman, should live in common publickly & notoriously with the same woman [1] must shock everyone, but to my feelings is repugnant beyond the power of expression. I bear these men no ill-will, I will not however live with them. Yes. I am a very religious man. It is not the canting Puritanical religion of Lady Elgin [2] : the false hypocritical doctrine of Lord Hervey [3] : the silly weak Methodistical praying of Lady Macartney, the dangerous & bigoted zeal of Monsignor Erskine, [4] but a cheerful religion undisturbed by a bad conscience. The situation in which I stood with my daughter Charlotte [5] has kept me from the altar for three years, but now on my return to Town I shall certainly take an early opportunity of performing that solemn act of my belief with a pious &, I trust, a safe conscience. What, I wonder, will be your opinion of my mind after reading this, after noticing to yourself the unbounded confidence I have in you ? Will you think me better or worse ? For my own part I think I am better : roused & animated by these plagues the natural vigor resumes its wonted firmness, & I again bid defiance to the shock without the aid of Physicians or their tribe. . . .

[1] The clue is lost.
[2] Lady Elgin, wife of the fifth Earl of Elgin, and governess of the Princess Charlotte of Wales. She died 1810.
[3] Lord Hervey became first Marquess of Bristol, 1803.
[4] Monsignor Erskine (afterwards Cardinal), informal nuncio between England and the Vatican. A kinsman of the future Lord Erskine, and distantly connected with Coutts.
[5] Lord Bute's daughter Charlotte married in 1797 Sir William Homan and died his widow in 1847.

" Many thanks to Mrs Coutts for all the kind messages sent through you. I give them the completest credit, which is the strongest thing I can utter.

" As to Miss Coutts' unwillingness to write, it does not proceed from that but a charming part of her character, to which you & I are able to do justice. And let us say boldly to ourselves, it is not every Father, every Friend, who can, who know how to do justice. I mean the never-ceasing delicacy & propriety which distinguishes & graces the whole tenor of her conduct throughout."

Within eight months of his first wife's death Lord Bute married Fanny Coutts (September 17, 1800).

In 1802 the Coutts family circle was clouded over by the death of the infant Lord North (January 25) and of his father Lord Guilford (April 1).

Sir Francis Burdett cannot have been entirely at home in the *milieu* of Stratton Street. We have seen that in 1798 he was a great admirer of Fox; but he was far more Radical than Fox in his outlook, and on June 5, 1798, he was black-balled for membership of the Whig Club and denounced as a firebrand.

He was present at the celebrated dinner held at the Crown and Anchor (June 24, 1798) to commemorate Fox's birthday, when the Duke of Norfolk gave such dire offence to the Government by proposing " The health of our Sovereign—the Majesty of the people." [1]

In the mock account of this dinner given by the *Anti-Jacobin*, allusion is made to the unfortunate shyness that existed between the Whig Club and the Corresponding Society, and Burdett, who knew the haunts of the latter, is described as being despatched to Smithfield with dinner tickets for its members.

The fact was so. Burdett was in touch with people at

---

[1] The Government retaliated by dismissing the Duke of Norfolk from his position as Lord Lieutenant of the West Riding. When Fox repeated the toast at the Whig Club (February 6 and May 1) his name was struck off the Privy Council.

the very opposite end of Society from those with whom he associated in Stratton Street.   He was on familiar terms, for example, with the shoemaker, Thomas Hardy, secretary of the Corresponding Society, whom he supported by a pension for many years before Hardy's death in 1831. His acquaintance with that " consequential tailor," the radical Francis Place, dates from a few years later (1807). But he was in with many of the Extremists, and was still in 1802 a friend of Colonel Despard, and more than a mere friend of Roger O'Connor, the Irish patriot and traitor. Burdett's revolutionary fever reached its peak in 1803, when he was thirty-three.   From that point it declined.

His general outlook on life about this time was rather anarchic.   Since his return from France in 1791 he had constantly railed against the conventions of Society.   We have seen at the end of Chapter II his letter to Coutts, in which he had described marriage as " the grave of love " and asserted that all the ties of Society are calculated to obstruct human happiness.   I think this letter must mark the point at which he and Lady Oxford had yielded to each other's charms.   But this outlet to his nature possibly made him a more easy and companionable person at home.

Things did not even yet move altogether smoothly, for Eliza Burdett,[1] writing to her fiancé, James Langham, from her brother's house at Wimbledon, could still say, "This house does not afford the best example of conjugal felicity " (March 28, 1800).   But Sir Francis was soon to discover that even if marriage is the " grave of love," it is none the less the cradle of affection, and whatever his infidelities may have been, from this time onwards his letters show ever-increasing affection for his wife.

Something must be said about Lord and Lady Oxford. To all accounts they were an ill-matched pair.

Edward Harley, fifth Earl of Oxford, was born in 1773, and at an early age succeeded his uncle, the fourth Earl.

[1] Eliza Burdett, sister of Sir Francis, married James (afterwards Sir James) Langham on May 26, 1800.

In consequence of friendships formed at Oxford University, he quitted the Tory Party, to which his family since Queen Anne's reign had been attached, and for the greater part of his life was a steady Whig. He does not seem to have had any of the talents which would enable a man to rise from a lower to a higher class. He belonged to that class of men of whom, when they are gone

> " No one asks
> Who or what they have been."

But, if we are to judge from various protests he entered in the Journals of the House of Lords (1795–1798) against measures of Government, he seems to have been quite sensible. He was not, however, able to control the affections and the conduct of his wife. Jane Scott (*b.* 1772), whom he married in 1794, was the daughter of the Rev. James Scott, vicar of Itchin near Southampton, and chaplain to the King. She may have made the acquaintance of the Earl through her brother (afterwards her blackmailer), William Scott, who was the Earl's contemporary at Oxford. As pourtrayed by Hoppner, she must have been a beautiful creature. "Monk" Lewis wrote (? 1810), "Lady Oxford's long fair hair is the most beautiful I ever beheld; she is like one of Guido's fair Magdalens—that is to say in appearance." But she was a lady of easy virtue, and though she presented a number of children to her husband, the paternity of these children was so doubtful that, in the language of the "ton," they came to be known as "the Harleian Miscellany."

Burdett seems to have been her first, and Lord Byron her last lover.[1] For eight months in 1813 Lord Byron and

---

[1] The Radicals were taunted by the *Anti-Jacobin* for the freedom of their views about marriage, "that two-headed monster Man and Wife."

> " Of Whist or Cribbage mark th' amusing game,
> The partners *changing*, but the SPORT the same.
> Else would the gamester's anxious ardour cool,
> Dull every deal, and stagnant every pool,
> Yet must ONE man with one unceasing wife
> Play the LONG RUBBER of connubial life ? "

Lady Oxford were infatuated with each other, and it was touch and go whether they would elope. Finally Byron only went as far as Portsmouth, and in 1813 the Oxfords went abroad for several years.

Others reputed to have been lovers of Lady Oxford were Lord Archibald Hamilton and Lord Gower. The Duke of Cumberland was said to have been on too intimate terms in 1809. But throughout the whole period 1798–1813 Burdett was in the constant society of the Oxfords and from 1810 to 1813 they all formed part of the entourage of the unfortunate Princess of Wales—by then separated from her husband.

The Oxfords were travelling on the Continent from 1802 to September 1804. They visited Paris (1802), Italy (1803), Vienna, Dresden (1804), and returned to Eywood, Herefordshire, in September 1804. On this tour Henry Bickersteth (afterwards Lord Langdale, Master of the Rolls) acted as travelling physician to them (1803–1804). In Italy he met William Jones Burdett, brother of Sir Francis, and it was through Jones Burdett that he afterwards made that acquaintance with Sir Francis which soon ripened into an intimate friendship. In 1835 Bickersteth was united by closer ties to Lord Oxford, for he married one of his daughters, Lady Jane Harley.

From 1804 to 1813 the Oxfords remained in England, but in 1813 they again went abroad to Italy, making Naples their headquarters, where they were in close touch with Murat and his Court, but were seemingly very hard up. They remained there at any rate till December 1814. We read in Talleyrand's " Memoirs " (Vol. II, p. 504) that as Lord Oxford was passing through Paris en route to England he was on some pretext or other arrested, but no proofs were found on him of any conspiracy between him and Napoleon (December 1814).

We are told in the " Farington Diary," [1] on the authority of Aytoun the artist, that Lord Oxford's " mission to

178084   [1] Vol. VII, p. 276.

England was to obtain from the English Government a promise to support *Murat* as *King of Naples*."

Lady Oxford died on November 20, 1824, but Lord Oxford survived till December 28, 1848, dying in the house of his son-in-law, Lord Langdale.

Most of our knowledge of the Oxfords is derived from : (1) the Memoirs of Lord Langdale, but Lord Langdale, as married to a daughter, is very discreet. Everything he says redounds to their credit. Lady Oxford, as a devoted wife, hardly ever leaves her husband's bedside when he is seriously ill at Eywood in 1805, and Lord Oxford is said to be extremely popular in the countryside. In the "Farington Diary" (Vol. IV, p. 31) she is also represented as being very strict in the upbringing of her children. "Lady Oxford shews the greatest attention to the education of her children. She is constantly with them from 10 o'clock in the morning till 1 during which time they receive instructions. Lady Oxford never allows a book of any kind except such as she may have read and approved to lay in a room to which the children have access. Novels and such-like are not permitted to be seen." (2) The "Diary" of Lady Charlotte Campbell (Bury), which represents Lady Oxford as a wholly discreditable character, dragging down the Princess of Wales. (3) "The Conversations of Lord Byron." However great a poet Lord Byron may have been, he was no " gentleman " in his relations with women. In affairs of gallantry to " give away " a woman is unpardonable. Yet this is what he did. In 1813, under the spell of Lady Oxford's charms, he rejected the infatuation of Lady Caroline Lamb (the wife of the future Prime Minister, Lord Melbourne), and in Lady Blessington's "Conversations " (p. 255) he is reported as saying, " Even now the autumnal charms of Lady—— are remembered by me with more than admiration. She resembled a landscape by Claude Lorraine with a setting sun, her beauties enhanced by the knowledge

LADY OXFORD.
From a portrait by Romney in the National Portrait Gallery.

that they were shedding their last dying beams, which threw a radiance around. A woman is only grateful for her first and last conquest. The first of poor dear Lady ——'s was achieved before I entered on this world of care : but the last, I do flatter myself, was reserved for me, and a *bonne bouche* it was."

Again, in "Medwin's Conversations" Byron is represented as saying (pp. 93, 94), "There was a lady at that time, double my own age, the mother of several children, with whom I had formed a liaison that continued without interruption for eight months. The autumn of a beauty like hers is preferable to the spring in others. She told me she was never in love till she was thirty, and I thought myself so with her when she was forty. I never felt a stronger passion, which she returned with equal ardour. . . . She had been sacrificed, almost before she was a woman, to one whose mind and body were equally contemptible in the scale of creation : and on whom she bestowed a numerous family, to which the law gave him the right to be called father. Strange as it may seem, she gained (as all women do) an influence so strong over me, that I had great difficulty in breaking with her, even when I knew she had been inconstant to me, and once was on the point of going abroad with her, and narrowly escaped this folly."

A final tribute is paid to Lady Oxford by Uvedale Price in a letter to Samuel Rogers in 1824 ("Rogers and his Contemporaries," Vol. I, p. 397) :

"Poor Lady Oxford. I had heard with great concern of her dangerous illness, but hoped she might get through it, and was very grieved to hear that it had ended fatally. I had, as you know, lived a great deal with her from the time she came into this country (*i.e.* Herefordshire) immediately after her marriage, but for some years past, since she went abroad, had scarcely had any correspondence or intercourse with her, till I met her in Town last spring. I then saw her twice, and both times she seemed so overjoyed to see an old friend, and expressed her joy so naturally and cordially, that I felt no less overjoyed at seeing her after so long an absence. She talked with great satisfaction of our meeting for a longer time this next spring, little thinking of an eternal separation. There could not, in all respects, be a more ill-matched pair than herself and Lord Oxford, or a stronger instance of the cruel sports of Venus, or rather of Hymen—

> cui placet impares
> Formas atque animos sub juga ahenea
> saevo mittere cum joco.

It has been said that she was, in some measure, forced into the match; had she been united to a man whom she had loved, esteemed, and respected, she herself might have been generally respected and esteemed as well as loved; but in her situation, to keep clear of all misconduct required a strong mind or a cold heart; perhaps both, and she had neither. Her failings were in no small degree the effect of circumstances : her amiable qualities all her own. There was something about her, in spite of her errors, remarkably attaching, and that something was not merely her beauty. ' Kindness has resistless charms,' and she was full of affectionate kindness to those she loved whether as friends or as lovers. As a friend I always found her the same; never at all changeful or capricious. As I am not a very religious moralist and am extremely open to kindness, ' I could have better spared a better woman.' "

How and in what circumstances Burdett met Lady Oxford the records do not reveal. But the connection was in origin probably political. Lord Oxford and Burdett held similar views on Ireland. However that may be, in the famous cartoon of Gillray on the " New Morality " Burdett, Arthur O'Connor, and Lady Oxford are closely connected (August 1, 1798). Burdett is represented as holding a placard emblazoned with the words "Glorious Acquittal, Arthur O'Connor, dedicated to Lady Oxford." And in a further cartoon of the same year (December 13, 1798), referring to the substitution of a ten per cent. tax on income for the tripling of the assessed taxes, Burdett is represented as protesting, "Dam' me, if my Lady Oxford must not leave off wearing trousers, and take care of her little ten per cent." In 1801 the Oxfords had a house at Ealing, for we read in the "Creevey Papers" [1] of a curious dinner given by Lady Oxford: "Lady Oxford, who then had a house at Ealing, had by Lord Thurlow's [2] desire, I believe, at all events with his acquiescence, invited Horne Tooke to dinner to meet him. Lord Thurlow never had seen [3] him since he had prosecuted him when Attorney-General for a libel in 1774, when the greatest bitterness was shown on both sides, so that the dinner was a meeting of great curiosity to us who were invited to it. Sheridan was there and Mrs. Sheridan, the late Lord Camelford, Sir Francis Burdett, Charles Warren, [4] with several others and myself. Tooke evidently came prepared for a display, and as I had met him repeatedly and considered his powers of conversation as surpassing those of any person I had ever seen in point of skill and dexterity (and, if at all necessary, in *lying*) I took for granted old grumbling Thurlow would be obliged to lower his topsail to him. But it seemed as if the very look and voice of Thurlow scared him out of his senses, and certainly nothing could be much more formidable. So Tooke tried to recruit himself by wine, and tho' not a drinker, was very drunk. But all would not do; he was perpetually trying to distinguish himself, and Thurlow constantly laughing at him."

[1] P. 60 of the one-volume edition.

[2] It was of Thurlow that Fox said, "No man ever was so wise as Thurlow looks." Pitt had insisted on his dismissal from the Chancellorship in 1792.

[3] But Stephens, the biographer of Horne Tooke, says that it was at the house of Timothy Brown that Tooke renewed his acquaintance with Thurlow.

[4] Charles Warren was a Radical lawyer, a friend of Burdett.

After the preliminaries of peace between England and France had been signed on October 1, 1801, there was an exodus of all who could to see the altered condition of Paris under the new regime of the First Consul. Among others Fox and Erskine went. So did Burdett.

Fox left England for Paris on July 29, 1802, and en route halted at Calais. Finding Arthur O'Connor there, he entertained him at dinner. It was reported to Fox's party, while lodging in the inn at Calais, that " Sir Francis Burdett, on landing at Calais, had been designated with a design to flatter him as a friend of Mr. Fox, and that he had turned round and instantly corrected the expression by saying, ' No, that he was *l'ami du peuple.*' "

Trotter, Fox's secretary, who was present, in his memoirs of Fox [1] makes scathing remarks on Burdett for his action, and then talks of Burdett's " vanity, his tinsel glare, etc." But Walter Savage Landor in his " Commentary " on Trotter's Memoir [2] rightly defends Burdett for his words at Calais, and pays him a high tribute : " Sir Francis Burdett is not censurable for choosing to rest his claim on his own basis. Mr. Fox and Sir Francis might have been friends and yet Sir Francis might prefer some other designation than merely the friend of Charles Fox." He proceeds : " I have seen this gentleman [Burdett] not among mobs, nor at public dinners, but in the society of his friends, and I observed no tinsel or vanity; yet these are sooner seen than anything else about a man."

Burdett had gone to Paris in May 1802. He was there introduced to most of the celebrated men, but absolutely declined any introduction to Napoleon,[3] declaring that the

[1] Trotter's " Memoirs," p. 43.
[2] Landor's " Fox," p. 104.
[3] Napoleon seems to have thought a good deal of Burdett. Dictating to Montholon at St. Helena in 1820 he said that, if he had conquered England, " he would have abolished the English House of Lords, reformed the Commons, proclaimed liberty, equality and popular sovereignty and summoned *Sir Francis Burdett* to draw up a Constitution."

friends of freedom ought not by their homage to recognise a usurpation begun by dismissing the representatives of the people at the point of the bayonet.[1]

Here is an undated letter from Sir Francis at Paris to his wife. It must have been written in May 1802 :

Sir F. Burdett to Lady Burdett.

Paris, Monday. [May 1802].

At length, my dearest Love, the sight of your handwriting has blest my eyes & the contents of your letter my heart, which began to languish for want of the refreshing dews of affection. Post after Post arrived without bringing me any news of my Sophia & her little ones. I was full of anxiety, of doubt, of suspicions, of I knew not what : for love is a plant of that tender nature that the slightest appearance of neglect withers it, as the blighting East the early violet : my eyes devoured every line of your letter, every kind expression as eagerly as the thirsty plant of the desert drinks the grateful dew of the morning. . . . Having thus indulged myself, let me now give you some account of myself.

I am perfectly well & much gratified by this tour, & if you was with me should be tempted to stay some time to examine this curious scene which is before my eyes & which so few Englishmen have eyes to see.

Paris itself is greatly improved instead of being in a state of devastation & ruin, & the general appearance of the people, I think, improved, & though far from well better than I expected after such a Revolution & such a War, & better than before. Last night, Sunday, the Tuileries & the Champs Elysees were crowded with people all decently dressed, I mean by " decent " good cloaths, dancing singing & playing at all kinds of games. The Louvre is magnificent beyond description, & the arrange-

---

[1] Mrs. Stirling's " Coke of Norfolk," p. 299.

ment of the pictures done with much taste according to
the different Schools of the Painters : the gallery of statues,
where is the Apollo, is also fine, & everything thrown
open for the Public, which pleases me more than all the
rest.

I saw Bonaparte review the troops. He passed twice
close to me. I think him much better looking than he is
generally described. I have also seen & conversed with
most of the remarkable persons of all parties & upon the
whole am exceedingly gratified by my journey & altho' I
cannot help wishing I was with you, still I would not
upon any account have missed coming here.

N.B.—Pray send to Tooke, tell him I am well & shall
return in a few days.

Other letters of this time to Lady Burdett suggest that
there had been some *redintegratio amoris,* and it is noticeable
that although the Oxfords also were in Paris in 1802,
Burdett was not present with them when they attended a
dinner given by Benjamin West, President of the Royal
Academy, to some thirty-seven people. ·In August 1803
we find Burdett writing (with a voluptuous penitence) :

" Ah my sweet Sophia, what dismal havock hath my
rugged barbarous folly made. How ass-like have I wan-
dered from the freshest, fairest, loveliest pastures to pick
up weeds & thistles on a common, a goose would have
had more sense—shame and remorse—but 'tis too painful,
& reflection leads to I know not what—& yet your image
on that blessed Friday will spite of efforts cross reflection's
eye, that day which gave you full of health, spritely, gay,
confiding, (alas, ill-placed confidence) to my undeserving
arms—to look at the reverse of this picture after 10 years
marriage, I cannot, dare not. Oh for one drop of that
oblivious stream which washes from the brain all memory
of the past, but soft, ah no, I would not part with the

recollection of all those joys, those dear but unmerited delights derived from you, to escape the torments of the damned, & at this moment I feel something perhaps not very inferior. One drop of consolation however sweetens this bitter cup, the idea of your mind being free from these corroding thoughts, & that best of hearts warm with the sunshine of perpetual peace. You will easily conceive knowing my present feeling, how little importance I can attach to the base calumnies of a corrupt intimidated press, & how little I am vulnerable by newspaper abuse, especially as I am sure by their being so angry that I have done my duty."

He wrote verses also. But about Sir Francis Burdett as poet or as lover, perhaps the less said the better. The best of him went into his politics, where he was much less like Meredith's Sir Willougby Patterne, and not a little like Meredith's Beauchamp. The next chapter must be devoted to the personage who answers to Dr. Shrapnell in " Beauchamp's Career."

CHAPTER VI

JOHN HORNE TOOKE

In 1796 Burdett had taken a house at Wimbledon, and there he became a devoted friend and disciple of John Horne Tooke. He lived and moved and had his being in the society that centred round Horne Tooke, and there can be no question that Tooke's influence was of critical importance in the development of his political views.

Horne Tooke was a puzzle to his contemporaries, and is little less inscrutable to-day. When Lord Chief Justice Eyre in Tooke's trial for treason (1794) was summing up, he said : "One should imagine that Mr. Horne Tooke, with his principles, his habits, and his infirmities, would in truth be the last man in England that could justly be suspected of being engaged in a conspiracy of this kind; I am at this moment totally unable to develope his character and conduct."

The Lord Chief Justice was not singular in his inability to understand Tooke. Without the equation of *intelligent sympathy* it was difficult to grasp Tooke's meaning. For he was in the habit of saying more than he really meant. His words always had a meaning behind them and were intended to be φωνάεντα ξυνέτοισι ("vocal to the wise "), but how much exactly he did mean was not altogether clear to "the wise," and perhaps not even clear to himself. As for "fools," he never suffered them gladly, and for them his words had the wrong meaning, because they took them *au pied de la lettre :* "I wants to make your flesh creep," he might have said to them, like the "fat boy " on a famous occasion in "Pickwick " ; and he delighted in doing so.

108

John, born 1736, was the third son of Horne, a London poulterer, to whom Frederic Prince of Wales died owing some thousands of pounds. John was from his childhood an " original." Sent to Westminster in 1744 and to Eton in 1746, he was conspicuous neither at work nor at play. An anecdote of his Eton life shows him already the possessor of a pretty wit. A group of boys were boasting about their parentage. One said he was the son of the Earl of B——, another that he was the son of Sir Robert A——, and, turning to Horne, they asked him who his father was, to which the poulterer's son replied that his father was " an eminent Turkey merchant " ! !

In 1754 Horne entered St. John's College, Cambridge, and in 1758, as Senior Optime, graduated B.A. His own tastes inclined him to the Bar, and his instinct was right; for there is little doubt, in view of the forensic skill he afterwards displayed, that if he had followed his natural bent he would have become a distinguished lawyer. He entered at the Inner Temple in 1756 and was there on intimate terms with Dunning (afterwards Lord Ashburton) and Kenyon (afterwards Lord Kenyon).

But Horne's father was determined that John should be a parson. So he bought for him the presentation to the new church at Brentford, and John took priest's orders in 1760. He did his duty, but was regarded as too fond of cards and society, and never settled down. By 1765 he was already dabbling in politics on the side of the notorious John Wilkes against the Court. In that year he went bear-leading round the Continent a youth named Taylor; he doffed his clerical clothes at Calais, and formed a personal intimacy with Wilkes at Paris. They agreed to correspond. Horne took his pupil to Italy : they spent some months at Genoa, where Horne acted as *cicisbeo* to a noble Italian lady, Signora Durazzo. Her kinsfolk did not approve, but, mistaking another Englishman for Horne, they nearly killed him, while Horne escaped scot-free. He won a good deal of money by gambling at various places, and from Montpellier on January 3, 1766, he indited the letter to Wilkes (at Paris) that was used with so much effect against him at a later date.   The letter began : " You are now entering into a correspondence with a *parson*, & I am greatly apprehensive lest that title should disgust : but give me leave to assure you that I am not *ordained*—a hypocrite.   It is true I have suffered the infectious hand of a Bishop to be waved over me, etc."

In May 1767 Horne returned to his parish at Brentford, leaving with Wilkes at Paris five suits of fashionable clothes, and resumed his clerical duties and dress.

In 1768 Wilkes reappeared in England and fought his famous Middlesex election against the Court and Ministerial influence.   Horne plunged into the fray, and pledged all he was worth to get control of the best public-houses in Brentford (the polling-station) in the interest of Wilkes.

The election was a gigantic rag, and though all was quiet at Brentford, the roads from the city to Brentford (Piccadilly and the Oxford Road) were blocked by Wilkite crowds, who insisted on everyone travelling west wearing in their hats a card " Number 45,[1] Wilkes and Liberty." Even the pompous Austrian Ambassador was hauled out of his carriage and " No. 45 " chalked on the soles of his feet.   In the evening all windows that refused to illuminate on the popular side were smashed.   Horne had no small share in the triumphant return of Wilkes.   He had declared that " in a cause so just and so holy he would dye his black coat red."

Into the sequel it is unnecessary to enter in detail. Wilkes was expelled from, and declared " ineligible " by the House of Commons, and finally, after various elections, Luttrell, who had a minority of votes, was declared by the House of Commons the duly elected Member for Middlesex.

[1] The Court hostility to Wilkes had arisen from *North Briton*, (No. 45), a magazine in which Wilkes accused the King of having told a deliberate lie in his Speech from the Throne (1763).

In 1769 Horne and Wilkes took a leading part in the foundation of the " Society for Supporting the Bill of Rights," and it was at Horne's suggestion that a subscription was opened for the payment of Wilkes' debts.

Horne is said to have composed the Address which the City presented to the King on March 14, 1770, praying him to dissolve Parliament and dismiss his Ministers. The King roughly handled the deputation in his reply to the Address, and when he had " dressed " it down, turned to his courtiers and burst out laughing. Horne sent an account to the *Public Advertiser*, and added, " Nero fiddled whilst Rome was burning."   In an account of a subsequent Address by the City on May 23 Horne apologised for the offence he had given in his account of the first Address and said he was ready to admit that " Nero did not fiddle when Rome was burning."

But soon Horne quarrelled with Wilkes on very good grounds. He did not see why all the funds at the disposal of the " Bill of Rights Society " should be used exclusively for the payment of Wilkes' debts and diverted from " the Cause." He accordingly moved the dissolution of the Society in 1771, and when this motion was rejected by twenty-six votes to twenty-four, he and the large minority seceded to form the " Constitutional Society."

An unseemly wrangle between Wilkes and Horne followed in the *Public Advertiser*, and all their dirty linen was washed in public, Wilkes publishing the letter that Horne had written him from Montpellier about " the infectious hand of a Bishop," while Horne accused Wilkes of having pawned the five suits of clothes he had left with him in Paris in 1767, and embezzling a quantity of wine, etc.[1]

The quarrel did no good to the popular cause, and made Horne, as his biographer confesses, " one of the most odious men in the kingdom," because he was thought

[1] Junius to Horne July 24, 1771. "What a pitiful detail did it end in.   Some old clothes ! a Welch poney ! a French footman & a hamper of claret."

to be deserting the side of the people. " Junius " joined in the attack against him, but Horne retorted with effect, and he has been described as " the only knight that returned with his lance unbroken from a combat with ' Junius.' "

In 1773 Horne resigned his living at Brentford and took to the study of philology (in which he acquired distinction) and to reading for the Bar.

The year 1774 was critical in his career. One William Tooke, a gentleman of Radical sympathies, was the original Treasurer of the " Bill of Rights Society." When Wilkes and Horne quarrelled, Tooke was one of the minority who seceded with Horne to found the Constitutional Society. He was a man of considerable wealth, owning land in Norfolk and property in the West Indies. He had lately bought an estate near Purley in Surrey, and he had fallen foul of his near neighbour, Thomas de Grey, who, as Lord of the Manor, had tried to deprive Tooke of his right to fatten sheep on the neighbouring downs. A lawsuit followed, but de Grey, who was brother to Lord North's Attorney-General, thought to settle the matter in his favour by promoting an Enclosure Bill in the House of Commons. The affair seemed a foregone conclusion, when Horne, with characteristic readiness, suggested a plan of defeating de Grey, that was welcomed by Tooke. He wrote a scurrilous letter to the *Public Advertiser* accusing the Speaker, Sir Fletcher Norton, of gross partiality in the matter of the Enclosure Bill. The letter was a flagrant breach of the privileges of the House of Commons, and the publisher, Woodfall, when haled before the House, gave the name of Horne as the author of the letter. The Rev. John Horne was ordered to attend the House on February 16, 1774, but when February 16 came, instead of John Horne there arrived a letter begging the House not to address him by the title of " Reverend," which he no longer recognised. When Horne appeared before the House on February 17 no proof other than hearsay was

forthcoming that he was the author of the letter, and the
Commons had to discharge both him and Woodfall. Fox,
who had taken a prominent part as a member of Lord
North's Tory Government, incurred Horne's lasting resentment. But as a result of Horne's action, de Grey's Enclosure Bill was subjected to special attention, and modified
so as to meet W. Tooke's objections.

Thus began an intimate friendship between J. Horne
and W. Tooke.

In 1775 the Constitutional Society voted a subscription
"for our beloved American fellow-subjects . . . inhumanly
murdered by the King's troops." Under a thin subterfuge
this vote was proposed by Horne, and it was published by
his authority in the newspapers. As a result he was tried
before Lord Mansfield for libel (1777), convicted and sentenced to a fine of £200 and one year's imprisonment in
the King's Bench Prison. We learn from him that the
King's Bench Prison was far more unhealthy than Newgate,
as the basement was below the Thames' basin, damp and
insalubrious. But the confinement was not very confined.
He was allowed to rent a house weekly " within the rules,"
to dine with his friends at a tavern " The Dog & Duck,"
and even to take occasional holidays right away from the
prison.

After his release Horne made three separate attempts to
be " called " at the Inner Temple in 1779, 1782, 1794, but
was rejected as being in priest's orders. In 1782 his
application was rejected by a bare majority of the Benchers,
seven to six. It was a tragedy, as Horne's natural aptitude
was for the Bar, and there was no position in the legal
profession to which he might not have risen. In 1794 no
Bencher moved for his " call."

In 1782 Horne took the additional name of " Tooke,"
after his friend and benefactor William Tooke. It has
always been asserted (*e.g.* in the " Dictionary of National
Biography ") that the change of name was made at the

request of William Tooke, and signified that Horne was
to be William Tooke's heir. But this was vehemently
denied by Colonel Harwood (nephew of William Tooke)
in the action of Harwood *v.* Tooke and Burdett. Harwood
asserted that in 1782 Horne was anxious to obtain a post
under Lord Shelburne, that the name of " Parson Horne "
had fallen into such discredit that Horne was eager to
obtain some other name, and William Tooke reluctantly
consented to the adoption of his name by Horne. However
that may be, from 1782 the Rev. J. Horne was always
known as *John Horne Tooke.*

In 1786 Horne Tooke published an interesting philo-
logical work " Ἔπεα πτερόεντα or the Diversions of Purley." The latter title was a mere compliment to his friend,
for his real diversions at Purley were riding over the
downs by day and playing picquet at night.

Meanwhile Horne Tooke had not lost his political
interests. Both he and William Tooke had joined the
new " Society for Constitutional Information " (1782). He
had supported the opposition to the Fox–North Coalition
of 1783, and was seemingly a member, together with
William Pitt, of another Constitutional Club, with Reform
as its object.

At the Westminster election of 1788 he issued a pamphlet
" Two Pair of Portraits," in which he drew a violent
contrast between the two Foxes (Lord Holland and his
son, Charles James Fox) and the two Pitts (Chatham and
William Pitt) to the disadvantage of the former. In 1790
he himself stood against Fox at the Westminster election,
but was badly defeated, and his petition to the House
of Commons against Fox's return was dismissed as
frivolous.

In 1792 he retired to a country house at Wimbledon,
but by no means altogether from politics. In the moment-
ous years that followed the outbreak of the French Revolution (1789–1794) it is not easy to determine the real aims

of Horne Tooke in his rather tortuous course.   To many
he seemed to be " constantly treading upon the very verge
of crime," if not actually passing beyond the line.   And
the instinct of Government was right in regarding him as
the mind behind the activities of the " Corresponding
Society " and the " Society for Constitutional Information."
That was why they put not only Hardy but also Tooke on
trial for high treason in 1794.   Tooke was assisted by
Erskine as Counsel, but in large measure he conducted his
own defence.

The chief ground on which the Attorney-General based
the charge of high treason against Hardy was his scheme
for summoning a Convention, *i.e.* an assembly which should
be attended by delegates from other societies advocating
Reform.   This was represented as an attempt to overawe
and supersede Parliament.   Horne Tooke was accused on
the ground of assisting Hardy.   He had been appointed
by the " Society for Constitutional Information " as member
of a committee to meet a committee of the " Corresponding
Society " in order to discuss the summoning of a Convention.   But Tooke had no difficulty in showing that the
" Society for Constitutional Information " contained
members whose views varied indefinitely.

The great mass of the evidence tended to show that
Tooke was very moderate in his views.   The veteran
Reformer, Major Cartwright, bore witness that Tooke had
always been an opponent of universal suffrage and had
illustrated the difference between himself and extremists by
a quaint simile drawn from the stage-coach.   " If I and
several men are in the Windsor stage, when I find myself
at Hounslow I get out; they who want to go farther may
go to Windsor or where they like; but when I get to
Hounslow (applying it to the House of Commons), there
I get out; no farther will I go, by God."—Tooke had
always said that his quarrel was not with the Monarchy,
nor with the House of Lords, but with the House of

Commons, which as then constituted had ceased to represent the people.

Sheridan declared in evidence that at a meeting held at the "Crown and Anchor" on July 14, 1790, to commemorate the anniversary of the fall of the Bastille, with Lord Stanhope in the chair, when a vote congratulating the French on their Revolution was proposed, Tooke moved a rider "That this meeting feels equal satisfaction that the people of England, by the virtuous exertions of their ancestors, have not so hard a task to perform as the French have had, but have only to maintain and improve the Constitution which their ancestors have transmitted to them."

There are two stories told in connection with the trial that show Tooke's power of repartee.

One night, as he was returning from the Court to the prison, a lady admirer, pressing forward, put a scarf round his neck. "Pray, [Madam," he said, "be careful, for I am rather *ticklish* at present about that particular place."

When a daughter of one of the jury which had acquitted him offered congratulations, he replied, "Then give me leave, Madam, to call you 'sister,' for your father has just helped to give me life."

Hardy having been already acquitted, the verdict was a foregone conclusion, and the jury, after a retirement of eight minutes, declared him "Not Guilty."

Tooke then made a short speech, in which he asserted that he had rarely been present on those occasions on which his name appeared on the minutes of the Society. His sole anxiety had been for the safety of a very honest but not a very able man. (He meant Hardy.) "He frequently brought to me papers which were ordered for publication—and when I saw a word which was capable of causing a prosecution for libel I struck out the exceptionable words and inserted others. . . . Upon this has been built up all that suspicion of the direction and originating of Societies, etc."

After 1794 Tooke tended more and more to live in retirement in his beloved garden at Wimbledon, with his two natural daughters, Mary and Charlotte Hart. His personal friends and others who sympathised with him on public grounds bought him a considerable annuity. But in 1796 he once more unsuccessfully contested Westminster, and in 1801, by the influence of Thomas Pitt, second Lord Camelford, he was returned for the rotten borough of Old Sarum. His right to sit, as he was in Holy Orders, was challenged by Lord Temple; and in the course of the debates Tooke made a characteristic sally. If he had been deprived of his Orders for misconduct, he would, according to his opponents, have been eligible to the House of Commons.

" I am," he said, " in the situation of the young woman who asked for admission to the Magdalen. When questioned as to her previous history, and her life discovered irreproachable. ' Go about your business,' said the head of the Institution, 'you must qualify before you come here.' "

Tooke himself was allowed to retain his seat till the Dissolution of 1802. From that date he became an oracle at Wimbledon, where Burdett then had a house; his views on life were mellowed by age and his utterances more guarded in character.

Sir Francis Burdett was introduced to Horne Tooke by a Colonel Maxwell and R. C. Fergusson. Their houses at Wimbledon were a stone's throw apart, and their acquaintance soon ripened into a lasting friendship. Tooke was over sixty, and Sir Francis was a young man of twenty-six : so the relationship was that of master and disciple.

Stephens, the biographer of Horne Tooke, writes that towards Burdett Tooke " always exhibited a marked regard, an unvarying attention, and the most tender solicitude.

He was zealous for his welfare and seemed to participate in his growing fame and popularity. . . . He seemed to cherish for him all the affection of a fond father for a darling son, and is said to have been occasionally as jealous of his regard as if he had actually been a beloved mistress. He was afraid of all things lest he should get into the hands of the Whigs, and when he heard on the first contest for Middlesex that the Duke of Bedford had subscribed £1000 towards the expenses of the election, and had gone down to Brentford, Mr. Tooke immediately set off for the hustings in express opposition to his original intentions. . . . Sir Francis was in the constant habit of repairing to Mr Tooke's during many years. . . . At the Sunday dinners he was generally placed on the right hand of his host, and on other occasions took his seat anywhere without ceremony. He always appeared to me modest, unassuming, and rather taciturn."

That Horne Tooke had great influence on the development of Burdett's political views is an unquestioned fact, but that influence took the form not of changing or perverting Burdett's views, but of confirming their natural evolution. Each of them ploughed a rather lonely furrow.

Horne Tooke was not a believer in the wisdom of "the ignorant mob." Indeed he had slight opinion of its wisdom, having suffered from its desertion in the 'seventies. He disliked the writings of Tom Paine; he never believed in universal suffrage. Burdett agreed.

Horne Tooke and Burdett were both believers in the Monarchy and the House of Lords. Their complaint was that the Monarchy, no less than the people, suffered from the borough-mongering faction. Their quarrel was with the House of Commons " as at present constituted." It represented nothing but the "borough-mongers." In no sense did it represent the people, whose money it took largely to provide sinecures for the adherents of " the system."

Horne Tooke and Burdett had profound distrust of both

the historic political parties—Whigs and Tories. These were simply the " ins " and the " outs," both adherents of " the system," eager for the loaves and fishes of office. The Whigs had a tradition of " freedom " and " resistance to oppression " from the Revolution of 1688. But in practice the tradition had been perverted. It was they who, in the eighteenth century, had organised " the system of corruption," and their record in 1806–1807 went to show them just as much the adherents of " the system " as the Pittite Tories. In the matter of sinecures the most princely offenders were the Grenvilles.

Both Tooke and Burdett were believers in what they called " the ancient principles of the Constitution." Hence their essential Conservatism. They disliked the abstract and *a priori* reasoning of a Rousseau or a Paine. They conceived that the House of Commons had once been really representative of the " people." They appealed to Magna Charta. Most singular delusion! The " myth " of Magna Charta was an invention of the early seventeenth century : it was only at the end of the nineteenth century that Magna Charta was revealed in its true light as a feudal and reactionary document. But it is the sort of delusion that has appealed to Reformers in all ages. They read back the Reforms they wish to establish into the actuality of a distant past. The " freedom " that " the man in the street " was believed to have enjoyed in the thirteenth or fourteenth century never existed.

Both Tooke and Burdett hated oppression, with its attendant suffering, especially when inflicted under the sanction of the laws, or by the authority of the Government, or by the fiat of the House of Commons. Tooke had even rescued Luttrell from the fury of the mob in 1768. Burdett violently protested against flogging in the Army; the sufferings men endured in prison [1] were attacked

---

[1] Tooke altogether spent in prison 519 days : 1774, House of Commons, 8 days; 1777–8, King's Bench, 336 days. 1794, Privy Council, three days; Tower, 148 days; Newgate, 30 days.

by both, and the general truth of the statement is evidenced by the whole of their careers.

Something must now be said about the social life and the " Court " which surrounded Tooke in his later years at Wimbledon, where, Samuel Rogers said of him : " His present manners and conversation remind me of a calm sunset in October."

The house he had taken in 1792 was a commodious dwelling with a large garden and two fields in front, on which he kept cows. He had small and select parties in the middle of the week, but it was at the Sunday dinner at 4 p.m. that he entertained a miscellaneous crowd of cour-tiers. There was no telling whom you might not meet : for Tooke had all sorts of connections endeared to him either by their sufferings or their service. It might be an ex-Lord Chancellor, or a peer, or Sir Francis Burdett, who usually sat at the right of his host, or a pauper, or a barrister, or a banker, or a University Professor, or a millionaire, or a clergyman that sat next to you at table. It might be some one whom Tooke had befriended by legal advice, or it might be some one who had stood in the dock with Tooke when tried for his life. Thus it is related that at one of the parties a Mr. Baxter was announced. Tooke had no recollection of him, but on going into the hall he found that Baxter—a working man—was one of the people who had been in the dock with him on the charge of treason in 1794, and Baxter was immediately brought, with all possible honour, to the dinner-table. It was an odd assortment of people. A banker would have to find a common ground of conversation with a man of letters, an atheist with a clergyman, a professor with a merchant. To attend one of Tooke's dinners was in itself a liberal education. Everything went off splendidly; for Tooke was a charming host, full of jokes and jibes, that gave the guests an appetite. In case of disputes, appeal was made to the host, and unless the matter in dispute was one on which Tooke felt seriously, such as the law, religion, or the Constitution, the matter was settled by some jest which amused the company.

The dinner itself was sumptuous : soup, fish, white and brown meats, pies and puddings of all sorts, but, best of all, the vegetables and fruits that were the produce of Tooke's own garden—Alpine strawberries, Antwerp raspberries, and Dutch currants, grapes, etc.

Tooke was no mean gardener, and knew how to grow and preserve his fruit. The wines were Madeira, sherry, and port.

On the Sunday morning guests used to arrive from 11 a.m. : they were to be seen diagonally crossing Wimbledon Green, or going round by the two sides of the parallelogram in order to call first at the mansion of Sir F. Burdett. Another peculiarity in Horne Tooke's *ménage* was that he had no silver. His service was earthenware, china, and pewter. This was due to the fact that most of his silver had been the spoil of burglars. Thereupon he had sent the remainder to the Bank, with the exception of a fine silver tankard, which he had promised to bequeath to and therefore presented to Scott, the brother of Lady Oxford.

It was stated by James Paull, after he had quarrelled with Tooke and Burdett, that these dinners were in the nature of an ἔρανος or picnic, and that everyone who attended them made Tooke a handsome present at the end of the year. But the statement in the *Gentleman's Magazine* is probably more correct, that " the expense of Mr. Horne Tooke's Sunday dinners was defrayed by Colonel Bosville and Sir F. Burdett alternately."

Among those who constantly enjoyed Tooke's hospitality were many distinguished men. Among them were the following :

Thomas Erskine, the great advocate. He had voluntarily defended Tooke on his trial for treason (1794). At the private dinner given every year on the anniversary of the acquittal, Erskine attended, even after he became Lord Chancellor in 1806.

Colonel Bosville of Gunthwaite, Yorkshire. His sister was Lady Dudley, and he was great-uncle to Sir George Sinclair, the devoted friend and disciple of Burdett in his later years. Bosville's ancestor had come over with the Conqueror from Normandy, no doubt from the place now called " Blossville " (about ten miles from St. Valery). Bosville, after leaving Harrow, had taken a commission in the Guards, and served in the American war. Though he never rose above the rank of lieutenant, he was always styled " Colonel " by his friends. After leaving the Army he travelled with Lord Hawke's son in Morocco. Bosville said to a certain Moor, " If your Emperor were to leave off frying in oil and impaling alive, this would be a fine country to live in." The Moor rejoined, " A Moor does not dread the rope like a European, and if His Majesty were to leave off frying in oil and impaling alive, neither I nor any honest man would choose to live here."

Bosville had been a member of the " Society for Constitutional Information," and was a generous contributor to all kinds of " Radical " funds. When attacked by a French *émigré* for his supposed disloyalty and by an English writer who asserted " that his very slumbers are disturbed with treasons," he simply said, " I hope these gentlemen are in good credit with their printers, for the world will think me of no consequence the moment they leave off abusing me." But Bosville was no more a revolutionary than Tooke. In the " Diversions of Purley, Part II " (published in 1805, and written in the form of a dialogue between Tooke and Burdett), Tooke says, " You know that your friend *Bosville* and I have entered into a strict engagement to belong for ever to the established government, to the established Church and to the established language of our country, because they are established. Establish what you please. Do but establish : and whilst that establishment shall last, we shall be perfectly convinced of its propriety."

Bosville was a good raconteur. He was fond of telling how he happened to be at Rome during the last illness of Pope Clement XIV, and the bulletins ran—

"His Holiness is very ill."
"His Holiness is worse."
"His Infallibility is delirious."

Bosville every week drove a party from London to dine with Tooke at Wimbledon on Sunday. He was a person of very good manners, generous and obliging, and essentially a *bon vivant*. The dinners he gave in Town to his friends were famous. He was immensely rich, and is said to have spent £3000 a year on his dinner-table alone. Every day he entertained twelve persons at dinner. But the party was formed in an original manner. A slate was placed in the hall, and any one of his friends could write his name on the slate, till the tale of twelve was complete. No further names could be added. The dinner was served at 5 p.m. *exactly*. No guest was admitted if he arrived a moment after five. He was dismissed from the door by the porter with the words, " Sir, the Colonel has taken his chair." We are told in the *Gentleman's Magazine* that even Sir Francis Burdett on arriving after five had been dismissed. Bosville never visited his estates in Yorkshire, but he was a generous landlord. During this period, when rents were constantly rising, he never raised a tenant's rent. He used to say, " As I found them, so I'll leave them." He died in London December 16, 1813, and Sir Francis was a trustee under his will.

Porson, the famous Greek scholar, Professor at Cambridge, was frequently present at Tooke's dinners. It is well known that Porson's great weakness was drink. On one occasion, being asked why he had been so silent during dinner, he replied that " Addison was never himself until after the second bottle."

On another occasion Tooke asked Porson for a toast, and Porson replied, " I will give you the toast—of the man who is in all respects the very reverse of J. H. Tooke." Some altercation ensued, and Porson actually threatened to *kick* and to *cuff* his host. Tooke displayed the brawn of his own physique, but proposed to settle the matter by a different sort of combat. Putting aside the port and sherry, he ordered two quarts of brandy. By the time the second bottle was half emptied Porson fell vanquished under the table. Tooke, taking hold of Porson's limbs, in turn exclaimed, " This is the *foot* that was to have kicked, and the *hand* that was to have cuffed me." Then, drinking another glass to the toast of Porson's recovery, and giving orders that " great care should be taken of Mr. Professor Porson," he withdrew to his coffee as calmly as if nothing had occurred.

Tom Paine was frequently at Wimbledon, but was never liked by Tooke, who sneered at his writings. Tooke had a very exalted idea of learning, and despised " ignorant men : far better calculated to pull down than to build up governments." He disapproved of Paine's extreme views, thinking that the " original " Constitution of England was excellent.

Mr. William and *Mr. Hobbes Scott*, the brothers of Lady Oxford, were at one time accustomed to repair almost daily to Mr. Tooke's. A painting of Hobbes Scott was placed in the parlour, and part of the garden was actually converted into a hop ground out of compliment to him. A coloured print of Lady Oxford hung for some years over the chimney-piece.

Joel Barlow (1754–1812) was another intimate friend. He was an American graduate from Yale. Coming to London, he joined the " Society for Constitutional Information," and his work " Advice to the Privileged Orders " (1792) was proscribed by the English Government. It was

through Tooke's influence that he was accredited to France
with an address from the society. We know that he was
present at the dinner given by the painter Benjamin West
at Paris in 1802. During Pitt's second administration he
was allowed to return to England. Thence he went to
America. He was sent by the American Government as
Minister to Napoleon, and died in Poland from exposure
during the retreat of the French Army in 1812.

Among other visitors at Wimbledon were Sir James
Mackintosh, the lawyer and friend of Fox, Humphrey
Davy (not yet famous) and Count Alvise Zenobio. Zenobio
was a Venetian noble, the son of an Admiral in the Venetian
service. He had come to England, and foolishly (so far
as his own interests were concerned) had become a member
of the " Society for Constitutional Information." In 1801
Thomas Coutts had applied to the Earl of Chichester, as
Secretary of State, for leave for Zenobio to return to
England after the wreck of his fortunes in Venice. This
was seemingly granted. He gave Tooke much foreign
information, but, for " powerful and honourable " reasons,
did not visit Tooke after 1807.

Such, then, was the circle in which Burdett spent his
time at Wimbledon.

His intimacy with Horne Tooke involved him in a
protracted law-suit, arising out of the death of William
Tooke in 1802. William Tooke died a bachelor, having
admittedly quarrelled with his relations. Nevertheless
from 1787 Colonel Harwood, William Tooke's nephew,
and a great-nephew, John Baseley, saw much of the old
man, and Horne Tooke claimed to have brought about the
reconciliation. They are said to have entered into arrangements guaranteeing to Horne Tooke a provision for his
natural daughters, and Harwood signed a promissory note
for £4000 to Horne Tooke, which the latter promptly
lodged with " T. Coutts & Co." On the security of it
Burdett undertook to provide the annuities.

On William Tooke's death his will was opened and it

was found that he had left to Horne Tooke a mere sum of
£500. The assets, about £60,000, were to go between
Harwood and Baseley. Harwood promptly sought to
repudiate the note which he had given, and wrote to
Burdett in that sense. Burdett replied:

To W. T. Harwood Esq.

Bath. 31 Oct. 1803.

SIR,

　　　　The concern & regret you rightly suppose I must
feel on reading your letter can only be equalled by the
surprise with which it was attended. I can be no judge of
any transaction between yourself & Mr Tooke, but cant
help expressing my conviction of his being incapable of
acting dishonorably towards you. I have known him long,
seen him much & think this credit due to a life of tried
integrity & almost unexampled persecutions. As to the
note lying at Mr Coutts' all I know about it is that I consented to grant Mr H. Tooke an annuity & one to each of
his daughters, & to receive that Note in part payment:
whether it is good, or whether it is bad, or why you gave
it, or how he obtained it, or what passed between you, are
all matters of which I am totally ignorant. I remain, Sir,

　　　　　　　　　your most obedient honorable servant,

　　　　　　　　　　　　　　　F. BURDETT.

From the following letter it would seem that Coutts was
not so sure of Tooke as Burdett was. It will be remembered that the note had been deposited with " T. Coutts
& Co." on July 9.

Sir F. Burdett to T. Coutts (in London).

Bath.
26 Aug. 1803.

MY DEAR SIR,

　　　　. . . I have only one word to say about Tooke:
whenever any man shall, ceasing the base practice of

calumniating, bring proof of his having ever in the course of a long & narrowly watched life been guilty of a dishonourable action, my friendship will cease also; but He is one of those Men who will do honour to their Country, when the miserable ephemeral politicians of the day shall be buried in the common grave of oblivion, tho' their baseness & corruption will leave lasting mischeifs upon their Country. I remember in the times of the Caesars the friends of Brutus were suspected Persons, Seneca too was a suspected Person in the time of Nero, Sidney & Russel in the time of the Stuarts, & the great Milton publicly insulted by the pensioned House of Commons; it is very fit Tooke should be suspected in the time of George III, & tho' his friendship can be nothing but disadvantage, I am prouder of it than F. can be of his office, nor is it to be moved like a straw by tainted breath.

When the note became due, on March 25, 1804, Burdett, the holder of the note, began an action in the King's Bench against Colonel Harwood, and caused him to be held to bail for the sum of £4000.

Harwood urged in the course of the pleadings that the £4000 had been granted to buy annuities for Tooke's daughters; but as the money was in large measure used to buy an annuity for Tooke himself, the money had been obtained under false pretences, and there had been a breach of trust.

On May 19, 1809, the Court of Chancery gave its decision in favour of Sir Francis Burdett, and ordered that the money should be paid over to him.

The money transactions of Horne Tooke, it must be admitted, leave " a nasty taste in the mouth," and are the shadiest part of his career. What, it might be asked, had Horne Tooke done, that he should receive £3000 from Felix Vaughan, £9000 from W. Tooke, £4000 from Har-

wood, and I don't know how much else from Burdett,
Bosville, and others? A man with a delicate sense of
honour would, I think, have felt uneasy at being the
recipient of such sums for no very apparent reason.

Of the part played by Tooke in Burdett's elections for
Middlesex and Westminster something will be said in
succeeding chapters.

The friendship between the two men was remarkable,
and could not *a priori* have been predicted. For in temperament they differed widely. True, they were both lacking in reverence for everything except Magna Charta and
the " ancient Constitution " ! But hard, dry materialism
was the characteristic of Tooke, while Burdett was " senti-
ment " personified. Burdett was by nature a poet, with
the whole of Shakespeare and Pope and other poets at his
command. He was by temperament imaginative, while
Tooke's texture was one of prose and keen logic. Burdett
was fastidious : Tooke was often lacking in delicacy of
taste. Tooke was a man of cool self-possession; if he
talked treason, it was always " with a saving clause." He
" chafed others into madness," says Hazlitt, " while remaining himself unmoved " : Burdett was often extravagant in
his language, and let his tongue run away with him.
Burdett was deficient in a sense of humour : wit, " sprung,"
says Hazlitt, " from his excess of logical faculty " was
distinctive of Tooke. Burdett shone as a public speaker,
but in private life was often taciturn : on the public platform
Tooke was a failure, but he shone in private conversation.
He delighted in " mischief " : there was no end to his
amusing anecdotes, his happy repartees, his irony and love
of paradox, his powers of ridicule and banter and caricature.
Samuel Rogers, the banker-poet, in his " Table Talk,"
has preserved some of Tooke's witticisms and of his more
serious aphorisms. When Judge Ashurst said, " The Law
is open to all men," Tooke replied, " And so is the
London tavern."

SIR F. BURDETT.   HORNE TOOKE.

Being advised one evening " to settle and take a wife," he replied, " With all my heart, and pray what man's wife would you advise me to take ? "

When they were talking one night of the Princess of Wales and William Austin (the unknown boy whom she adopted), " Oh," said Tooke, " the old story of Moses in the bulrushes being found by Pharaoh's daughter."

When Charles Grey said, " If I was compelled to make a choice, I should prefer despotism to anarchy," Tooke retorted, " Then you would do as your ancestors did at the Reformation : they rejected Purgatory and kept Hell."

Among his more serious sayings two, that referred to the leaders of the " system," Whig and Tory, may be mentioned :

" There are men who pretend that they come into the world booted and spurred to ride you."

" When a pension is given or a salary, a draft is issued on the tiller of the soil."

Tooke had the great gift of being able to laugh at himself. He hung in his back parlour the caricature of himself as the " Old Man of the Sea carrying Sinbad (Burdett) on his Back to Destruction."

" One of the first times," writes Stephens, " I ever saw Sir Francis Burdett in his (Tooke's) house, he invited him to hear a satire composed for the express purpose of vilifying both. Our host then sat down and read aloud the most aggravating passages against them, commenting on the poetry and examining the merits of the production, which he had now seen for the first time, with a clear calm unruffled brow, as if wholly unconcerned. When any of the lines proved feeble or impotent, he tried both to mend the versification and point the irony; and if a passage was written with more than ordinary ability, he was sure to recite it twice and that too in such a manner as to produce additional effect by means of appropriate emphasis and intonation."

The devotion shown by Burdett to the old man during his last years—years of suffering—was really touching. In a letter to Lady Burdett dated Ramsbury Cottage, August 8, 1809, Sir Francis wrote : " It was very kind of you to send the venison to my dear Tooke, who I now fear will never get up again—I really grow quite out of heart about him, & very sick at heart it makes me. I endeavour to encourage hope, or drive off thought from the subject altogether, as the event I dread whenever it takes place will be sufficiently painful without anticipation. Whenever he dies, an able, injured, undauntedly honest man is lost to the Country, whose character will hereafter be an honour & reproach to it. I shall have the melancholy satisfaction of having done him justice, & the never-ceasing recollection of his irretrievable loss."

If, as Hazlitt said, Burdett was " the Educator of his countrymen," it was Horne Tooke who trained him to be so.

When Stephens visited Tooke on October 7, 1810, he found him in an invalid chair drawn by Sir Francis in front, the Miss Harts pushing behind. They visited the mausoleum that Tooke had prepared for himself in his own garden, made from enormous blocks of black Irish marble. The inscription on the top ran :

JOHN HORNE TOOKE
late proprietor,
and now occupier of this spot
was
born in June 1736
and
died
in the   year of his age.
Content and Grateful.

And his desire was that at his funeral Burdett should deliver a classical oration.

Horne Tooke died on March 18, 1812. On March 24 Burdett wrote to Samuel Rogers :

Sir F. Burdett to S. Rogers Esq.

> Piccadilly.
> March 24, 1812.

MY DEAR MR. ROGERS,

Our friend Horne Tooke used to express his desire that his few real friends should accompany him to that " everlasting mansion ", which, like Timon, he had prepared for himself. As I know he counted you one of that number, & as I believe you would like to pay this last sad tribute to his memory, I take the liberty of acquainting you that his remains will be deposited in his garden at Wimbledon on Friday next the 27th.

> yours very sincerely,
> F. BURDETT.

This arrangement was not carried out. After the grave in the garden had been opened and all the preparations made, it was determined, in view of the deterioration of value that would be caused to the property, that his body should be interred at Ealing, where the funeral took place in the ordinary way. His nephew, Mr. Wildman, and Sir Francis were the chief mourners.

CHAPTER VII

THE MIDDLESEX ELECTIONS

1802–1806

THE Parliament that met in 1796 was dissolved on June 29, 1802. Sir Francis Burdett, utterly disgusted with politics, even had thoughts of migrating to France, when he received the following invitation to stand for Middlesex.

To Sir Francis Burdett, Bart.   26 June 1802.

SIR,

       Having heard from various quarters of an intention in many freeholders to offer you their votes at the general election, as a fit person to represent the County of Middlesex in the next Parliament, we are anxious to know whether in such event you will stand forward in compliance with their wishes. Our own votes as well as our exertions among our friends depend on your answer : for assure yourself we feel as you feel with respect to the late Ministers & their measures.

       As Englishmen we concur in your abhorrence of the use & management of such a prison as that in Cold Bath Fields. As freeholders we desire an occasion to express the sentiments we entertain of your manly opposition to the establishment in Middlesex.

       In any case we trust a majority of our fellow freeholders will agree with us that Sir.Francis Burdett is more worthy than Mr Mainwaring to represent the interests, deliver the sense, & support the rights of the first County in England.

We remain, Sir,

your obedient servants

W. TOOKE.

M. PEARSON, etc.

W. Tooke was now well over eighty years of age. This
letter must have been written shortly before his death.

Michael Pearson is one of his four contemporaries mentioned by name in " The Diversions of Purley " by Horne
Tooke : " Michael Pearson my gentle and amiable
friend : forty long years my steady and uniform accomplice
and comforter in all my treasons : equally devoted with
myself to the rights and happiness of our countrymen and
our fellow-creatures " (" Diversions of Purley," Vol. II,
p. 193).

Pearson was an apothecary, and member of the " Society
for Constitutional Information." A glowing tribute is
paid to him in the anonymous " Memoirs of Sir Francis
Burdett " (1810).

To this letter Sir Francis sent the following reply :

June 26, 1802.
78 Piccadilly.

GENTLEMEN,

I will freely acknowledge to you, that I have for
some time past relinquished all thoughts of a seat in Parliament, & have consequently declined very many overtures
for that purpose. If the people of England are pleased &
contented with what has passed, with their present situation,
& with the terrible changes which have been made in the
laws, constitution, & manner of governing this country,
let statues be erected in each County through the land, to
Lord Liverpool, Mr Pitt, & Mr Dundas, to whom principally they are indebted for the blessings.

I shall not desire to overturn them, but will remove from
such odious & disgraceful objects, confessing myself not
fit for the society of such a nation.

Yet, though disgusted, I do not despair; I think our
country may still be saved, but by one means only—by a
fair representation of the people in parliament. By that
alone can we possibly obtain the restoration of those

invaluable rights which have been ravished from us, or the security of what little good remains.

If the County of Middlesex, which from circumstances is likely to be more free, informed, & independent, than any other county in England, shall be pleased *upon this principle* (& I wish for no support upon any other principle, holding all palliations nugatory & destructive)—If *upon this principle* the County of Middlesex shall be pleased to intrust to my hands a portion of their present small & inadequate share of representation, I will cheerfully & zealously devote myself, my life, & my fortune to their service.

I am, Gentlemen,
your obedient humble Servant,
Francis Burdett.

It is to be noted that the reply of Sir Francis was made from 78 Piccadilly, which remained his town house till 1816. He had let Ramsbury Manor to a Mr. Bailey, and his country residence was at Wimbledon, when he was not at Foremarke. In Town he seems to have lived for a time at 8 Stratton Street.

Thomas Coutts in February 1796 had acquired 1 Stratton Street, and he gradually bought up other freeholds in the same street. Throughout the earlier part of 1802 he was looking out for a Town residence for Lady Burdett, and he finally, in June 1802, fixed on the house adjoining his own, 78 Piccadilly (till that time known as Littleton House).[1] A subterranean passage seems to have run between the two houses, 1 Stratton Street and 78 Piccadilly, but this was now closed up, and a door of inter-communication between them on the first floor was substituted for it.

No. 78 was not ready for habitation by the Burdetts on June 26, the day on which Sir Francis accepted the Middle-

[1] Lady Burdett-Coutts, the daughter of Sir Francis, at a later date used the two houses as one. No. 78 was afterwards re-numbered No. 80 Piccadilly.

sex invitation, but Coutts put at his disposal the ground floor of the house, fitting it up for the purpose of the election with some tables and chairs. And hence Burdett's reply to the invitation was dated from 78 Piccadilly. Various alterations in the house had to be carried out, and the Burdetts only took up their residence in it at the close of the year.

The Middlesex election continued from July 13 to 28. The candidates were Mr. Byng, a Whig; Mr. Mainwaring, a banker, and chairman of the Middlesex Bench of magistrates; Sir Francis Burdett. The two former had in the preceding Parliament represented Middlesex. Byng's election was a certainty, and the real contest lay between Mainwaring and Burdett.

The three candidates dined together with some of their friends at Uxbridge on July 8, but a jarring note was struck, when, on Mainwaring's health being proposed, one of the company proposed that the health of Aris should be coupled with it. Mr. Mainwaring said the proposal was unkind and ungentlemanly. Burdett then said, " Sir, you confess that you are ashamed of your friend." To which Mainwaring replied, " No, sir, I always considered him an honest, humane, and upright character."

Every election at this time in an " open " constituency was by unwritten law a time of licensed and unbounded ragging, which in the absence of any real police force ran the risk of developing into a regular riot. " The proceedings at an election," says Halévy,[1] " were a periodical reminder that riot formed part of the political traditions of the English people." Rowdyism, in which voters and non-voters alike participated, was traditional, scenes of drunkenness and violence were all too much in evidence, and electoral contests were regarded " in the light of a national sport as popular as, indeed more popular than, horse-racing." [2]

[1] Halévy, Vol. I, p. 132.   [2] Ibid., p. 137.

The Middlesex election of 1802 beat all previous records, even that of 1768 in Wilkes' time.

On the first day of the poll, July 13, at 8 a.m., Sir Francis started from 78 Piccadilly with an enormous cavalcade. Twenty butchers in white jackets, with their marrow-bones and cleavers, marched in front. Banners streamed, flags waved with the inscription "Burdett and no Bastile"; bands of music played—all these interspersed amid a never-ending line of carriages. The chariot of Sir Francis himself was attended by gentlemen outriders. The procession moved onwards amidst the huzzas of the populace wishing him success. His dark-blue cockades were to be seen everywhere, the lower classes, and especially the women, being violent in his favour. When Kew Bridge was reached at 9.30 a.m., the populace took the horses from Burdett's carriage and drew it into Brentford amidst immense cheering.

The hustings were said to have been the most spacious ever built : the mere cost of their erection, apart from the timber used, had been £300. After some preliminary proceedings, the three candidates were proposed and seconded. Burdett was recommended by his proposer on the grounds of his independent fortune—he would therefore not be exposed to temptation—and his independent mind. Mainwaring was attacked as having supported all the "gagging" Acts of Pitt and as the defender of Aris— a man worse than Robespierre. After the other two candidates had spoken, Burdett declared that he intended to fight the election chiefly on the question of the Cold Bath Fields Prison. Mainwaring was the abettor and defender of all the cruelties and atrocities committed within the walls of that Bastile. He was therefore not a fit person to represent Middlesex. Burdett wished the father of Mary Rich to tell them something of the enormities practised in the prison, but the Sheriffs ruled that Rich should not be allowed to speak.

Meanwhile some *tableaux vivants* were presented in front of the hustings—a man in a smock frock whipping a hand-bill that portrayed a prisoner, a man whose hands were tied with a rusty chain acting all the agonies of an exhausted victim, etc. After the close of the first day's poll Burdett returned with the same cavalcade as that in which he had come. There were many fracas, the public-houses were crowded, and many of the drivers and passengers returned " half-seas over."

The second day of the poll was the anniversary of the fall of the real Bastille (July 14) and there was much semi-rioting. After the close of the poll on the sixth day Burdett's supporters had a dinner at the " Crown and Anchor." [1] The healths of Charles Fox, and the Duchess of Devonshire and other female canvassers were drunk. It would there-fore appear that the whole of the Whig interest was exerted on Burdett's behalf.

The election continued from day to day, and while Burdett accused the Government of exercising undue influence, Mainwaring's friends retaliated by accusing Burdett and his partisans of treasonable practices. " Arthur O'Connor & Colonel Despard were his friends." On the thirteenth day of the poll a great meeting was organised by Charles Fox and Lord William Russell at the " Crown and Anchor " in support of Burdett, and enthusiastic crowds filled the streets. " By 10 a.m. the Strand, Pall Mall, St. James Street, Piccadilly were literally blocked with the population of this great capital, whilst the windows exhibited a display of beauty, which we believe no other country can rival." The windows of the house where Mainwaring dined in Brentford were broken.

During the first thirteen days of the poll Burdett had been some 400 or 500 votes below Mainwaring, but at the end of the fourteenth day he was only fourteen votes

[1] For a description of the " Crown and Anchor," see " Farington Diary," Vol. II, p. 234.

behind, and at the close of the poll on the fifteenth day the tables were turned, the final result being :

Byng 3848
Burdett . . . 3207
Mainwaring. . 2936

The successful candidates, Byng and Burdett, were "chaired" in the usual style; the Revolutionary song " Ça ira " was sung in front of the King's Palace at Kew; the horses were removed from the carriages, and in tremendous triumph the populace drew them back the whole way to London. The line of carriages four abreast was three miles long; enormous crowds accompanied them on foot; the windows and tops of houses were crowded with spectators. Even tempestuous storms of rain did not damp the enthusiasm, and when the procession stopped before the residence of Sir Francis in Piccadilly, and the house of T. Coutts & Co. in the Strand, the crowds wildly cheered. The day ended with a dinner at the " Crown and Anchor " attended by some 600 people.

That the election was marked by bribery, perjury, drunkenness, and ruffianism of every kind is an undoubted fact. In a contemporary caricature—" The scum upper-most, when the Middlesex porritch-pot boils over "—the Devil is represented as finding Brentford too hot.

" Brave B . . . tt, adieu you've blown up a fine flame :
'Tis so hot, I'll return to the place whence I came,
    And tell my grim Quorum,
    With how much decorum
Your tag-rags of Middlesex drive all before 'em.
'Twill be long ere my Blackbirds attain such perfection,
What's Hell when compar'd with your BRENTFORD
    ELECTION ? "

It was at this time that the neat anagram on Sir Francis Burdett's name—Frantic disturber—was coined. But *pace* the " Annual Register " of 1802 there was little to choose between the two sides.

On his election Burdett issued an address to his constituents, dated from 78 Piccadilly on July 29.

To the Independent & Public-spirited Freeholders of
the County of Middlesex.

GENTLEMEN,

Mr Mainwaring has endeavoured to make the
public believe that our opposition to his reelection was an
attack upon the Government, & that his numbers on the
poll would be a justification of his political conduct.

His numbers on the poll do not in the least incline me to
believe that even those freeholders of Middlesex approve
his conduct, but only that some of them were not sufficiently
acquainted with it. But I do acknowledge, & I wish all
the freeholders had been sooner aware of it, that an opposition to his reelection was in effect an opposition to any
government by secret & concealed torture.

Gentlemen, when I assert that secret imprisonment, secret
trial, & secret execution, are the never-failing engines of
oppression & tyranny, & that innocence can have no
security but by public trial, public execution & public
custody in the sight of day & before the eyes of the country
at large : when I assert this, I am conscious that I stand
upon a rock, from which I cannot be removed by any hired
Magistrates, Parliaments, or Kings. . . .

I heartily congratulate you, Gentlemen, on the tedious &
protracted contest : for it has given an opportunity to the
independent & public-spirited freeholders of the Metropolitan County, deliberately to declare their sentiments of
the present system of torture in the dungeons of Cold Bath
Fields & their opinion of Mr Justice Mainwaring & his
humane friend,

" THE STEELED GAOLER, WHO SELDOM IS THE FRIEND
OF MAN."

The election of 1802 was the cause of a great flutter in

the soul of Thomas Coutts, and led him to write a number
of rather undignified letters to Pitt and others.   It made
him quite ill that Lord Hawkesbury (afterwards Lord
Liverpool, the Prime Minister) should have withdrawn
some of the Foreign Office accounts from the Bank.   Yet
the accounts were not withdrawn because of anything that
Sir Francis did or said in the course of the election.   The
actual election only began on July 13, but the letter of
Thomas Grenville to Lord Grenville on July 12 shows that
the accounts had already been withdrawn.   The only
ground of offence can have been that Coutts was the father
of Lady Burdett, and was said to have canvassed for his
son-in-law.   The accounts were restored to T. Coutts &
Co. by Charles James Fox in 1806.

Thomas Coutts to Rt. Hon. William Pitt.

Petersham

25 July, 1802.

Sir,
        In case you are so kind as to take any notice of the
hardship with which I cannot help thinking I have been
very undeservedly treated at this time, I beg leave to state
to you that some time ago my family having some suspicion
of Sir Francis Burdett transferring his fortune & residence
to some foreign country, which made us all very unhappy,
I endeavoured to encourage by any means in my power his
continuing in Parliament, as the most likely way of preventing a measure which struck so deep at our comfort, by
removing from our society my daughter & her lovely
children, at the very moment when we were suffering by the
recent loss of Lord Guilford.

        We were all in good hope (as he is by no means void of
talent & understanding) that time would give moderation
to his opinions & conduct, & that his associates who we
considered (though totally unacquainted with them) as very
bad society, would by & by appear to him in the light they

are seen by other men of sense & experience, so that he would of himself withdraw from such connections. My endeavours however proved vain, for he repeatedly told me he was positively determined to be in Parliament no more. To my knowledge seats, by purchase & in various modes, were offered to him, but he declined them all. I had therefore quite given up the point, when he came to me one morning, & surprised me much by saying he was to stand for Middlesex. He did not consult me, for this unexpected communication was made to me on the morning of the day it appeared in all the newspapers. I was truly sorry for it, not because I conceived it would be obnoxious to Government, which never occurred to me as being worth their attention (neither for the first week did I ever hear they took any part or troubled themselves about it), but because it appeared that the expense must be *great & certain*, & the success at least very doubtful. I never intended *myself* to take any part, or ever dreamt of my having any influence : & as to voting myself, I neither intended it, nor have I voted, or mean to do so. But, on the commencement, various people of various ranks came to ask my wishes about it : to which I answered that I must naturally wish well to so near a connection. And indeed I very much wished it, for the same reason that I had before so much endeavoured to induce him to come in, in a quiet way. I made some efforts to get him votes after this, when it was pointed out to me where I might hope to succeed, but certainly with no great degree of animation or success. It was a scene I had never been acquainted with, & for which I really felt great detestation, & if I got him a dozen votes I believe it will be found the outside of the issue of my exertions, which have been blazoned forth as of so much consequence that I have heard it was even supposed by Government that Sir Francis must have given up the contest long ago but for my support. Nothing can be further from the truth, & it is well known by those near me that on the second day, & every day since, I have always said the 500 majority must be decisive of the ultimate fate of the election, & that it was absurd to go on & could answer no good purpose,—was very expensive & might endanger the quiet & good order of the metropolis & its environs, which it was as much my interest as any man's & still more my inclination to maintain.   Had I actually been one of His Majesty's Ministers, I do not see how I could have acted otherwise towards my daughter's husband, living with her, & she & her mother & sisters in the most affectionate style surrounding me.   And surely it must arise from these gentlemen having been misled by some very false impressions of my conduct, that they have taken such unprecedented steps against me, which I do not think would have been taken against any man for such a reason under your Administration.   They are very much mistaken indeed if they considered me an enemy to them, & still more if they considered me as a man of any dangerous principles —which I am sure the few that know me, & those who know me the most, will be most ready to contradict. Indeed I do not believe my enemies, if I have any, have ever ascribed any such opinions or conduct to me.

Sir Francis's house, which I bought & let to him with a very innocent view of keeping him from emigration, & to have my daughter & grandchildren close to me—being at next door—I believe has favoured the idea of my taking a violent part.   It is possible too, as I have been told, that envious & malicious people have forwarded it for their own interested views, & the Council & Committee of Sir Francis, none of whom I either know or ever will have any intercourse with, may have taken unwarrantable liberties with my name.   In every view of it I hope you will think I have been cruelly treated.   Heaven knows except for the reason I have given I do not care a straw for the event of the election, nor did I ever, unless for private affection, ever take any part in my life in anything of the kind.   I hope,

Sir, you will be satisfied of the honest truth of all I have stated, & with the kindness you have often shown me, shield me from further injury. I have been obliged to leave Town on account of great indisposition, & it is with difficulty I have written this or can assure you of the sincere respect with which I remain, Sir,

your faithful humble servant,

THOMAS COUTTS.

To the Strand, *private*, will be my best direction, if you are so good as to write to me.

The two following letters [1] suggest that Coutts was not so innocent as he wished to be thought:

Duke of Devonshire to T. Coutts.

July 8, 1802.

SIR,

In consequence of the note the Duchess received from you yesterday, I write this to let you know that I have given directions that whatever interest I have in the County of Middlesex shall be given to Sir Francis Burdett & Mr Byng.

I am, Sir,

your most obedient humble servant,

DEVONSHIRE.

Duke of Northumberland to T. Coutts.

Northumberland House

7 July, 1802.

SIR,

I shall at all times be happy in seeing Sir F. Burdett; but, if his intended visit is upon the subject you mention in your letter, I should be sorry he gave himself that unnecessary trouble at a moment, when his time must be so

[1] I am indebted for these two letters to Messrs. Dobell, Booksellers, of Bruton Street, London. Mr. Dobell thought that the letters came from the " Melville Papers."

much occupied : as I have for particular reasons fully determined to take no part whatever in the present contest for the County of Middlesex.   I have the honour to be, Sir,

your obedient servant,

NORTHUMBERLAND.

Among the Coutts papers is a memorandum, unsigned but obviously from some person in the Addington Government, which shows the Ministerial point of view :

" They admit it is hardly possible for a man so enviably situated as Sir Francis Burdett is, & still less for you, to have any designs of this nature, but that the Power which they contend you once had is now out of your hands, & that if Sir Francis's present Counsellors get a little more ascendancy, it will be torn from his when the consequences may be extremely distressing.   Under these circumstances they say no person ought to be surprised at their shewing in the most decided manner their dissatisfaction with any one whom they consider as having been the means of bringing forward a Contest (even though unintentionally as to the mischievous consequences) more alarming from the encouragement it gives to what they consider a disaffected Party than any thing that has been done for many years."

Another letter, to J. Home, pictures the amiable banker's confusion :

Stratton Street
19 Aug., 1802.

MY DEAR SIR,

. . . During my illness Piccadilly has been in a continual mob with my son-in-law's election.   Fortunately it has not produced the mischief that seemed almost unavoidable.   At least I have heard of nobody having been hurt.   Government took no part the first week, & when the question was between two individuals it was very natural for me to prefer my daughter's husband to a stranger, but when I found it was considered an object to Government I desisted . . . yet envy & malice has been attacking me by every possible means in newspapers—representing me as a Jacobin. . . . Believe me when I tell you . . . I hold all Jacobinical principles in abhorrence. . . . No man is more sincerely attached to the King & Constitution than I am . . . & as to money I never either did or ever will advance any or was ever asked to do so. . . . Neither does Sir Francis Burdett owe me a shilling or ever did borrow from me any money in the whole course of my acquaintance with him—nor did he ever ask any from me, neither (for anything I ever knew of his affairs) have I any reason to believe he stood in need of it . . . most faithfully yours,

T. COUTTS.

Mrs. fitzherbert to T. Coutts.

[July or August 1802.]

MY DEAR SIR,

I do assure you, my good Friend, *we* did not want an explanation of yr conduct, as *We* were perfectly persuaded that nothing but malice could have fabricated the reports that have been propagated about you.—However I am not sorry I have under yr own handwriting a confirmation of what I was myself convinced of before. Nobody can be more yr advocates or feel more properly towards you than both the Prince & Duke of York, the latter has been here for a few days, & yesterday the Duke of Clarence left us. The three brothers are everything you could wish, & one & all feel much hurt at the conduct of the D. of C (umberland), who I cannot forgive for what he has done towards you, what could induce him to behave so, it certainly cannot be of any consequence to you, & whatever *he may think* I am certain nobody thinks him of *any sort of consequence whatever*, tho' I believe his Ideas of himself are very different.—He has been very busy in implicating the Prince in the Business of the Election, & has done & said everything he could to his prejudice on the occasion, no reason could be assigned for such a conduct but the love of mischief, & sowing dissensions in his Family, thank God he has not succeeded. The Prince bids me assure you of his best & kindest wishes, you have not had a better friend upon this occasion than he has been, being perfectly persuaded that your conduct has been perfectly the reverse of what was so industriously propagated concerning you. I was very often tempted to call at yr Door before I left Town to talk to you upon this Business, but I did not dare do it, I assure you no one has felt more for you than I have done. . . .

M. F.

Of all the contests in the General Election of 1802 that of Middlesex excited the greatest interest. Pitt wrote to his successor, the Prime Minister Addington, on July 29 :[1] " I shall be impatient to hear the result of Burdett's triumphal entry, though I think it will end without his being proclaimed first consul : & as to his being member for Middlesex I do not suffer myself to think there is any chance of it, unless his mob decrees the repeal of Grenville's bill [2] & appoints Horne Tooke to decide, in the name of the sovereign people, all controverted elections."

Burdett's election, as Pitt felt sure, was challenged; but the Mainwaring mill ground slowly, and it was not till November 23, 1803, that Mainwaring presented a petition to the House of Commons claiming the seat. He alleged, among other things, that the Sheriffs had shown great partiality to Burdett by admitting people to vote who had no right to vote, thus giving him " a colourable & apparent majority."

The Select Committee of the House reported on July 9, 1804 :

---

[1] Pellew's " Life of Sidmouth," Vol. II, p. 72.
[2] The Grenville Act of 1770 by which disputed elections were to be determined by a Select Committee of the House of Commons.

MIDDLESEX·ELECTION. 1804. — a Long Pull, a Strong Pull, and a Pull Altogether

HORNE TOOKE.   BURDETT.   SHERIDAN.

(1) That Sir Francis Burdett was not duly elected for Middlesex. The Sheriffs wilfully, knowingly, and corruptly did admit to poll for Sir Francis Burdett upwards of 300 persons claiming to vote as proprietors of a mill purported to be situate in the parish of Isleworth and called " The Good Intent Mill," by which means a colourable majority was obtained for Sir F. Burdett.

(2) That W. Mainwaring ought to have been returned by the Sheriffs as member for Middlesex.

(3) That W. Mainwaring did by his agents commit acts of treating, whereby he is incapacitated to serve in Parliament upon such election.

The House of Commons therefore ordered a new election. But in consequence of the Report the Sheriffs, Sir W. Rawlins and Robert Albion Cox, were on March 11, 1805, voted guilty of a breach of privileges and committed to Newgate. They were only released on May 10, 1805, after a severe reprimand, which was entered on the Journals of the House.[1]

From July 23 to August 6, 1804, Middlesex was plunged into a new election fight. The candidates on this occasion were Sir Francis Burdett and G. B. Mainwaring, the son of the former candidate.[2] In character the election of 1804 was similar to that of 1802. Burdett was again supported not only by the Radicals, but also by the Whigs. All the Whig leaders upheld his cause, including the Dukes of Norfolk,

---

[1] Henry Hunt declared that Burdett never visited Cox in prison, and that Cox in consequence was disgusted with " Radical " politics.

[2] The chief authorities for the election of 1804 are : (a) A letter to the freeholders of Middlesex by an " Attentive Observer " (1804), written against Burdett. The " Attentive Observer " was J. Bowles. Bowles was a " Commissioner for Dutch claims," and is said to have made thereby £30,000. He belonged to the class of " war profiteers," whom Burdett loathed. (b) " A Full Report of the Speeches of Sir Francis Burdett at the late Election (1804)," written on Burdett's side.

Bedford, and Devonshire, Lord Lansdowne, Lord Moira, Grey, Sheridan, Whitbread, while Fox [1] took the warmest interest in his success. Burdett in the course of the election, while preserving his independence, almost proclaimed himself a Whig—" I have ever been a steady supporter of what is called the Whig interest. Without being a Party man, I have always given the Whig interest my support, because I believe that the Whig principles are those which must save the country . . . a creed calculated for freemen. But if the Whig interest deserts its principles, or if the Tory interest abandons its errors, then you will find me supporting the Tories." Fox he described as " the man who is universally acknowledged to be the greatest character in this country, whose virtues and abilities are so transcendent as to hold him out at this moment, not to this country alone, but to the world, as an object of esteem and admiration."

But the Whigs were not to be alarmed by too close a contact with the " Correspondists " (*i.e.* the Extremists).

There are among the Burdett papers of this date (1803—1804) three letters in the same handwriting, two of which are signed "Notary" and " J. Notary." The first of these refers to the trial of Colonel Despard in 1803 [2]; the second is a letter to the freeholders of Middlesex signed " A Freeholder of Middlesex," comparing the claims of the two candidates in this election to the advantage of Burdett, and dated July 18, 1804; the third, of the same date, gives us some insight into the working of the election. Here it is :

---

[1] Henry Hunt, " Memoirs," Vol. II, p. 139 : " I remember sitting in the Library with Mr. Fox (at Cheltenham) on the morning when the news arrived by the Post that Sir Francis Burdett was elected for Middlesex by a majority of 1. Fox was greatly elated with this momentary success of the Baronet, but he expressed his doubts upon the final issue of an inquiry before a Committee of the House of Commons. This famous contest for Middlesex had caused considerable anxiety throughout the country, and a party of us, including Fox, used to assemble daily on the arrival of the Post at the Library to hear the state of the Poll."

[2] See below, p. 165.

18th July 1804.

DEAR CITIZEN,

I am employed in a curious department, namely as an Agent for Printing Bills, Songs, etc. etc. & as such have employed our freind Seale. The Bills are to be made in my Name, & I am to pay them, but Bonney [1] is to remunerate me on this account.

Mr Knight of Grosvenor Sqr. is the Agent for Triumphal decorations, State Coach, Horse trappings etc. etc. Others are to hire Coaches, Some to Bribe & Treat, while our Hero & his avowed Agent are to be as pure & unspotted as Caesar's wife.

Hobbs Scott is commissioned to get *Heron* to stir up the Spital Fields Men on Monday, & I have been repeatedly exhorted to raise as many as possible. Bully Robinson is returned from Aylesbury, & entered our Service. Captain Gawler [2] is gone to Scotland, but his Brother Henry is shortly expected in Town. There is to be a dinner of Byng's Friends this day at 78, but the Correspondists are kept in the background, lest the Whigs should be alarmed.

yours in civic esteem

NOTARY.

Mainwaring's supporters attacked Burdett for his friendship with traitors such as Arthur O'Connor and Colonel Despard, who had been executed for treason in 1803 and for certain seditious language he was said to have used at a dinner given in July 1803 at the "Crown and Anchor" to celebrate his return for Middlesex in the preceding year. But the "Attentive Observer," who gives an account of the election, had to admit that Burdett was still "the idol of the mob": "their enthusiasm for him was greater than

[1] John Augustus Bonney was one of those who, with Hardy and Tooke, were put on their trial for high treason in 1794.
[2] Captain Gawler, afterwards known as John Bellenden Ker, second to Burdett in his duel (1807). His brother Henry was Burdett's solicitor.

ever"; "he retained complete possession of their minds."

The contest was neck and neck. Pitt, who was staying at Cashioberry with Lord Essex, had the numbers of the poll brought to him every day. One of the few jocose remarks ever assigned to him was in this connection: "Being offered some cowslip wine he at first declined it, but immediately after said he would drink success to Sir Francis Burdett in *Cowslip*." [1]

On the fifteenth and last day of the poll (August 6) the Sheriffs promised that such of the disputed votes as could not be examined before the close of the poll at 3 p.m. should be examined later, and, if found good, admitted. After 3 p.m. the Sheriffs examined the disputed votes, and found that if the good votes were admitted Burdett would have a majority of one. But Mainwaring protested. The Sheriffs on August 7 heard Counsel on both sides, and finally decided that the poll must be declared as it stood at 3 p.m. on August 6, and therefore they returned Mainwaring as the duly elected Member for Middlesex by a majority of five votes.

To this date must surely belong the letter from Burdett to Creevey which Sir Herbert Maxwell in his edition of the "Creevey Papers" dates as 1802.

Sir F. Burdett to Mr Creevey.

Piccadilly,
Aug. 18, [1804].

MY DEAR CREEVEY,

I look upon your advice as excellent, & intend consequently to follow it. You know by this time the Petition is taken out of my hands in a manner most flattering & honourable. The conduct of the Sheriffs I believe quite unprecedented, but whether they will be punished, protected, or rewarded, exceeds my sagacity to foretell, perhaps

[1] An allusion to Lady Oxford. "Farington Diary," Vol. II, p. 283.

both the latter. I regard the issue of this contest exactly in the same light as you do—a subject of great triumph & not of mortification. My friend is compleatly satisfied. I have done my duty & the Public acknowledge it—surely this is sufficient to satisfy the ambition of an honest man.

Sherry is quite grown loving again; he came here yesterday with all sorts of (illegible) from the Prince, Mrs fitzherbert etc. etc. It is a year & a half I believe before this Election, since we almost spoke. Mrs Sheridan came one day on the Hustings, & was much delighted & entertained at being hailed by the multitude as Mrs Burdett . . . yours sincerely,

F. BURDETT.

On January 25, 1805, Freeholders of Middlesex petitioned the House of Commons against Mainwaring's return on the ground that the Sheriffs ought to have taken into account the disputed votes.

On March 5, 1805, the Select Committee of the House reported that Sir Francis ought to have been returned as duly elected.

Thereupon Mainwaring presented a petition accusing Sir Francis of bribery, corruption, impersonation, etc. (March 13).

On May 6, 1805, the Speaker read a letter from Burdett informing him that he was not in a position to defend his election, and finally on February 10, 1806, the Select Committee reported in favour of Mainwaring; who was then declared the duly elected member for Middlesex. But by this time the Parliament was drawing to its close.

The sum of money spent by Burdett on these two elections was enormous—anything between £56,000 and £100,000. But such outlay was characteristic of the age. Coke of Norfolk is said to have spent no less than £500,000 on his elections.

CHAPTER VIII

SOMETHING must now be said about general politics in these years 1802–1806. They were in a state of considerable confusion. The Addington Government had mismanaged the Peace (of Amiens, March 1802), and Addington "the Doctor", though full of sublime self-conceit and regarded by the King as an ideal Minister, was altogether unequal to the position.

> " As London is to Paddington,
> So is Pitt to Addington,"

was the witticism of Canning.

Pitt had promised George III that he would never again raise the question of Catholic Emancipation during the King's life. He had given an even more foolish pledge to Addington, that he would support his Ministry, and he had induced a number of his followers to become members of it. Grenville, Windham, and Canning had, however, refused to do any such thing. The incapable Addington Ministry found itself confronted with formidable enemies. The " Old Opposition " under Fox enthusiastically welcomed the Peace, though they criticised the mismanagement shown in its negotiation. The " New Opposition," Grenville, Windham, and Canning, denounced the Peace as a complete surrender of British interests and clamoured for war. Pitt gave the Peace his blessing, but without enthusiasm.

Napoleon soon showed that his intentions were anything but peaceful. In violation of the Treaty of Lunéville, he had himself elected President of the Italian Republic, and overran Switzerland; he broke the Franco-Dutch Convention of 1801 by not withdrawing French troops from Holland; he annexed Piedmont; he refused to renew commercial treaties with England; he schemed for the formation of a French Empire in the West (Louisiana); he sent Decaen to India to stir up the natives against England; he published in the *Moniteur* of January 30, 1803, a bellicose report of Sebastiani about Egypt, clearly instigating its reconquest by the French. He complained of attacks upon himself in the London Press and demanded the expulsion of the Bourbon Princes from England. The Addington Government therefore announced that England would not restore Malta (as she had promised in the Peace of Amiens) to the Knights of St. John. It would simply be handing it over to France. England had made the promise in the belief that Napoleon intended to carry out the provisions of the Treaty of Lunéville and the Franco-Dutch Convention of 1801. But the situation had been altered in vital respects by Napoleon's subsequent encroachments in Italy, Holland and Switzerland, and England was justified in demanding equivalents. Clearly the renewal of hostilities was imminent. War was declared on May 18, 1803.

Pitt approved of the Declaration of War. Fox agreed that, *if* Napoleon was the unscrupulous and aggressive tyrant that he was represented as being, war was inevitable. But of Napoleon's character and aims he was not certain, and he held that the negotiations had been woefully mismanaged. Grenville, Windham, etc., were fierce supporters of the war policy, and Fox, Grenville and Windham were all agreed on the incompetence of Addington to conduct the struggle. Pitt held curiously aloof, giving Addington at first a qualified support; he refused to join with Grenville, Fox and Windham in a united opposition to the Government. Grenville and Windham, unable to move Pitt, then turned to Fox and entered into a policy of active co-operation with him. Pitt's support of the Ministry soon dwindled away, and finally he was found in open opposition. The situation was further complicated by a recrudescence of the King's insanity (February to April 1804) and the dangerous illness of the Prince of Wales. The following letters illustrate the position of affairs in the early part of 1804 :

Mrs fitzherbert to T. Coutts (at Bath).

18 Feb. 1804.

The Prince, thank God, is well, he has had a very severe & dangerous illness, every unpleasant symptom is totally removed & nothing but a degree of lowness & weakness remains which he daily gets better of. The present state of affairs are such as to distress him very much, but by keeping as quietly as he possibly can, I trust he will be able to encounter the many difficulties I see approaching. He has not seen a creature of any description either publick or private acquaintance except the King's Ministers, who he is obliged to receive daily to report the state of His Majesty's health, & as he belongs to no party & has never been consulted he feels he has nothing to do but remain passive & quiet. What is to become of both the King & him, time must determine.

Burdett set out his thoughts on the situation at length in a letter to Coutts—which begins with some reflections about his own possessions. Coutts had proposed a tenant for Ramsbury who was also a possible purchaser. Burdett accepted the tenancy, but added :

Sir F. Burdett to T. Coutts (at Clifton).

London.
6th March 1804.

My DEAR SIR,

. . . As to selling, unless it was for the purpose, which I have often had in view, of placing money in America (a very wise step) I shd. never think of parting with land; for, if once converted into money, it wd. fall away like friends in adversity from a person of my habits & disposition, there being nothing so irksome to me as thinking upon that subject, & if money is not thought about, as well as used, with prudence, it is a very evanescent possession : land is best for a man who places his supreme good in leisure, liberty & command of his own time, which are my Penates or household Gods. . . .

I am going to dine with the Duke of Bedford today, Sunday. Mr Fox is to be there, & I suppose the whole party; we had a late debate the other night in the house, which only tended to confirm me in my opinion of the stupidity, or I shd. rather say insanity, of the war, which, it seems agreed on all sides, we are unable to make although we have declared : for certainly it cannot be called making war " ubi tu pulsas, ego vapulo," where you give & I receive all the blows, merely exposing yourself to attack with a confessed impotence of attacking your enemy, & entertaining great apprehensions & doubts as to your power even of efficient means of defence.

Mr Pitt made some very foolish propositions, as I thought, for mending the volunteer system accompanied with great encomiums upon that body, great abuse of the French & indeed of every nation in Europe to whom the Volunteers were to set an example, which was to stimulate them to emulation & to shake off the French yoke. This unmeaning declamation, this inflated inanity, & low solicitation of the narrowest & most contemptible national prejudices, which a boy in the fifth form of Eaton School wd. despise, passes in the assembly of the collected wisdom of the country for statesmanlike ability, & I believe has convinced them that Mr Pitt is a much greater general than Bonaparte. I heard several members expressing their surprise at Mr Pitt's military ability. But how low England must have sunk when the ground of panegyric is her possibly being able to defend her own shores against the French. We seem to be undergoing the fate of Greece, which was ruined by a set of venal orators, who spent their whole time in talking as their interest prompted, whilst Philip matured his plans for their destruction. But we shall never believe this possible till it happens, & those who have the power will prefer running all risks to taking the steps necessary for securing the country, because with the danger wd. be destroyed the corruption to which they cling, in which they live move & have their being.

Messrs Pitt, Fox, Windham, etc. appeared all to agree in uniting their efforts to turn out the present Administration; all (except Mr Pitt) are believed with good reason to have coalesced for that purpose. I own I am sorry for it, & I am fearful Mr Fox will injure himself in public estimation, & participate the just odium that party have incurred, nor do I see what possible advantage he can reap from it. Should the King recover, the Administration [1] would in my opinion be rather strengthened than weakened by it. Should he die, or a Regency be formed with the Prince at the head, Mr Fox might probably come in but with less popularity & more incumbrance for his new friends.

As Launcelot says, " We were Christians enough before, e'en as many as cd. well live one by another; if we grow all to be pork eaters, we shall not shortly have a rasher on the coals for money." [2] Mr Pitt stands cunningly aloof from all these arrangements unencumbered, eying attentively the doubtful balance & dealing out his flattery to both parties, the scales once fixed he will settle on the winner, sharing the triumph & the spoils of victory, & perhaps in a little while be again joined by his former associates,[3] who will make no scruple of abandoning Fox & abusing him as much as ever, which he will bear with his usual good temper, retire once more to St Annes, & be as ready to forget & forgive as before, & remain an unexampled instance of

[1] *i.e.* the Addington Government.
[2] " Merchant of Venice," Act 3, sc. 5.
[3] Burdett was wrong, Grenville did not desert Fox.

splendid talents & aimiable dispositions rendered useless
by indiscretion & want of firmness.   Jago's speech to
Othello [1] is perhaps not quite inapplicable.   " If you forget,
the World will call you wise : if you forgive, the World will
call you good ; if you shd. take her to your arms again, the
World will call you very very very—good."

As for me I am so convinced of the necessity of some
strong measures far beyond a mere change of Administration (about which I am very indifferent) that having done
my duty in speaking plainly & fairly against this war & this
system at a time when it is possible it might have availed ;
not partaking the feelings of any set of public men, whose
views appear to extend no farther than the walls of St
Stephen's, or efforts beyond a seat on the Treasury bench,
partaking none of their views or wishes, I think my wisest
way is to be quiet, neither attempting to advance or obstruct
any set of men in pursuit of such objects alone—which
seem to me to fall short, very far short of what the times &
situation demand.   Whether this mode of seeing things
proceeds from any defect of judgement arising from habits
of abstract speculation, bookish theory & want of practical
knowledge, is not for me to determine.   I heartily wish it
may be the case, for I had much rather be in error by myself
than in danger with all, & the country in reality be so shamefully treated as to me it appears.   At the same time, when I
examine my own breast & am unable to discover any latent
interested motive or selfish consideration misleading me,
but on the contrary see plainly how opposite are my sentiments & opinions to my interests, I cannot avoid concluding that they have a rational, as I am sure they have, an
honest foundation.   Wise or simple therefore they must
remain the rules of my conduct, by observing which I can
alone preserve that proud feeling of conscious rectitude,
which is the chief ingredient of my notion of happiness, &

[1] The quotation is not from Shakespeare's " Othello."   I have not
been able to trace it.

the only good out of the power of all-controlling fortune.
Adieu.

Love to all, yours sincerely,

F. BURDETT.

Addington, in view of his crumbling majority, resigned
on May 10, 1804, and Pitt resumed office as Prime Minister
at a time of terrific strain, when invasion was continuously
threatened from Boulogne. He proposed to the King the
formation of a " national " Ministry that would include
Fox, Grenville and Windham, but the King would not hear
of the admission of Fox.

In view of the fact that George consented to receive Fox
as a Minister in January 1806, it is probable that if Pitt had
applied the requisite pressure the King would have given
way. As things were, Grenville and Windham refused to
join a Ministry based on a principle of " exclusion," and Pitt
is said to have declared that he would teach that proud man
(Grenville) he could do without him.

Political parties had become disintegrated into groups.
There was "the Old Opposition" under Fox, the Grenville–
Windham group who co-operated with Fox, an Addington
group of some fifty M.P.'s, and the followers of Pitt. One
half of Pitt's Cabinet belonged to the Addington group, and
Addington himself joined Pitt's Ministry as Lord Sidmouth
(January to July 1805).

With none of these groups except that of Fox had
Burdett the slightest sympathy. When the Parliament
elected in 1802 met in November, a renewal of hostilities
already seemed imminent, and Burdett denounced the
policy of war. Speaking on the Address, he said : " The
formidable position now occupied by France must be
contemplated by every Englishman with dismay. But was
it not extraordinary that those, who have accumulated
against us this mountain of dangers,[1] should be the most

[1] Grenville, Windham, etc.

forward to exaggerate them : that they should be the loudest in stating the result of their own conduct and counsels, and the most studious in detailing the perils with which their imprudence, their obstinacy, or their infatuation, have encompassed the country. Nothing surely could be more extraordinary except the advice they now offer us. They advise us to do, what ?   Why, to pursue the same mad career they themselves had run before, and to choose the same person [1] for our guide who has plunged us in all the perils & perplexities, which they now so pathetically, but so preposterously deplore. . . .

" But what is the blame imputed to Ministers ? [2]   That they made peace without foreseeing what advantages France would derive from peace, and that they do not now hold a bold and blustering language, while it is confessed that, if they again tried the chances of war, there would scarcely be any hope of their doing anything effectual. . . . But if any faults or blame attended the negotiation of peace, they were not fairly ascribable to Ministers : for they arose out of the nature of the war itself, and the principles upon which it was conducted."

Burdett then gave his more particular objections to the proposed Address. " . . . It seemed to indicate that we should catch at an opportunity of renewing hostilities. This he considered imprudent, for it argued an inclination without a consciousness of ability to give it effect. . . . Ministers ought to exert every means to conciliate the confidence and affections of the people. . . . If it was really their wish to rally and unite all honest men in defence of the country, let them hold out some principle for which they will fight : a principle that can win their hearts and gain their understandings. For his part he believed the principle of Reform would have great weight to that effect, and under the present circumstances he did not see that any other principle would enable the country to cope with France."

[1] Pitt.   [2] The Addington Ministry.

Napoleon was a Sphinx-like riddle to Whigs and Radicals. They did not know what to make of him. In a sense he was the " heir " of the Revolution, upon which they had bestowed their blessing. He personified the abolition of privilege and all the " social " work of the Revolution. On the other hand, by a *coup d'état* he had cashiered the representatives of the French people. But it was only by slow degrees that he came to be recognised by them as a despotic ruler at home and an aggressive conqueror abroad. The orientation of politics in England gradually changed. The former war had been regarded by all Radicals as an attack by the despotic powers on freedom and liberal principles; all advocates of freedom had opposed the war. But if France had " boxed the compass," and if Napoleon was simply an aggressive despot, the heir not of the Revolution, but of Louis XIV, why, then, it was possible for English Radicals to support the new war. The Lake poets show the change of attitude. Wordsworth, who had once regarded the French Revolution as the dawn of the Millennium, could write,

> " But now, become oppressors in their turn,
> Frenchmen had changed a war of self-defence
> For one of conquest, losing sight of all
> Which they had struggled for."

And as the sun of Freedom set over the Continent, leaving it under the night of tyranny, he gave to the world his " Poems dedicated to National Independence and Liberty."

On the other hand, many Radicals continued for a time to regard Napoleon as the spirit of the Revolution personified, and Burdett seems still to have viewed him in this light.

Burdett's Radical fever reached its climax about this time and got him into strange company.

On November 19, 1802, just after the meeting of Parliament, Colonel Despard was arrested on the charge of high treason. We have met with Colonel Despard before. He was one of those imprisoned in Cold Bath Fields Prison on suspicion of treason under the Habeas Corpus Suspension Act in 1798, and on his release in 1801 Burdett had been a security for his good behaviour. Something further must now be said about his history.

The youngest of six brothers, who all, except the eldest, became soldiers, Edward Marcus Despard was an Irishman born in 1751. In 1779 he served with distinction in the West Indies, when, in company with Nelson, he was sent on an expedition to capture San Juan, in Central America. The commander of the expedition, Captain Polson, wrote: "There was scarcely a gun fired but what was pointed by Captain Nelson or Lieut. Despard, chief engineer, who has exerted himself on every occasion." The thanks of the King were conveyed to Despard (1782), and those of the Assembly of Jamaica were voted to him in 1783. In 1784 he was given the governorship of what is now called British Honduras, with the title of " Superintendent of His Majesty's Affairs " within the district. His salary was a paltry £500 a year. Disputes arose between the old settlers and the new log-wood cutters, who were authorised to ply their trade by the treaty of peace with Spain (1783). Despard took the side of the newcomers, and there were many complaints of his highhanded action, but he was supported by the Governor of Jamaica and the Secretary of State, Lord Sydney. Then there arose "a new king who knew not Joseph " in the person of Lord Grenville, who succeeded Sydney as Secretary of State. Despard was recalled in 1790, and kept waiting for a dreary period of two years in the lobbies of Whitehall. In 1792 he was informed by Grenville that his office as " Superintendent " was abolished, and he was given no further employment: the monetary compensation to which he thought himself entitled was refused. He brooded over his real or imaginary grievance, and drifted into revolutionary companionship. He is mentioned in the " Castlereagh Correspondence " in connection with the " United Irishmen," and it was doubtless on the ground of this connection that under the Habeas Corpus Suspension Act he was imprisoned in Cold Bath Fields Prison, and only released at the beginning of 1801. His soul had been still further embittered by imprisonment, and on November 16, 1802, he was arrested on a charge of high treason.

Sir Francis Burdett pitied Despard because he was poor and persecuted by Government, and, so far as the world knew, an innocent man. Lord Moira from the same feeling of pity sent him £50 only a few days before his arrest.

Despard's case has been compared by Sir Charles Oman with that of Sir Roger Casement in the Great War (1914–1918). They were both Irishmen who had served the Crown with distinction in high official posts and been rewarded with promotion. But there is this difference— that Despard had, while Casement had not, a grievance. The most charitable view to take is that both men had suffered from a " touch " of the sun in tropical climates, and were in consequence not wholly responsible for their actions.

Despard was accused of a conspiracy to seize the Bank and the Tower, and to assassinate the King on his going to open Parliament " by gaining possession of the great gun on the parade before the Horse Guards in St James' Park, loading it with chain shot and firing it at His Majesty's carriage." The plot has been generally regarded as wild and extravagant. How could Despard have expected, without arms, without money, without any force—for the total number of conspirators was some fifty people, drawn from the riff-raff of the population, some disaffected private soldiers and common labourers—how could he have hoped to overthrow the Government ? Sir Charles Oman takes a more serious view of the plot. He recalls the fact that in the absence of a proper police force London as late as 1780 had been for three days in the hands of a riotous mob (the

Gordon Riots). Some of the companies of the Grenadier Guards were " riddled with sedition," and Despard himself is said to have declared that the working classes in all the large towns were ready to revolt. But the Government was well served by spies, and on November 19 a police force surprised the conspirators in an obscure tavern known as the " Oakley Arms." Some thirty people were arrested, all of the lowest class, with the solitary exception of Colonel Despard. Despard and twelve others were put on their trial for high treason. A Special Commission under Lord Chief Justice Ellenborough was appointed to try the accused men. The case of Despard was taken first on February 7, 1803. The Attorney-General, Spencer Perceval, prosecuted, and Serjeant Best (afterwards a Judge) was leading Counsel for Despard. The prosecution rested its case on the testimony of some of the conspirators who had turned " King's evidence." And it must be admitted that there was little corroboration. Counsel for the defence explained Despard's presence at the " Oakley Arms " by saying that certain soldiers with a grievance, knowing that Despard was also a soldier with a grievance, had invited him to meet them and discuss the situation. Counsel then proceeded to blacken the character of the witnesses for the prosecution. " Where are the two credible witnesses? The witnesses for the Crown are, on their own showing, the most wicked and abominable of mankind. They try to redeem themselves from destruction by swearing away the life of Colonel Despard."

Lord Nelson, Sir Alured Clarke (who had been Governor of Jamaica in 1790) and Sir Evan Nepean were called to testify to Despard's character.

Lord Nelson spoke up strongly for his old comrade-in-arms.[1] Referring to the year 1779, he said, " We went on the Spanish Main together; we slept many nights together in our clothes upon the ground; we have measured the height of the enemies' wall together; in all that period of

[1] Shorthand report of Despard's trial by J. and W. B. Gurney.

time no man could have shown more zealous attachment to his Sovereign and his Country than Despard did. I formed the highest opinion of him as a man and an officer. Having lost sight of him for the last twenty years, if I had been asked my opinion of him, I should certainly have said, if he is alive, he is certainly one of the brightest ornaments of the British Army." But Nelson had to admit that he had never seen Despard since April 29, 1780.

The jury, after an absence of twenty-five minutes, found Despard guilty, but added a rider, "We do most earnestly recommend him to mercy because of his former good character and eminent services." The Judge in passing sentence referred to the plot as "a treasonable conspiracy of enormous extent and most alarming magnitude."

Lord Nelson, even after Despard's conviction up to the morning of his execution, February 21, used every influence in his power to save his life.[1] If Despard was guilty, it was not the fault of Nelson, Moira or Burdett that Despard, goaded into madness by desperation, embarked on a wicked scheme of treason.

Henry Hunt in his Memoirs [2] professes to believe that Despard was innocent. Henry Clifford [3] in 1801 had cited to him Despard as an instance of tyranny and injustice carried out under forms of law. If Hunt is correct, Despard must have been removed from Cold Bath Fields to the Tower; for he describes a visit that he and Clifford paid to Despard in the Tower at the beginning of 1801. Clifford in 1801 said to Hunt that if Despard on his release were troublesome, Ministers "will stick at nothing, and I should not be the least surprised, if they were ultimately to have some of their spies to swear away his life." Hunt therefore

---

[1] "A Full Report of the Middlesex Election of 1804," Introduction, p. xx.

[2] Hunt's "Memoirs," Vol. I, pp. 476, 494, 500. Cf. "Farington Diary," Vol. II, p. 83 : " Lady Abercorn told Laurence this afternoon that she had been to-day at Sir W. Hamilton's, where Mrs. Despard was in another room in great distress. She came there to urge Lord Nelson to make further application to Government, Feb. 10th."

[3] For Clifford see note on p. 166.

professes to believe that Despard fell a victim to spies and
agents provocateurs employed by Government.

The following letter, written by " J. Notary," is of
interest as referring to Despard's trial, and as showing the
survival of the old British Jacobin propaganda into the
nineteenth century. It seems to describe a belated meeting
of the " Society for Constitutional Information." None of
the people mentioned in the letter was a member of Colonel
Despard's entourage.

Monday morning, Feb. 7th (1803).

DEAR CITIZEN,

I was employed the whole of Saturday for our
friends, & in the evening attended Committee, where little
worthy of note transpired. Hardy,[1] Le Maitre,[2] & myself
form a kind of secret Committee, & we met previous to the
other Committee & arranged our matters. Our object is
to look after the expenditure, to protect Palmer [3] in his
claims, & to issue out the money entrusted to us as we deem
expedient. Most of the supplies come from the circle of Wimbledon, & very trifling from any other quarter. Yesterday
I attended Head Quarters, & received instructions relative
to Fowkes. Such an infamous character of a man I never
heard, & the last words uttered to me, when I took leave,
were " Remember the rascal Fowkes." Burdett, Gawler,[4]

[1] Presumably Thomas Hardy the shoemaker. Prosecuted 1794;
supported by Burdett for last nine years of life, 1823–1832.

[2] Le Maitre, see Cobbett's " Political Register," May 16, 1807.
He was several times imprisoned, 1794–1795, 1796, 1798, 1801. He
helped Paull in the Westminster election of 1806.

[3] Palmer was the originator of Reforms in the Post Office mails.
See p. 221.

[4] Henry Gawler was Burdett's solicitor. His father was John
Gawler of Ramridge, near Andover, Hants. His mother was Caroline,
eldest surviving daughter of third Baron Bellenden. His brother was
John Gawler, compelled to quit the army in 1793 owing to sympathy
he displayed with the French Revolution. He changed his name to John
Bellenden Ker (Burdett's second in the duel 1807). William, seventh
Baron Bellenden and fourth Duke of Roxburgh, tried to divert the
succession to him, and entailed his estates on him. But both the
entail and his claim to the title were, after much litigation, set aside

Gunter Browne,[1] Clifford,[2] Michael Pearson,[3] John Pearson, Moody, Rogers,[4] Morgan, & Knight [5] were

---

by the House of Lords in favour of James Innes-Ker, fifth Duke of Roxburgh May 11, 1812.   He died 1842.

[1] Gunter Brown, " Farington Diary," Vol. I, p. 118.   He was one of those indicted with Lord Thanet for attempting to rescue A. O'Connor in 1798.   Lord Kenyon directed his acquittal as there was no real evidence against him.

[2] Henry Clifford.   See Hunt's " Memoirs," *ad lib*.   He was a lawyer cadet of a Roman Catholic family in Staffordshire; wrote a pamphlet (when twenty-one) insisting on right of English Roman Catholics to nominate their Bishops.   Tooke had a great opinion of Clifford's abilities, and told Stephens " he had got acquainted with that gentleman in consequence of a disagreement : that Mr. Clifford, who would allow no one to abuse him but himself, had afterwards fought a duel on his account."   He visited frequently at Wimbledon. His dates were 1768–1813.   He took a prominent part in the O. P. riots at Covent Garden Theatre, 1810.   Covent Garden Theatre was destroyed by fire September 1808 and Drury Lane in February 1809. Covent Garden was reopened by Kemble with " Macbeth " in September 1809.   The rise in prices was small.   Riots continued till the middle of December, when the original prices were restored.

Holland's " Further Memoirs of the Whig Party," p. 55 : " They (the public) thought an undue advantage was taken of that entire monopoly which the hopeless state of Drury Lane Theatre conferred on Covent Garden.   Riot when headed by Mr. Clifford, a Roman Catholic lawyer of considerable name, seemed likely to swell into political sedition. . . . Mr. Clifford was a man capable, both from temper and talents, of harbouring and executing very mischievous designs.   Impatience of the unjust disabilities under which his sect labours had reconciled him to violent opinions in politics : and unrestrained habits of in-temperance had inflamed the malignity of a disposition not originally amiable, without impairing the very acute perceptions and strong intellect with which nature had endowed him.   He was, however, pacified by the submission of the Managers, seemed to bear his triumph meekly, and if he entertained any project of engrafting further designs on the popularity to which he had raised himself, he did not live to develop them.   The drams which were unable to extinguish his spirit or drown his reason undermined his bodily constitution."

[3] Michael Pearson was one of the signatories of Middlesex free-holders who invited Sir Francis Burdett to contest Middlesex in 1802 (See " Memoirs," p. 20).

[4] Samuel Rogers, the banker-poet.

[5] Richard Payne Knight, M.P. (see Edmonds' " Poetry of Anti-Jacobin," p. 139).   He had sat more than once in Parliament; possessed a considerable landed estate, and had served the office of High Sheriff of his county; became acquainted with Horne Tooke in 1792.   He advanced money to Tooke when his situation was un-comfortable.   Tooke mentioned his kindness with heartfelt gratitude (Stevens' " Life," p. 332).

of the party. The latter said he had been pricked down
for Sheriff in Wales, & came for instructions from the
High Priest. He gave me a draft on Ransom & Co. for
£20 to be applied as follows : £12 for Mrs Graham wife
of one of the prisoners, & the remaining £8 to the general
stock. I also received subscriptions from Gunter Browne
& Rogers. Gawler will give me another £50 from Burdett,
whenever I call for it. Another £100 he said was carried
on Saturday Evening from the same party by his brother
to Le Maitre for the Colonel's defence. Burdett appeared
to be under apprehensions of his name being brought up in
the course of the trials, which he said would be damned
awkward. Tooke recommended strongly to blacken the
characters of the five material witnesses, or he said the
prisoners [1] would all be hanged. After dinner he gave as a
Toast " The innocence of the virtuous Despard." The
whole of the conversation related to two objects—the State
Trials now approaching, & the characters of the Royal
Family, which were severely satirised by Tooke & Burdett.
I was surprised to hear such pitiful & malignant aspersions
cast on the individuals belonging to that Sacred Family.
The Duke of Kent was most scandalously aspersed by Tooke,
Burdett, Gawler, & Browne, & the former compared him
to Nero & other tyrants. Tooke said that Cartwright in
his last pamphlet had mentioned that there was little chance
of a reform until the Heir Apparent ascended the Throne :
which he considered a good idea to promulgate, for, says
he, " it will make the vain fellow pledge himself to such a
thing, & that will do some good." Burdett, Tooke
attacked Clifford & charged him with attempting to draw
them into a junction with the Whigs. Tooke entered into
their history for the last 43 years & painted them out in the
most odious colours. Rogers gave Burdett some names of
several good fellows, to be introduced as Commissioners
into an Act now pending before the House, & which
Burdett promised to give to the Clerk to be entered in the

[1] Twelve others were tried with Despard.

Bill. The idea of the Colonel being fettered shocked Burdett very much, & he attributed it to private orders given to the gaoler. The whole company seemed to think his case desperate, unless the witnesses could be discredited, & therefore I was charged to spare no exertions on that score.

Stewart the Ci-devant Secretary to the Constitutional Society was denounced by Tooke as a corrupted rascal & Rogers was ordered to avoid him at the Stock Exchange. Burdett said that Government had bestowed 200 per annum on the scoundrell's wife for betraying the members of the C.S.

You will perceive by my late letters that the Junto entirely support our indicted friend, & indeed every other scheme whereby there may be the most distant chance of distressing TYRANNY. The Junto have the most rooted aversion to the persons as well as functions of sacred characters, & as such they must be ever well looked after. To use Tooke's own words, " Whigs want titles & Places, but the Citizens want a restoration of their Rights & the full enjoyment of Freedom," by which he means an entire Revolution. Barrère [1] underwent a severe castigation in his character from the High Priest to the great entertainment of the auditory. Burdett told me " there were so many Committees before the Middlesex Committee, that it would be a long time indeed before his cause could be heard : besides he had many other chances in his favour, viz. litigation, change of Ministers, death of Mainwaring, dissolution of Parliament etc. etc.

Today at two I attend my duty at Horsemonger Lane as one of the Committee of Defence. Last night there was a meeting at Slaters but I did not attend . . . You will of course excuse my punctual attendance on these low Committees, when I explain to you that in all probability it might injure

[1] Barrère was a member of the " Society for Constitutional Information " (Rose, " William Pitt and the Great War," p. 167).

my reputation with the higher orders, especially after what
has happened to the Colonel; for they will be careful of
associating too intimately with the lower Class as their
friends in future; besides I have never been used to connect myself with such men as Nichols,[1] Pemberton, Farrell,
Blythe, Aitchison etc. etc.   At present I have their confidence, & have established it by the part I have taken in
the Subscriptions etc. etc.   Therefore by not going so often
among them as I have hitherto done, I shall be more sought
after & my advice considered as more valuable than when I
am so very familiar with them.   I saw Nicholls on Saturday
night & he is highly disgusted with his journey.   The
Country Patriots are lukewarm & frightened, & we have
been much deceived in point of their numbers.   He has
brought to London only £3—13—6 in addition to the
£10—10—0 sent per post, & the Committee advanced him
£5—5—9 to prosecute his journey; so that after travelling
many hundred miles he has only profited us £8—13—6.
So much for Country Civism,

yours in civil esteem,

J. NOTARY.

To Mr Bruce, 45 Little Russell Street, Bloomsbury.

Sir Francis Burdett did not take a prominent part in the
Parliament of 1802–1806, perhaps because his Middlesex
seat was so insecure.   But the extreme nature of his views
is shown by his declaration in Parliament on July 18, 1803,
that " the only way to give spirit and energy to the people
and to make the country worth defending was to repeal
every act since the accession of His Majesty," and by a
speech he made at the " Crown and Anchor " at the end
of July 1803, when his election for Middlesex was com-
memorated.   He hated the money-jobbers who made
money out of the war, as no true Englishmen—" Wherever
money is, there is their Country," and he rightly con-

[1] See Edmonds' " Poetry of Anti-Jacobin," p. 91.

sidered that when great sacrifices were demanded from the people, reforms should be carried through to satisfy their just claims and augment their zeal. But he expressed himself in unguarded language, that gave a handle to his opponents. " If your Government want sailors to perform a particular act, though on most occasions tardy justice they do them, yet they hold out something to amuse them, either the prospect of a more equal distribution of prize money or some other object." " Men should not fight till their grievances are redressed." " I have no hesitation in declaring that in the present situation of the Country, viewing the conduct of Ministers in the light I do, I think it impossible for an honest man to come forward in their defence, or to be justified in lending an assisting arm in defence of their Country." Such language cannot be defended, but its object was to secure the adoption by Ministers of a line of conduct which must have roused the people to resist Napoleon to the utmost by enhancing the value of the object for which they fought. Sir Francis Burdett felt that he and the ordinary Englishman had a stake in the country, which the financial jobbers had not.

Pitt had resumed office as Prime Minister on May 10, 1804. But his Ministry was by no means a complete success. The 10th Report of the Commissioners appointed by the Addington Government to inquire into naval abuses contained grave charges against Pitt's colleague, Henry Dundas, Lord Melville, first Lord of the Admiralty. Melville resigned and was impeached, and only acquitted after Pitt's death (January 1806).

If the absolute supremacy of England at sea was established by Nelson's victory at Trafalgar (October 21, 1805), the third Coalition of England, Austria and Russia was on land a total failure. The whole Austrian army was captured at Ulm (October 20, 1805), and the Russians were crushed at Austerlitz (December 2, 1805). The shock of these events, coupled with gout, was too much for Pitt, who died on January 23, 1806.

The following, hitherto unpublished, letter of the Duke of Clarence (William IV), written six weeks before the Battle of Trafalgar, is of some interest, and reflects credit on him for his estimate of the naval situation :

Duke of Clarence to T. Coutts.

> Thursday night
> (5 Sept. 1805).
> Bushey House.

DEAR SIR,

Yours of 4th instant from Christ Church reached me this evening & in answer I am to observe that the courage of Sir Robert Calder [1] cannot be doubted; as for the separation of Admiral Stirling it requires explanation : if ordered by the Admiralty, Sir Robert is cleared : if not, it is an error in judgment : I never was apprehensive of either our East or West India Fleets : the French never go to the right or left but implicitly follow their orders : I was always of opinion that the object of the Toulon squadron was to proceed by the West Indies to Ferrol, which object has been clearly defeated by Sir Robert : they suffered so much in the action & were of course so short of provisions that, Ferrol not supplying them with what they wanted, necessity has drove them to Cadiz, where I trust the remainder of this war they will remain blockaded. At the time of the French leaving Toulon their object was the invasion of these realms, & the Texel fleet was part of the plan in which they never could have succeeded : for of late years the channel is become so narrow that one ship only at a time can come out & only at a spring tide : therefore with common attention the Texel is easily watched; still it is my opinion Bonaparte would have attempted the invasion, unless the events on the Continent had taken the turn they

---

[1] Calder was court-martialled and severely censured for having failed to intercept Villeneuve from Ferrol. On the whole subject see Corbett's " The Campaign of Trafalgar."

have & must produce a general war. I understand the treaty between this country Russia & Sweden is actually signed : it is expected Austria & Denmark will join. I do not know what part the King of Prussia will act : nothing in my opinion but a general war can produce a permanent peace.

Your letter has given me sincere pleasure by informing me I am not forgot by you & yours to whom I must for so many reasons be attached : my best wishes & Compliments (to use your own words) attend the Ladies, old young & middle aged, & I hope you are fully persuaded that I am & ever will be,

Dear Sir,

Your best Friend,

WILLIAM.

CHAPTER IX

THE MINISTRY OF ALL THE TALENTS AND THE ELECTIONS
OF 1806

ON Pitt's death the King was at last forced to have recourse
to the Whigs. Lord Grenville formed an Administration
known as the "Ministry of all the Talents," and Fox
became Secretary of State for Foreign Affairs. In the
Ministry the "new" and the "old" oppositions were
balanced. If Grenville was First Lord of the Treasury,
Fox was Foreign Secretary; if the Tory Lord Chief Justice
Ellenborough was in the Cabinet, the Whig Erskine became
Lord Chancellor. Lord Sidmouth also joined the Cabinet
as Lord Privy Seal. Sheridan, without a seat in the
Cabinet, was Treasurer of the Navy.

An effort was made to conclude peace, and Lord Lauderdale was despatched to Paris for the purpose, but it soon
became clear that any accommodation with Napoleon was
impossible. Referring to Sicily, Fox said to Lord Holland :
" It is not so much the value of the point in dispute as
the manner in which the French fly from their word that
disheartens me." It was therefore necessary to continue the
war. The following letter refers to Lauderdale's mission :—

Sir F. Burdett to Rev. R. N. French.[1]

Piccadilly,
18 Aug. 1806.

DEAR FRENCH,

Whether Parliament will be dissolved or not is
more than I know, but I fear at all events I must give up
visiting Foremarke. I know not what to say about success

---

[1] Burdett's chaplain at Foremarke.

at another Middlesex Election. I fear no Minister will be inclined towards me, at the same time I think they cannot now openly use the same exertions as formerly against me, but I begin to think that & all other things now of little consequence; I fear the die is cast & that this country is marked for the destroying angel. The malice of a priest you know is proverbially implacable, how much more that of a Saint, & I have sinned past redemption : no, we can hope for nothing but Saintlike zeal against the ungodly : for even our best actions, you know, partake of the nature of sin. Fox is said to be somewhat better, but I have not seen him a long time. I am sorry you have had no Cobbetts sent & shall take care in future. I dont know what we should do without him. As to peace you see the Funds sink, but I cannot help believing, & so does Tooke, that peace will be made, because it must, a base & dishonourable one it will be. Indeed any Peace is so under our actual circumstances, nor do I see that we have the power or inclination to mend them. Ld. Lauderdale's travelling day & night to get it is neither dignified nor the way to succeed in his negotiation. I begin to think we have no choice but submission or revolution, & I believe our luxurious sheep-breeding gents. would much prefer the former. . . .

yours sincerely,

F. BURDETT.

Fox's health had entirely given way, and on September 13, 1806—eight months after the death of Pitt—he passed away. The only great achievement of " The Talents " Ministry was a Bill for the abolition of the slave trade, which passed into law after Fox's death.

The " Ministry of all the Talents " was regarded by Burdett and other Radicals as an " acid test " of the Whig Party, and in their view it stood revealed as an imposture. They had expected a change in the " system," but lo and behold, the " system " was continued, the only difference being that a Whig was substituted for a Tory personnel. And really, even if we allow for all the difficulties of the situation, the record of the Ministry was bad. Lord Grenville, who received £6000 a year as First Lord of the Treasury, was allowed to retain the sinecure office of Auditor of the Exchequer at £4000 a year (though it is true that a deputy was appointed). Thus he would audit his own accounts. The Lord Chief Justice, Ellenborough —*pessimo exemplo*—became a member of the Cabinet in order to support the interest of Sidmouth. Thus it would have been possible for him as member of the Cabinet to order the prosecution of, and then, as Judge, to try, a defendant. To justify his appointment there was the precedent of Lord Mansfield, and the excuse has been put forward that he was appointed in view of the " delicate investigation " that had to be made into the indiscretions of the Princess of Wales. But the appointment was bad, and no Lord Chief Justice has since this date been given Cabinet office.

Nothing whatever was done for Reform or Catholic Emancipation. The Income Tax was raised from $6\frac{1}{4}$ to 10 per cent., and, in a time of frightful stress, the incomes of the younger branches of the Royal Family were raised from £12,000 to £18,000 a year.

Burdett was utterly sickened with what he regarded as want of principle in the Whigs. But he was not the only politician on whose mind this effect was produced.

The outlook of Cobbett on politics was similarly transformed. First and last Cobbett was Burdett's enemy, but in the middle period of 1806–1819 he was Burdett's friend.

Born of peasant stock, Cobbett[1] was entirely self-educated, but never became a " gentleman." He enlisted

---

[1] Apart from the " Political Register," Cobbett is famous as the author of the " Parliamentary Debates," afterwards taken over by Hansard and, as the author of " State Trials," afterwards taken over by Howell.

(1784) in the 54th Regiment of Foot, and after service
with his regiment in Nova Scotia he obtained his discharge
(1791). In 1792 he migrated to America, and there gained
distinction as a pamphleteer, attacking the Radicals Priestley
and Tom Paine, and defending his own country through
thick and thin in her struggle against revolutionary France.
Having got into trouble in America by reason of his writings, he returned to England in 1800. His fame as a
vigorous pamphleteer had preceded him, and Windham
became his patron. At a dinner given by Windham he
met Pitt and Canning, and he was offered the control of a
Government paper, but, preferring independence, he
started, with Windham's help, a paper of his own, "The
Political Register," which with few interruptions he edited
till his death in 1835. He wrote in terse vigorous English,
"racy of the soil." In 1802 he was fiercely monarchical
and anti-Gallican; he followed Windham in his politics,
denounced the Peace of Amiens, and applauded the renewal
of the war in 1803.

At the time of the Middlesex election in 1802 he denounced Burdett as "a leader of thieves against the Magistrates." "We declare our abhorrence of a man, who in
alluding to the British Government speaks of 'hired
Magistrates, Parliaments, and Kings.':[1] we detest, and loath
Sir F. Burdett: we would trample on him for his false,
base, and insolent insinuations."

But at the Middlesex election of 1804, having parted
company with Pitt, and approving of Windham's opposition to the Government, he gave Burdett a qualified support. The opponents of Burdett had raised the old cry of
"Jacobinism," and had not scrupled in the odium of the
cry to connect with Burdett "the whole of the Opposition—a connection for which the appearance of the
Cavendishes and Russells openly in the cause of Sir Francis
furnished a tolerably good ground." Such action appeared

[1] See p. 139.

to Cobbett inimical to the national interest.   He regarded
Jacobinism as an extinct issue.   What was needed was a
" union of all hands and hearts."   Now that France had
become an Imperialist nation, even a Radical could heartily
approve of the war.

The fact was that Cobbett's point of view was changing.
Sprung from the soil and with agricultural sympathies,
Cobbett no less than Burdett felt antagonism to the commercial and " funded " interests.   He had begun to hate
" corruption " and " sinecurists."   His attack on Grenville as the typical sinecurist gave offence to Windham,
and the friendly relations of Windham and Cobbett came
to an end in 1806.   Cobbett remembered " the rock from
which he had been hewn."   From that date onwards he
was a Radical.

On the death of Fox (September 13, 1806) a bye-election
for Westminster became necessary and Burdett was
approached to know whether he would stand for the
vacant seat.   But he replied in the negative, saying that
he had promised his vote to Lord Percy.   He added :

" I am besides bound in gratitude and honour to the
independent freeholders of Middlesex, and never will on
any personal account forsake them.   But for any advantage to be derived from it to the public I would cheerfully
resign all my pretentions to-morrow.   Nor would I ever
have presumed to be a candidate for the County, but that
I am persuaded that in order to rescue the Country from
its present calamitous and disgraceful thralldom, we stand
more in need of integrity than talents."

Westminster was one of the few large " open " seats
that existed under the old electoral system.[1]   It reached
from the City on the east to Kensington Palace on the

[1] The poll-book of the Westminster election of 1812 shows that
some 11,000 voters actually polled.   They were mostly small shop-
keepers and artisans.

west, from Oxford Street on the north to the Thames on
the south. Its population in 1801 was over 150,000, and
the number of its Parliamentary voters was some 11,000.
It has been well described as being at this period the
" storm-centre of English politics." The Houses of
Parliament were within its area, and this fact kept its
citizens alive to all the political issues of the day.

On Burdett's refusal to stand for Westminster at the
bye-election of September 1806, Lord Percy, son of the
Duke of Northumberland, was put forward by Government to contest the seat. A false hare was started in the
candidature of Sheridan, but Sheridan presently withdrew
by arrangement, and Lord Percy was returned unopposed.

Francis Place has described the shame with which he
witnessed the corruption of the mob by the Duke of
Northumberland—" lumps of bread and cheese " being
thrown " among the dense crowd of vagabonds," " coal-
heavers ladled the beer out of butts with their long-tailed,
broad-brimmed hats." " The butts were upset and the
beer flowed along the gutters." [1]

The Radicals had not been ready with a candidate to
rescue Westminster from its " disgraceful thralldom," but
Lord Percy only held the seat for one month, as Parliament
was dissolved on October 24.

On this occasion the Radicals were prepared. The
poll for Westminster continued from November 3 to 19;
that for Middlesex from November 10 to 26; [2] and the
history of the one election is interwoven with that of the
other, many of the same people taking part in both. Thus
at Westminster, Burdett, who had refused to stand himself
for Westminster, nominated at the hustings on November 3
James Paull as the Radical candidate.

Born in 1770, the second son of a tailor at Perth, James

[1] " Place Papers," quoted by Graham Wallas in his " Life of Place."
[2] The chief authority for the elections is " A History of the Westminster and Middlesex Elections in the Month of November 1806."

SIR S. HOOD.   WHITBREAD.   SHERIDAN.   PAULL.   COBBETT.   BURDETT.   BOSVILLE.

WESTMINSTER ELECTION, NOV. 1806.

Caricature by Gillray.

Paull matriculated at the University of St. Andrew's; going to India in 1788, he became a prosperous merchant at Lahore; in 1804 he returned to England with the reputation of having amassed a considerable fortune. The existence of the fortune may be doubted, as he died quite poor in 1808, indebted to his brother, and his poverty in 1808 can hardly be accounted for by the sums of money he spent on his elections and by the loss of £1600 at a gaming-table in April 1808. On his return to England in 1804 the chief *motif* of his public life was to impeach Lord Wellesley for his Indian administration, especially for his treatment of the Nawab of Oudh.

He became a friend of Windham (then in opposition), and through Windham a friend of Cobbett. Cobbett introduced him to Burdett, and Burdett gave him the *entrée* to Tooke's dinners.

Elected to the House of Commons as member for Newtown in the Isle of Wight (1805), he moved for papers that would show up Wellesley's dealings with the Nawab of Oudh. Paull was a quarrelsome fellow. A duel in India had already cost him the full use of his right arm. After the formation of " All the Talents Ministry," difficulties thrown in the way of Wellesley's impeachment by the coalesced Whig and Tory parties drove him into the arms of the Radicals. And as a Radical he stood for Westminster in November 1806.

The rival candidates were Admiral Sir Samuel Hood and R. B. Sheridan. Hood's return was certain : so the real struggle lay between Paull and Sheridan. The chief features of the election were the circulation of scurrilous songs and handbills, the use of offensive pageantry and personalities.

Paull was taunted with his low birth as the son of a tailor. Sheridan's " bludgeon men " escorted before the hustings " a banner-bearer carrying at the top of a long pole a cabbage surmounted by a smoothing iron. Next followed a man dressed in the character of an ape, borne upon a board and surrounded by the professional implements of a tailor."

Paull was attacked for his gross ingratitude to Lord Wellesley. "It was only at Lord Wellesley's special request that the Nawab of Oudh had permitted Paull's return to Lucknow in 1802." Paull had written a grovelling letter of thanks and eulogy to Wellesley "to whom no man ever complained in vain that complained with justice." Then he had turned and bitten the hand that fed him. He was ridiculed as a mere satellite of his "little god, Sir Francis Burdett." On the other hand, Paull and his supporters, especially Cobbett, were not behind hand in throwing mud at the manager of Drury Lane. Sheridan, they said, was nothing but the son of a play-actor sprung from a class denominated by the good old laws of England as VAGABONDS. He was represented as taking three bottles of port at dinner with Aris (!),[1] and then having recourse to brandy. He was a swindler who never paid his debts.

In one of his speeches Sheridan denounced Cobbett's suggestion to break faith with the national creditors (*i.e.* repudiate the National Debt). Thereupon a man from the middle of the crowd in a very distinct voice uttered the following words : " Hear, hear, hear, Richard Brinsley Sheridan DETESTS BREAKING FAITH WITH CREDITORS ! " It was stated—and the statement seems to have been substantially true—that the Duke of Northumberland had written a letter in which he had refused to let his son be a candidate in the election, lest he might be " contaminated by standing with the abandoned profligate " Sheridan. And Sheridan, on hearing this, was reported to have said (but he denied the report) that if the Duke of Northumberland had not been " an old cripple and a dotard " he would

---

[1] This placard was, of course, untrue : Sheridan was not a friend of Aris.

have chastised him.   But the chief charge brought against
Sheridan was that he the erstwhile friend of the people
was now an apostate place-man, drawing £4000 a year
for the sinecure office of Treasurer of the Navy, while his
son Tom held another sinecure of £2000 a year.

Whitbread, the brother-in-law of Lord Howick (Charles
Grey), was a prominent supporter of Sheridan in the
election, while Burdett took an active part on the side of
Paull, until his time was engrossed by his own Middlesex
election.   Burdett, in his early speeches on behalf of Paull,
definitely took up the line that the clause in the Act of
Settlement (1701) which laid down that no one holding
office or place under the Crown should be eligible to the
House of Commons ought to be re-enacted.   Sheridan, he
said, as a place-man holding a sinecure office of £4000 a
year, was quite unfit to represent the independent City of
Westminster.   How could the House of Commons act
as a control on the executive if its members were in the
pay of the executive ?   In his speech nominating Paull
he said :   " In my estimation a hundred mercenaries in
the House of Commons are much more dangerous than
500,000 mercenaries in military array headed by the
Emperor of France."

After the close of the election Cobbett was even more
outspoken about the Sheridans :   " . . . In a word, they
are a sort of State Paupers; like sturdy beggars, they tell
you, ' Here we are out of employment and without a
shilling; you must either find us work or maintain us
idle; in plain English, you must either give us places or
pensions.' "

Paull headed the poll in the early part of the election,
but Hood and Sheridan joined their interests on the fifth
day, and the final result of the poll was :—

Hood	.	.	.	.	5478
Sheridan	.	.	.	.	4758
Paull .	.	,	,	.	4481

Paull immediately announced his determination to present an appeal to the House of Commons against the election.

Meanwhile the poll for Middlesex had opened on November 10. The candidates were Sir Francis Burdett, Mr. Byng (the former member), and a Mr. Mellish, a banker-merchant (vice Mainwaring). This third election in which Burdett engaged for the representation of Middlesex was to be fought by him in a very different way from those of 1802 and 1804. On the elections of 1802 and 1804 he had spent a considerable portion of his fortune. He did not intend to spend more of it on such a purpose. In the earlier contests he had received the support of the Foxite Whigs, but now he was to stand entirely on his own. He was utterly estranged from the Whigs by their record since their coalition with the Pittite Tories in the " Talents Ministry." In office they had adopted all the abuses of the system, which in Opposition they had denounced.

The keynote to the contest was struck in Burdett's first election address issued at the beginning of November, which took an entirely new line.

GENTLEMEN,

Whenever the Leaders of contending parties and factions in a State unite, the history of the world bears evidence that it never is in favour, but always at the expence, of the People; whose renewed & augmented pillage pays the scandalous price of the reconciliation. Under these circumstances you are called prematurely & suddenly to a fresh election of your Representatives, if they can be called such. And a double imposture is attempted to be passed upon you. The watchword of one party [1] is, ' The best of Kings." The watchword of the other [2] is, " The

---

[1] The Tories.   [2] The Whigs.

best of Patriots." [1] But neither of these parties will choose to descend to particulars, & inform you what the best of Kings & the best of Patriots have already done, or will hereafter do, for you. What they have done for themselves, we know & feel; what farther they will do for us, we can only conjecture. They who have desired a new Parliament thus suddenly in our present situation undoubtedly have their own strong reasons for it, which they are not likely to disclose; but I am thoroughly persuaded, that all our present burdens & restraints, vexatious & galling as they are, will appear but as trifles when compared with what they will be at the close of this now-coming Parliament. I would willingly be instrumental in the rescue of my country at the certain expence of life & fortune. But it cannot be rescued, unless the majority of the Country be uncorrupt. It is fit that the experiment should be tried : & that at least the proportion of remaining integrity should be known. And I pledge my honour to you, Gentlemen, that upon the present occasion I do not desire the aid or countenance of any of the parties in or out of power; that I will not distribute, nor consent to the distribution even of a single cockade; nor will I furnish, nor consent to the furnishing of a single carriage. If the Freeholders of Middlesex feel the situation of their Country, & desire to redress its grievances, they will do their easy parts towards such redress by an uncorrupt vote. And if this spirit is not to be found in this County at this time, it is not likely to be found anywhere else at any time. Let the Freeholders of Middlesex do their easy duty; I will do mine, which will not be easy : & if it shall be their unbiassed choice, I will prove myself their uncorrupt, disinterested, & zealous Representative. I am, Gentlemen, with full assurance of your integrity & spirit, your most faithfull humble servant,

FRANCIS BURDETT.

[1] C. J. Fox.

This address brought down on Burdett a torrent of ridicule and abuse. " To ask no vote ! to distribute no ribband ! to excite no riot ! This is indeed a change," wrote a correspondent to the *Morning Chronicle*. " After the ribbands, the tumults, the carriages, the profusion of two elections, not a vote asked, a cockade distributed, or a carriage allowed ! Sir F. Burdett, the Idol of the rabble, all at once set up for a Coriolanus ! "

The whole Whig party was antagonised by Burdett's scoffing allusion to Fox as " the best of Patriots," and his denunciation of the Whig Party as an imposture.

When Byng declined to join his interest at the election to that of Burdett, the latter wrote to the Freeholders Club of Middlesex :

" This, Gentlemen, is the short statement of our situation. The politics of George Grenville, the father, lost us America. The politics of William Grenville, the son, have lost us all Europe. To these politics & to assist in carrying them on, the professing Whigs have lately joined themselves—to their own great emolument & to the just dismay of the public. In this conjuncture it is not surprising that Mr Byng, who belongs to those Whigs, should play into the hands of Mr Mellish, who belongs to that Grenville whom they have joined. I am perfectly aware, that, if I had been silent, I might have been returned for Middlesex without a contest. But I will have no compromise nor suspected compromise with such shabby politics. I will not by silence be guilty of the ruin which appears to be fast approaching. Gentlemen, I will never consent to be returned by the connivance of any Ministers : for I will never connive at their plunder. I desire no seat, but by the unbiassed votes of intelligent & uncorrupt Freeholders. If my principles differ from theirs, I am not fit to be their Representative, & shall not desire it. But I shall wait for their decision, regardless of the intrigues, misrepresentation, & influence of the coalesced factions. I shall ever remain, Gentlemen, faithful to the principles I avow, & to your honest service.

F. BURDETT.

But with both the party organisations employed against him, Burdett had no chance, and he got only 1197 votes as against 3215 for Mellish and 2304 for Byng.

The language that Burdett had used about Fox seems to have touched the Whigs on the " raw." Lord Holland, for example, in his " Memoirs of the Whig Party," wrote that " before Fox was cold in his grave, (Horne Tooke) prevailed on Sir Francis Burdett to insult and revile his memory in language uncalled for by any political object." If Lord Holland simply referred to Burdett's gibe at Fox as " the best of Patriots," his words seem exaggerated.

As a matter of fact, Burdett had been a great admirer of Fox (see p. 52). He had hoped for great things from the advent of Fox to power. Speaking about Fox in the course of the election on November 20 he said : " Gentlemen, the high opinion I undoubtedly entertained of Mr Fox, the great and transcendent abilities of Mr Fox, and the amiable private qualities of Mr Fox, were certainly of such a nature, as perhaps to induce men to pass over many political faults; and undoubtedly to make all men, who were witnesses to the exercise of his abilities, admire his talents; and those who had the good fortune to partake of his society, to love and respect him. In paying that tribute to the memory of Mr Fox, I must say he was the only person of that party, upon whom my hopes were founded. I must confess that, when he came into power, I did look to some of those great schemes of National Reform, which his great mind was well calculated to produce. I did so, as eagerly as the traveller in passing the thirsty desert looks for the moistening drops of Heaven." Burdett then proceeded to explain his bitter disappointment. Time passed by; no scheme of Reform was brought forward, no hint was given that former pledges and promises would be redeemed, and it would have been, he said, a treachery to the people if he had acquiesced in this surrender of principles.

Burdett had remained on terms of personal friendship with Fox till his death, and after Fox's death he showed affection for his memory by advancing large sums of money to his widow. The friendship between Mrs. Fox and Burdett continued unbroken till the former's death in 1842.

After the election, Samuel Whitbread published a long Open Letter to Burdett which dealt with Burdett's attack on a " place holding and place-hunting party." Whitbread was a prominent Whig, who received no office in 1806, and was a man of generally recognised honour. Burdett replied, with equal verbosity and with less courtesy. This letter produced a challenge from Whitbread to a duel, which Burdett declined. His refusal threw doubts on his personal courage, and this was one of the reasons why in the following year he accepted another challenge.

There can be no question that in this Middlesex election Burdett put his finger on the genuine evils of the day. It was the cause of his increasing popularity.

He denounced the ever-growing burden of taxation. His opponents asked him, how the country could be managed without taxes; if he (Burdett) had been a Minister, he too would have had to increase them. To this Burdett retorted that a large part of the taxation was unnecessary, because it was simply spent on corruption (pensions and sinecures). He had mentioned the Sheridans, but there was even a worse instance, viz. that of the Prime Minister, Lord Grenville, and his family. " I object to the emoluments derived by the Marquis of Buckingham, the brother of Lord Grenville, for the unreformed Tellership of the Exchequer " (£35,000 a year). " I complain also of the

plunder of the people in the emoluments received by my
Lord Grenville as Auditor of the Exchequer, holding as he
does an office really incompatible with his position as First
Lord of the Treasury." These were simply samples. The
whole list of sinecures and pensions was a scandal when
" our resources are all wanted for national defence."

Burdett's enemies taunted him with being an enemy of
the King and Constitution. And this charge gave him the
opportunity to develop his political and constitutional
ideal. He retorted on his enemies that they mistook the
abuses of the Constitution for the Constitution itself. He
was a firm believer in the Monarchy. " One of my strong
objections to the present parties has been that the prerogatives of the Crown are as much usurped upon on the
one hand, as the Rights of the People on the other. I am
not for a King ' of shreds and patches '—I am not for a
man of straw—I am not for a Name, which other persons
are to use or abuse for their own party purposes—but for
the efficient Magistrate, for the constitutional King of
England—the abuse of his prerogatives by Ministers being
checked, controlled, and guarded against by a fair representation of the People in Parliament. What I want to
obtain for the people is not a sword, but a shield against
official abuse."

" Some people," he said in 1804, " have charged me
with want of respect in speaking of the House of Commons.
To them I answer that towards the constitutional part of
that House no man living bears a higher respect than
myself. I esteem it. I revere it. In my estimation there
is more honour and dignity in sitting there, the real representative of two or three thousand freemen, the immediate
guardian of public liberty, than in having place amongst
nobles, or being seated upon a throne. But if there be
any part of that House which is not constitutional, I scruple
not to acknowledge that it moves and ever will move my
indignation."

By 1806 Burdett had become convinced that the only
way to remedy the abuse of a House of Commons whose
members were bribed with pensions and sinecures was to
re-enact the clause in the Act of Settlement (1701), " That
no person who has an office or place of profit under the
King, or receives a pension from the Crown shall 'be
capable of serving as a member of the House of Commons."

" What man on earth," he said, " ever yet contended
that it was fit the same attorney should manage a cause for
two contending parties ?   The representatives of the people
are the Attorneys of the people, and cannot also be the
Attorneys of the executive.   That a man should act as a
control upon his own conduct is absurd."

What is known to-day as the " American " or " Presi-
dential " system of government now became part of the
regular " platform " of the Reformers, and remained so
for several years.

The grievance that Burdett sought to remedy was a
genuine evil, but it may be doubted whether the probable
results of his suggested remedy had been thoroughly
thought out.   Interest in the proceedings of the House
of Commons would certainly have diminished, and time
was to show how deeply corruption would eat into American
politics.

It is amusing to note that, in spite of the hard knocks
that Burdett gave the Sheridans publicly in the course of
the election, in private he kept up friendly relations with
Tom Sheridan.[1]

Sir F. Burdett to Thomas Sheridan.

Hustings.

14 (Nov.) 1806.

" I am quite sorry that any circumstances should alter
our connection, but I cannot be silent under the most

---

[1] Tom Sheridan was the only son of R. B. Sheridan by his first
wife.   He died of consumption in 1817.   His three daughters were
famous for their beauty and talents.

unfair & false insinuations, nor can I alter my politics to suit the purposes of individuals or parties. Writing is so liable to mistake that I will write no more, but shall be glad to see you any time before 10 in the morning or from 6 to 10 in the evening, & shall at all times be happy, when in my power, to shew my regard for you, when it does not compromise my public conduct. I cannot forget the pleasant hours I have pass'd with you—but public principle is my God. Believe me, yours very sincerely,

F. BURDETT.

There was one other person who took a prominent part in the election—William Cobbett. This erstwhile enemy of Burdett had now been converted to the Radical cause and lent him his active support. In the " Register " he gave an interesting account of his change of attitude to Burdett. Here it is :

" It should not be forgotten that in 1802 I had been but about 18 months in England, after a long war carried on with great zeal against Republicans in a foreign country, where every Republican was a sworn enemy not only of the King of England but of England itself. Upon my return to England, I naturally fell into a literary acquaintance consisting entirely of men who were the political enemies of Sir F. Burdett. Several of these had corresponded with me, while I was in America : & it was not until long after my return to England that I found to my utter astonishment that *every one of them* had long been receiving in one shape or another considerable sums of money annually from the Government : that is to say, out of the taxes raised upon the people. Amidst such a circle it was not likely that with all my independence of mind I should soon arrive at the truth : & from them I imbibed what was, I dare say, their sincere opinion that Burdett in his denunciation of *Cold Bath Fields Prison* was

actuated by no other motive than that of regard for
the *Mutineers* confined there, & that this regard was
founded on an approbation of their treasonable designs.
That was why I opposed him at the first Middlesex Election
(1802). In the second Election (1804) I took little part,
because I approved of Burdett's action in Parliament,
because he was misrepresented by his enemies, who were
all placemen & pensioners. I had learned from Mr Reeves
a magistrate that the abuses in the Cold Bath Fields Prison
were really shocking.

"In March 1806 I met Burdett for the first time. I am
convinced that in the whole Kingdom there is not a man
more attached to the Kingly Government & the whole of
the Constitution of England than Sir F. Burdett. He
gave me information about Cold Bath Fields.

"Such are the reasons for my change of opinion about
Burdett, 'A gentleman calumniated more than any other
man that ever lived, but yet enjoying popularity unparalleled . . . popularity, which is by no means confined
to the rabble, but extending to the whole mass denominated
the People.

"This popularity I wish to see employed in *preserving* & not in *destroying* : That is why I deprecate the pro-
pagation of the idea that Burdett is an enemy to the King
& Constitution. For Burdett's ideas are popular with
the people, & if you succeed in persuading the people
that these ideas are inimical to King & Constitution, the
people will be persuaded that they themselves are also so,
& the only result will be to prepare their minds for Revolutionary measures. For Burdett ' amongst the really efficient
part of the people possesses more influence than all the
other public men in the kingdom put together.' If Union
is desired against the enemy, the calumniation of Burdett
is not the way to secure it.

"The phrase in Burdett's Address—' *the best of Kings* '—
is in its context not hostile to the King or Kingly govern-

ment of England. There is nothing in the Address of which any sensible man could disapprove. Is it for Sheridan & Co to talk ? Have not they for the last 17 years maintained the right of cashiering Kings & toasted ' *their Sovereign, the Majesty of the People* ' ? Why calumniate a man who is more loyal than they & is only hated because he has exposed their Corruption ? "

Cobbett in this phase of his career was very much a Burdettite.

CHAPTER X

WITH the death of Fox (September 13, 1806) the brightest
star in the " Ministry of All the Talents " disappeared.
The Ministry as reconstructed by Grenville was in a weak
position. The King bore it no good will, but bided his
time : the Prince of Wales, thinking himself neglected,
was indifferent to its fate; the whole of the reforming
party was alienated. On the Continent Napoleon had
trampled upon Prussia, and in the Peace of Tilsit (July
1807) had come to terms with the Tsar. The net result of
the arrangement was that Russia was to have a free hand
in the east and Napoleon in the west of Europe. England
was left in isolation to continue the war with France.

In March 1807 the fall of the Grenville Ministry was
precipitated by the Catholic question. An Act of the
Irish Parliament in 1793 had opened to Roman Catholics
all ranks in the Army up to and including the rank of
Colonel. From the higher staff appointments the Roman
Catholics were still specifically excluded. But difficulties
had arisen when Irish regiments were transferred to
England; for the Act of 1793 only applied to Ireland,
and Roman Catholic officers in regiments so transferred
rendered themselves liable to penalties in England. The
Grenville Government proposed to remedy this anomaly.
But misunderstandings as to the extent of the concessions
arose not merely between King and Ministers, but between
members of the Cabinet themselves. The King gave his
reluctant consent to the extension of the provisions of the

Act of 1793 to England, but when the Bill was eventually brought forward it was found to go further than the Irish Act of 1793, and to open *all* (even the highest) posts in the Army to Catholics. The King was understood to have given his consent to this proposal, and Lord Holland does not scruple to charge him with duplicity. But Ministers were soon undeceived. The King either had not realised the full extent of the concessions that were proposed, or else he said that he had not. (It is to be remembered that George III was nearly blind.) He now utterly refused his consent, and Ministers in consequence dropped the Bill; but they forwarded to him a Cabinet Minute, reserving to themselves the right of openly avowing their sentiments if a Catholic petition was presented, and of submitting to the King from time to time such measures as they might deem advisable. The King in his reply demanded from Ministers a pledge that they never would again raise with him the Catholic question, and, on their refusing to give such a pledge, dismissed them.

The erstwhile Whig, the Duke of Portland, became the new Tory Prime Minister, Lord Eldon returned to the Woolsack, Castlereagh became War Minister and Canning Foreign Secretary. This was the origin of Grey's profound distrust of Canning. For Canning, though a firm believer in Catholic Emancipation, now took office in a Government based on the exclusion of Catholic claims. The Parliament elected in November 1806 was dissolved after an existence of five months on April 30, 1807. The elections filled the month of May.

For Burdett, the month was marked by two important events: his quarrel and duel with James Paull,[1] and his first election as member for Westminster—a seat which he retained continuously for thirty years.

[1] The chief authorities for the quarrel are—Horne Tooke's letter to *The Times*, May 6, 1807; Paull's " Refutation of the Calumnies of Horne Tooke," 1807; " Place Papers," 27817, 805 (British Museum); Private papers.

It is difficult to pass an impartial judgment on the rights and the wrongs of Burdett's quarrel with Paull. The main facts are quite clear, but in many points the accounts are contradictory; and the aims and motives by which the different characters were actuated are difficult to determine.

Paull was eager to be returned for Westminster, but he was equally anxious that Burdett should be a joint candidate with him. He tried to rush Burdett by getting a requisition from electors asking Burdett to stand. Whether one of his motives was that Burdett might pay the expenses—as Horne Tooke asserted—must remain an open question.

Burdett's position is a little difficult to understand. On *Wednesday, April* 29, he definitely refused, in an Address to the Freeholders of Middlesex, to stand for Middlesex or any other constituency. "In this desperate situation of our affairs I cannot consent to become a candidate for any seat in Parliament."

On the other hand, a deputation from Westminster (Francis Place and Mr. Adams) asked him on the same day whether, if elected without his interference, he would accept the seat. He replied, "Certainly." And as a matter of fact this was the way in which Burdett was eventually elected for Westminster.

Further, it is difficult to understand his change of attitude towards Paull. In November 1806 he had nominated Paull in eulogistic terms as a candidate for Westminster; he had subscribed £1000 towards the expenses of Paull's election petition; he had given him the *entrée* to Tooke's Sunday dinners. If Paull's narrative is to be believed, there were only three Sundays between November 1806 and May 1807 that Paull had not attended Tooke's Sunday dinner, and only ten days within that period that he had not dined with Burdett.

It is true that by April 1807 Burdett had become wearied of Paull's requests for money. His protégé's election petition was proving a costly amusement. Apart from Burdett's contribution of £1000, the public subscription had only amounted to £200, and the petition was costing Paull £70 a day. In April 1807 he wrote to Burdett that the solicitors for the petition wanted an immediate £1000 and security for another £800; that he had " in vain applied to Jew and Gentile and could raise no money." He entreated Sir Francis to apply to Bosville to assist him. Burdett cursed the petition and said that he was peculiarly situated with Colonel Bosville, who had given four or five thousand pounds for coaches for the Middlesex freeholders, and that he could not for that and several other reasons with any delicacy apply to him.

It is difficult, too, to understand the malignancy with which Horne Tooke attacked Paull in *The Times*, though it must be remembered that these letters were written after the duel. There must have been something behind the complete *volte-face* of Burdett and Tooke. Was Burdett, as Gillray in contemporary caricatures insinuated, and as Henry Hunt openly asserted in 1820, moved by jealousy of the independent popularity which Paull had acquired in Westminster? Or was Paull a mere climber, who wished to use the Burdett money and the Burdett influence in his climb? It is a significant fact that after the duel practically all Paull's Committee deserted him and transferred their allegiance to Burdett. If the report of Place and Adams to the Westminster Committee is to be believed, Paull was throughout the election a prevaricator. They found him out in deliberate lies. I think the truth is that Paull was a cad, that Burdett discovered it, and that Paull found out that Burdett had discovered it. The knowledge infuriated him.

The critical week of the quarrel was April 26 to May 4.

On *Sunday, April* 26, Burdett and Paull were both present at Tooke's Wimbledon dinner, and it was on this occasion that Burdett undertook to nominate Paull on the hustings.

On *Monday, April* 27, Burdett and Paull both dined in London at Colonel Bosville's. Burdett had just received the Address of Mr. Fawkes taking leave of the Yorkshire freeholders, and under its influence he expressed regret that Paull was to stand for Westminster.

On *Tuesday, April* 28, Burdett wrote from Wimbledon his Address taking leave of the Middlesex electors and announcing his determination not to stand for *any* seat in Parliament. This letter was published the following day :

" In this desperate situation of our affairs (for such I esteem it) I cannot consent to become a candidate for any seat in Parliament. With the omnipotent means of corruption in the power of our spoilers, all struggle is vain. We must wait for our redress & regeneration till corruption shall have exhausted the means of corruption : & I do not believe that period very distant; the present ministers being most likely to be our best friends in hastening it. Till that time shall arrive, I beg leave to retire from all Parliamentary service : without the least abatement of zeal for the rights & liberties of my countrymen, to which I will always be ready to sacrifice my own interests, in any manner, whenever there shall appear the smallest prospect of success.

" I am, Gentlemen, with respect & gratitude,
" Your faithful servant,
" FRANCIS BURDETT."

On *Wednesday, April* 29, Burdett received from Paull an advance copy of two advertisements which appeared in the Press on *Thursday, April* 30 :

(1) " April 30. The Free and Independent Electors of Westminster, in the interest of Mr Paull are requested to dine at the Crown and Anchor

Tavern in the Strand to-morrow, to concert measures to insure to that gentleman his return for the said City. Sir Francis Burdett Bart. in the chair."

(2) "April 30. The Electors of Westminster are earnestly requested not to engage their votes: as the result of a communication with Sir Francis Burdett Bart. this day, will be made known to the Electors at large, at a public meeting to be called forthwith."

On *Wednesday, April* 29, Burdett wrote an indignant letter to Paul.

Wimbledon, April 29.

DEAR PAULL,

Your letter this morning occasioned me great surprise, &, to speak the truth, some displeasure. I must say that to have my name published for meetings (like " Such a day is to be seen the great Katerfelto " [1]) without any previous consent, or any application to me, is a circumstance I should really from any one else regard as an insult.

[1] As to Katterfelto, see Moritz, "Travels in England in 1782," p. 70: " Mr. Katterfelto gives himself out for a Prussian, speaks bad English, and understands beside the usual electrical and philosophical experiments some legerdemain tricks with which (at least according to the papers) he sets the whole world in wonder. For in almost every newspaper there are some verses on the great Katterfelto. . . . Every sensible person considers Katterfelto as a puppy, an ignoramus, a braggadocio, and an impostor: notwithstanding which, he has a number of followers. He has demonstrated to the people, that the influenza is occasioned by a small kind of insect, which poisons the air: and a nostrum, which he pretends to have found out to prevent or destroy it is eagerly bought of him. A few days ago he put into the papers: ' It is true that Mr. Katterfelto has always wished for cold and rainy weather, in order to destroy the pernicious insects in the air: but now on the contrary he wishes for nothing more than for fair weather, as His Majesty and the whole Royal Family have determined the first fine day to be eye-witnesses of the great wonder, which this learned philosopher will render visible to them ' Yet all this while the Royal Family have not so much as even thought of seeing the wonders of Mr. Katterfelto."

You were acquainted with my sentiments & determination not to do anything, even for my own Election : & should have been consequently aware of the impossibility of my coming forward in any one else's. I yielded to your desire that I should nominate you, although I should much rather avoid even that; but as I highly approve of your conduct, I did not object to that one act, as a public testimony of such approbation, in case you think it (which I do not) of any importance,—but to that single act I must confine myself, or be exposed to be reproached & justly with inconsistency or folly.

Yours notwithstanding, very sincerely,
FRANCIS BURDETT.

Paull replied by express stating his regret, and, according to his own account, received an answer that Burdett would see him next day at Bosville's.

Meanwhile Burdett's Address to the freeholders of Middlesex appeared to the Westminster Election Committee to be so contradictory to the statements that Paull was making about Burdett's intentions, that Place and Adams were deputed by the Committee to wait on Burdett and discover his real views. At Wimbledon they were received by Burdett. He told them that he refused to be a candidate, that he had written to Paull protesting against the use of his name and against Paull's advertisement. He had told Paull both on Sunday and on Monday that he would not stand. The deputation then asked him, whether, if elected without his interference, he would accept the seat ? Burdett replied : " Certainly. This is the right way : electors ought to seek representatives, not candidates solicit electors. If I should be returned for Westminster, for Middlesex, or any other place, I must and certainly shall obey the call, and will do the duty of a faithful steward; but I will not spend a guinea, nor do anything whatever, to contribute to such election."

On *Thursday, April* 30, Paull's first and second advertisements, as given above, appeared in the newspapers,
but, owing to the offence they had given Burdett, Paull
was requested by the Election Committee to postpone the
dinner. This he refused to do, but he sent to the newspapers a third advertisement, which appeared the following
day.

> " Mr. Paull's Dinner, Crown and Anchor, May 1st,
>   1807. As it is intended to move certain resolu-
>   tions, expressive of the opinions of the Free and
>   Independent Electors, that personally apply to
>   Sir Francis Burdett, Mr. Paull will be in the Chair
>   instead of the worthy Baronet. Mr. Paull en-
>   treats a numerous attendance of his friends, on
>   an occasion so highly important to the first
>   interests of the City."

On the Thursday evening Burdett and Paull met at
dinner at Colonel Bosville's. Paull's version of what
happened is this : " I showed Burdett the advertisement,
which had been drawn up in consequence of his declaration to Place and Adams. He made no objection. . . .
After dinner I handed him the resolutions, which were to
be moved at the Crown and Anchor, proposing us as joint
candidates." But there was obviously some misconcep-
tion. Burdett is represented by Mr. Cooper, Paull's second
at the duel, as saying to him just before the duel, " As it
was at the moment of going down to dinner Mr. Paull
put that paper into my hand, I certainly did not pay attention to the advertisement." And this was probably the
true explanation. Burdett was often, as we have already
seen, casual and absent-minded.

On the evening of *Friday, May* 1, the dinner was held at
the Crown and Anchor. Among those who came was
Jones Burdett, the brother of Sir Francis. " Jones Burdett," said Paull, " slunk into the room, and was only

discovered by me, as we were going into dinner, and I brought him up and placed him on my right hand." He said that he had brought a letter from Sir Francis to be read to the meeting, but he refused to divulge its contents beforehand. According to the account of Place and Adams, Paull " begged for God's sake they would interfere to induce him not to make the communication. For, if he does, by God he will ruin us."

As soon as dinner was over, the bomb was exploded, for Jones Burdett read to the meeting the following letter from Sir Francis :

To the Electors of Westminster Assembled at the Crown and Anchor.

Gentlemen,

I am exceedingly distressed by the disagreeable necessity imposed upon me to contradict thus publicly the implied import of the two advertisements by which you are called together this day. They were both inserted without any communication with me; & never should have been inserted, if any means had been afforded me of preventing it. As soon as I knew of the first advertisement, placing me in the chair, I wrote the following letter to Mr. Paull.

(He then read the Katterfelto letter.)

The Advertisement of this day is still more offensive to me, as it might, if not thus contradicted by me, lead many persons to suspect that I had a dissembled wish to be elected into Parliament, notwithstanding my public declarations to the contrary. I beg you, Gentlemen, to accept this explanation from me towards you, whilst it is one of strict duty towards myself,

your most obliged & humble servant,

F. BURDETT.

May 1, 1807.

This letter produced some consternation, but Paull tried to gloze over the situation by representing it as a slight misunderstanding between Sir Francis and himself that would soon be set right. Jones Burdett admitted that the letter just read did not prevent them from electing Sir Francis, who, if elected, would be their faithful steward. Resolutions—framed by Paull's Committee—were then passed by the meeting that Sir Francis and Paull should be jointly nominated as candidates for Westminster.

As soon as the diners had risen, Paull said to Place, " Well, how do you think I have managed this business ? " Place replied, " Very ingeniously, but, sir, you must allow me to say that your conduct has been such as to make it necessary to come to an immediate explanation and I beg you will appoint a time to-morrow morning to see Mr. Adams and myself on the subject." Mr. Paull said, " Well my good fellow, I am sorry to hear you say so, but we will not quarrel now." Place refused to get the resolutions passed by the meeting inserted in the newspapers.

Paull was seething with inward rage, and determined to demand satisfaction from Burdett. Retiring shortly before 10 p.m., he indited to the Press a letter giving Burdett the lie, that was published in the newspapers next morning (Saturday, May 2).

10 p.m. Friday night.

To the Free and Independent Electors in Westminster.

Gentlemen,

The letters that were read this night from Sir Francis Burdett, I have not time, nor have I inclination to comment on. I assert positively, that on Sunday last at Wimbledon not only did Sir Francis most cheerfully consent to nominate me, as he had done last November (which was at a dinner at the Crown & Anchor), but that he would also serve with me for Westminster, if chosen.

On Monday Sir Francis & myself dining at Col. Bosville's received Mr. Fawkes's Advertisement of Yorkshire;
& then for the first time, he expressed his regret that I
had resolved to stand for Westminster. Yesterday I
shewed the amended Advertisement to Sir Francis Burdett
(which he now says he disapproves of) : it then met his
highest approval. I subsequently shewed it to Col. Bosville; . . . Without any communication with me, Mr.
Burdett entered the Crown & Anchor. What occurred he
has undertaken to submit to the public, & on which I
shall make no further comment. Anxious to stand well in
your estimation, I subscribe myself, Gentlemen, your
devoted servant,

JAMES PAULL.

Then Paull with a certain Mr. Cooper drove down to
Sir Francis Burdett's house at Wimbledon, where he
arrived shortly before 1 a.m. (Saturday, May 2). The
sleeping Baronet was awakened, and Mr. Cooper explained
the purpose of his visit. He handed Burdett a letter from
Paull and according to his instructions set forth coolly
and deliberately the injury Paull had sustained both in a
public and in a private point of view. Several communications through Mr. Cooper passed between Sir
Francis and Paull (who remained in his carriage) between
1 and 4 a.m. But Sir Francis, feeling that Paull had no
claim to any kind of apology, informed him that apology
was out of the question. It was then agreed that they
should meet in duel at Kingston, as soon as Sir Francis
could procure the attendance of his friend Mr. Bellenden
Ker from Town.

The duel came off at twenty minutes past ten in Coombe
Wood. The first shots proved abortive, but at the second
shots both combatants fell wounded. Sir Francis was hit
in the thigh; Paull in the legbone.

The account of the duel may be told in Bellenden Ker's
own words :

DUEL BETWEEN SIR F. BURDETT AND JAMES PAULL.
Caricature by Gillray, 1807.

"On Saturday morning, May 2nd, about half-past five o'clock, Sir Francis Burdett's servant came to me with a note from Sir Francis, desiring me to come to him instantly to Wimbledon with a pair of pistols, as he had been called upon—by whom?—I could procure none, after trying in vain at two Officers of the Guards & at Manton's, none that were thought fit for my purpose. It occurring to me that going thus from place to place for pistols might at last be the occasion of bringing on more notice than I wished, I determined to proceed to Kingston without them, thinking that those who had called on him must have a pair at least, & that, if it was necessary, they might serve both parties. I arrived at Sir Francis Burdett's house at Wimbledon at about 8 o'clock, having been obliged to wait more than 2 hours for a chaise. He was gone on to the King's Arms, Kingston, having left a note for me to follow him there in his carriage. On entering Kingston, I saw Mr. Paull in a coach accompanied by another person. He called out to me on passing, & said something that I did not very distinctly hear; but I think he advised me not to proceed into the town, as the affair would be blown. I asked him where the inn was & went on. As soon as I had entered the room where Burdett was sitting, a person appeared who had followed me. On his entrance I asked Burdett who he was? He said it was Mr Paull's second. I then said, 'Whom have I the honour to address?' 'My name is Cooper.' 'Do you know him, Burdett?'— 'No, I have no doubt Mr Paull has appointed a proper person to meet me.' 'Sir, Sir, Sir,' was Mr Cooper's answer. I then said, as Burdett desired, that we should immediately follow them, if they would proceed to Coombe Wood, which seemed to be a proper place for the meeting. After Burdett had given me some letters & memorandums for different friends, & explained to me the subject of Mr Paull's demand, we proceeded to the place appointed; where, ordering the carriage to stop for us, we went into the wood for a considerable distance. I fixed on a proper

spot. During our walk Mr Paull frequently addressed me
on the subject of the quarrel. He said he was sure I had
not heard it rightly stated, & wished me to hear him. I
always replied that I had heard the whole from my principal,
& that I placed implicit confidence in what he said : for,
if I could not have done that, I should never have accompanied him there; & that from all I heard & had read
concerning the matter it was my decided opinion that
Burdett was the person most entitled to consider himself
ill-used; but at all events an apology from him was out
of all question; & that I had rather see him shot than
advise him to do so disgraceful an act. As Mr Paull did
not seem to have at all placed his opinions or cause in the
hands of his second, I found it in vain to talk to him on
the subject of accommodation. After we had stopped, I
asked for the pistols which were produced by Mr Cooper,
who declared that he had not expected things would have
taken this turn. I asked him if he expected that I should
advise, or that Burdett would consent to disgrace himself.
I then told him that we had been unable to obtain pistols,
& expected he would consent, as well as Mr Paull, that
we should use one of theirs. To this they both agreed.
He (Mr Cooper) told me he did not know how to load
them. I showed him how, & directed him to load Burdett's, while I loaded Mr Paull's. I then asked him what
distance he proposed them to stand at. He said he knew
nothing about the matter & left it to me. I measured out
12 paces, & placed the principals at the extremities of the
space. I then directed him to give Sir Francis a pistol &
I presented another to Mr Paull, at the same time assuring
him, as I had Mr Cooper, that Sir Francis came there
without the slightest animosity against Mr Paull, but that
he would fire at him as a mode of self-defence. I said
besides to Mr Paull, that I hoped he was thoroughly convinced that the injury he had received was of a nature not
to be satisfied with anything short of attempting the life

of my friend & risking his own. He replied he must do so, unless he had an apology. I then asked them if they would agree to fight by a signal I would make by dropping my handkerchief. They each did agree to it. I placed myself about 4 yards on one side the centre of the space between them, while Mr Cooper, on giving the pistol to Sir Francis, retreated very precipitately behind a tree at some distance. On the signal being made, they fired together but without effect. I then took Mr Paull's pistol from him & said, 'I hope, Sir, you are now satisfied.' He said, 'No,' he must have an apology or proceed. I said, to talk of an apology was absurd & quite out of all question. We then reloaded the pistols, & gave them as before. I again addressed Mr Paull, as I had at first : he answered with warmth, he must have an apology or proceed; & called God to witness that he was the most injured man on earth. Mr Cooper was then to make the signal; but he stood so far out of the way, that Sir Francis could not see him, although he had already called to him during his retreat & begged him not to go so far off, & to come forwards or words to that effect. . . . At last I saw Sir Francis did not see Mr Cooper nor his signal, & upon his making it, I called out 'Fire' to Sir Francis, as soon as I saw Mr Paull raise his pistol : they did so together, I believe upon my uttering the word. I should observe that, while they were waiting for the signal, I observed that Sir Francis held his arm raised, & his pistol pointed towards Mr Paull. Knowing this was not with the view of taking any unfair advantage, but the effect of accident, I said, 'Burdett, dont take aim; I am sure you are not doing so; drop your arm, as you see Mr Paull has his pistol pointed downwards.' Mr Paull then asked me why I advised Sir Francis not to take aim. I said anybody might see that I could only mean for him not to take aim or prepare to do so before the signal, & from a desire to see that they were upon equal terms. The consequences of the second shots have been already described. After speaking to each of them, I set off for the carriages. Both were put into Mr Paull's. I went on to Sir Francis Burdett's house to Lady Burdett & his brother, & also to procure a surgeon in Wimbledon. During the transaction, not one word passed between me & Sir Francis, except what I said about taking aim. Mr Cooper has constantly refused to sign any official account, to say where he lives, or what is his situation, which also was repeatedly requested of him by me, nor do I at this moment know anything concerning him."

(Signed) JOHN BELLENDEN KER.

Thus challenged, Cooper too gave an account of the duel. It is substantially the same as that of Bellenden Ker. But, while admitting that he knew little about the loading of pistols, he denied that he made " a precipitate retreat," or cut the absurd figure described by Ker, or ever concealed his name or residence.

Burdett and Paull were conveyed back to London in the same carriage, under the care of Mr. Landford, a doctor brought from Wimbledon. Sir Francis was taken to his house in Piccadilly, Mr. Paull to his house in Charles Street.

Paull seems to have been the more seriously wounded, and for some time it was thought that his leg would have to be amputated, but eventually this was found to be unnecessary. His wound did not, however, preclude him from prosecuting his candidature for Westminster.

Sir Francis was put in charge of the surgeon Mr. Cline, who extracted the bullet. Cline insisted that Sir Francis should be kept in absolute quiet, and that no communications from the outside world should be delivered to him. Hence, until May 15 Sir Francis knew nothing of the events that happened on the days immediately following the duel.

What happened was this.   Paull was repudiated by most of his supporters, and some thirty of Sir Francis' friends, without his knowledge, formed themselves into a Committee to put up Sir Francis as a candidate for Westminster and to secure his election free of all expense to himself.   The poll was taken from May 7 to 22.

We are informed by Place,[1] that on the morning of Friday, May 1 (*i.e.* the day of the dinner and the day before the duel), Paull's Committee, disgusted with his lies, and regarding his whole conduct since the Dissolution as " a continued fraud upon Sir Francis Burdett," had decided to retire from his support.   In entire ignorance of the duel, the Committee met again at nine o'clock on Saturday morning and unanimously resolved " to announce to Sir Francis that the duplicity and tergiversation of Mr Paull had induced them to withdraw their active support from him, and to apprise Sir Francis that in so doing they should endeavour to prevent the committal of his character by any further connection with Mr. Paull, and a deputation appointed for this purpose were actually in the house of the Baronet, when Mr Bellenden Ker entered announcing the duel and its consequences."

A meeting of electors favourable to the Radical cause was summoned to the Crown and Anchor for the evening of Monday, May 4.   But the meeting broke up in disorder.   Whenever a partisan of Burdett began to speak, his voice was drowned by cries of " Paull," " Paull."

" I know no word," writes Place, who was present, " so well calculated to confound an audience as the open sound Paull." [2]

The supporters of Burdett than retired to another room, formed themselves into an independent Committee, and

[1] Report of Place and Adams to the Electors of Westminster; " Place Papers," 27,817, 105 (British Museum).
[2] " Place Papers," 27,850, 68.   Cp. Wallas, " Life of Place," p. 45.

passed the resolutions of which these are the operative clauses :

> " That the recent Conduct of Mr Paull has been such as to induce us to withdraw from him our support at the ensuing Election.
>
> " That it would be to the immortal honour of the City of Westminster, and afford a great and glorious example to the Electors of the United Kingdom, that they should return Sir Francis Burdett to Parliament, free from every sacrifice and expence to himself, upon independent principles, consonant to the genuine Spirit of the Constitution of England, which declares that Elections shall be free and without Corruption.
>
> " That for this purpose a Subscription be now opened, etc., etc."
>
> (*Signed*) SAMUEL BROOKS, Chairman.

With a sum less than £200 at their disposal, the Committee entered upon an election, which had been known on former occasions to have cost £50,000; and this they did without any communication direct or indirect with Sir Francis Burdett. Francis Place represents himself as the chief organiser of the victory that followed; but, however important his services may have been, it is certainly true that Place always exaggerated his own importance.

The election began on May 7. It was in many ways unique. Sir Francis Burdett was not a *candidate* for the suffrages of the electors; he heard nothing of what was going on till May 17, and no official communication was made to him, till a deputation on May 23 announced to him his election as member. The electors sought him, not he the electors.

Another extraordinary feature of the election was that the total expense incurred on his behalf was only £780, of which not a penny was contributed by Sir Francis, but the whole of it by his supporters, mostly in half-crowns and shillings.

A still more extraordinary fact was the enormous majority which Burdett secured. The circumstances in which he started were not exactly auspicious. Sheridan and Elliott, the candidates of the two recognised parties, Whig and Tory, stood against him, but they were nowhere. Government influence was against him. It availed nothing.

In the absence of Sir Francis, Mr. Jennings acted as his locum tenens on the hustings, and the programme put forward was quite simple, viz.: (1) The freedom of elections; (2) the re-enactment of the clause of the Act of Settlement excluding pensioners and placemen from the House of Commons; (3) the disfranchisement of rotten boroughs. In the issue the two Radical candidates, Sir Francis Burdett and Lord Cochrane were elected, Burdett heading the poll by an enormous majority. After the third day it was for him a run-away affair. The figures were:

Burdett	5134
Cochrane	3708
Elliott	2137
Sheridan	2645
Paull	269

Poor Paull cut a sorry figure. Deserted by his supporters, on May 5 (two days before the poll opened), he issued an Address, endorsed by his Committee, retiring from the contest. Stung by the attack of Burdett's friends, he changed his mind, and on May 7 was nominated at the hustings. On May 13, however, he withdrew his poll-clerks and inspectors.

His subsequent history can be told in few words. He brooded over his political failure and his losses at the gaming-tables; finally, in April 1808, he cut his throat.

Cobbett by 1807 had become an enthusiastic supporter of Burdett in the " Political Register." On February 14— three months before the election—he bore witness to Burdett's wonderful popularity. Burdett had been given a dinner by his friends at the Crown and Anchor, and Cobbett wrote, " Name any other man in this kingdom, or that has of late years lived in this kingdom, who could find 1500 people voluntarily to give 10/6 each for the sake of dining with him."

Cobbett had also been a warm advocate of Paull in the months preceding the election. The situation was delicate, but he resolved to take no part in the quarrel of Burdett with Paull. While regretting the quarrel, he stated that for a long time past he had regarded Burdett as the man best qualified to represent Westminster. He wrote on May 16 to the electors : " If you succeed in causing Burdett to be returned to Parliament, you will have done more for the Country in the space of 14 days, than has been done for it during the last 100 years."

Again on May 23 he wrote in the " Political Register " : " To cherish those whom your mortal enemy fears and hates is a tolerably good rule of action. Had you therefore no other proof of Sir Francis Burdett's merit than that the Plunderers from the very biggest to the very least hate him more than they hate any other man, this alone would be a sufficient inducement for you now to exert yourselves to return him by an unexampled majority."

Having been elected senior member for Westminster by an overwhelming majority, Burdett on May 25 issued the following Address to the Electors of Westminster :—

GENTLEMEN,
        Next to the consciousness of endeavouring sincerely to serve my country, nothing can be more pleasing to my mind than the public approbation of my endeavours. Accept my grateful thanks.

At the same time forgive me feeling something like despair of any good to the country, whilst I see the regular expenses of corruption greatly exceed all the expenses necessary for any war which we can be justified in pursuing; whilst I see attempts to delude the public mind, by *comparatively* petty & insignificant inquiries into what is termed *peculation ;* whilst those inquirers themselves think it not dishonourable to seize greedily every opportunity of enriching themselves out of the public spoil, by any other means not termed by them *peculation.*

Such wretched notions of public honour & honesty can afford no signal benefit to the public, nor can give us any suitable redress. They appear to me to resemble the notion of chastity entertained by the prostitute, who boldly challenged any one to say—that she ever went out of the regiment.

According to them, all within the regiment, all within the *RED BOOK* is honourable & virtuous; & they insult us by declaring, that they have as good a title, by the *red book,* as any of the people can have to the fruits of their industry or to the inheritance of their ancestors; from which industry, & from which inheritance, be it remembered, & from them alone, the red book takes everything that it has to bestow : so that they pretend as good a right to all which they can contrive to take from us, as we have to the remainder—till they can take that too.

Such is my conception of the different corrupt ministers we have seen, & their corrupt adherents. And unless the public, with an united voice, shall loudly pronounce the abolition of the *whole* of the present system of corruption, I must still continue to despair of my country.

You, Gentlemen, by this unparalleled election have loudly pronounced your sentiments. May your voice be echoed through the land !

In the meantime, though an individual is as nothing in the scale, I will carry with me your sentiments into the

House of Commons.   And I assure you, that no rational endeavours of mine shall be omitted to restore to my countrymen the undisturbed enjoyment of the fair fruits of their industry; to tear out the accursed leaves of that scandalous *red book;* & to bring back men's minds to the almost forgotten notions of the sacredness of private property, which ought no longer to be transferred from the legitimate possessors by the corrupt votes of venal & mercenary combinations.

I will continue, Gentlemen, disinterestedly faithful to the interests of my country, & endeavour to prove myself
Your zealous representative,
FRANCIS BURDETT.

Meanwhile Burdett's Committee determined to continue its existence, and it became the " recognised authority " in Westminster politics.   Though twenty-five years would yet run their course before the Reform Bill was carried in 1832, Burdett's election in 1807 was the "handwriting on the wall " for the old electoral system.   It was a shadow of things to come.   The election was a quickener of life to Radical politics elsewhere.   It was now that Henry Hunt the Radical (Orator Hunt) began to rise into prominence as an agitator.   He tried to do in Bristol what Burdett had done in Westminster.   A dinner of Bristol electors, under Hunt as president, was held at the Trout Tavern in Bristol on June 2, 1807, when resolutions were passed exulting over Burdett's election as a triumph and as a lesson given by Westminster to other boroughs that they " may at length return members to Parliament, who shall be distinguished for patriotism and public virtue."

Hunt as the representative of Bristol Radicals opened up a correspondence with Burdett and various members of the Westminster Committee, and they responded.   But Hunt was not universally accepted among Radicals.

About this time Cobbett wrote a letter to his friend

Wright, which, though not published at the time, became later of some importance in the election of 1818.

" There is one *Hunt*, the Bristol man. Beware of him, he rides about the country with a whore, the wife of another man, having deserted his own. A sad fellow. Nothing to do with him."

But for Burdett no praise was too high. The " Political Register" of May 30, 1807, gives Cobbett's shout of triumph at Burdett's election address.

" ' Every one I meet,' said a person to me the other day in Oxford Street; ' every one I meet reprobates the Address of Sir Francis Burdett.' ' Which way did you come ? ' said I. ' Why,' replied he, ' from Whitehall, across the Parade, through St. James's Palace, and up St. James's and Bond Street.' ' Well, then,' added I, ' now go to Somerset Place, the 'Change, the India House, Lloyd's, the Custom House and the Excise Office, and you will meet with exactly the same cry. But when you have heard the hundreds at these places, then go and hear the thousands and hundreds of thousands in the manufactories, in the shops, in the work-shops, upon the river and in the gardens. Go and hear those, whose labour, whose ingenuity, and whose industry in every way are taxed to support the clamorous whom you have heard; go hear the laborious father whose means of provision for his children is taken away by the income tax; go hear the merchant, who is compelled to make an exposure of all his most private concerns, and who by the taxers is frequently not believed upon his oath; go hear the numerous annuitants from whose scanty means of subsistence one-tenth is annually taken in a direct tax; go hear in short all those, who have nothing but their labour, of one sort or another, to subsist on, and who have no share in the taxes; go hear these, and then come and tell me, on which side you find the majority.'

"Well may there be clamours against Burdett's Address. Look at the Red Book. Only look at the outside of it—swelled to the thickness of a duodecimo Bible—bigger than both army and navy lists put together, its numbers surpassing, perhaps, the number of persons employed in the agriculture of the kingdom. . . . To deny the truth of the facts seems to have been thought unnecessary. It was more easy to assail the Address with a misrepresentation. To represent it as a declaration of a wish to overturn the kingly government, because forsooth *the names of the Royal Family are inserted in the Red Book*. What a scandalous misrepresentation. These misrepresenters know that Burdett has no such wish, and that his Address contains no such meaning. They know that he wishes to overturn nothing which belongs to the Constitution of England. They know that his wishes are to restore and preserve and not to destroy. They know that he wishes to deliver the King from the arbitrary power of any and of every faction; and that he would not, if he had it completely in his power, deprive him of any one prerogative which the Constitution has given him. It is against the factions, which each in its turn has ruled by the means of a Parliament both King and people in the manner that we have seen, that Sir Francis Burdett is at war, and not against the establishment of Royalty, much less against the person of the King, to whom he has never attempted to impute any degree of blame. . . .

"Not a single 'agitator' interfered in the Election. It was carried on by the People themselves. . . . There were no appeals to the Passions, no revilings of any one. 'You *know* Sir Francis Burdett, choose him if you will,' was the substance of all that was said."

Sir Francis only recovered slowly from his wound, and

on June 29, when his chairing as Member eventually took place, he was scarcely yet able to move about even with the aid of crutches. London had never seen such a triumphal progress as that given him. The procession started from Covent Garden about noon, headed by marrow bones and cleavers, four and four. There was the usual display of flags and banners inscribed with suitable mottoes such as : " Burdett and our Country," " Purity of Election," " Burdett the Choice of the People," " The

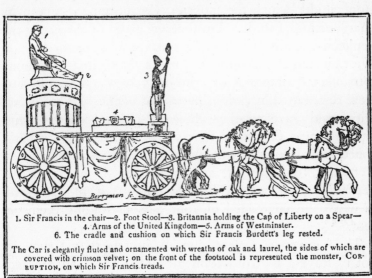

1. Sir Francis in the chair—2. Foot Stool—3. Britannia holding the Cap of Liberty on a Spear— 4. Arms of the United Kingdom—5. Arms of Westminster. 6. The cradle and cushion on which Sir Francis Burdett's leg rested.

The Car is elegantly fluted and ornamented with wreaths of oak and laurel, the sides of which are covered with crimson velvet; on the front of the footstool is represented the monster, CORRUPTION, on which Sir Francis treads.

Triumph of Westminster," " The Sense of the People." There were bugle-boys and trumpeters and bands of music. Electors, marshalled under the flags of the different parishes of Westminster, marched four and four. There followed the triumphal car of Sir Francis, and the procession was closed by horsemen and carriages. The cavalcade reached 78 Piccadilly about 2.30 p.m., and Sir Francis, unable to walk, was carried to the car by two gentlemen. He wore a blue coat, white waistcoat, nankeen breeches, white stockings, and he held in his hand a white beaver hat. The triumphal car was constructed, we are told, after the ancient classical models. "It was surmounted on four wheels, superbly ornamented. On the more advanced part was the figure of Britannia, with a spear crowned with the Cap of Liberty. In the centre was a faggot firmly bound, the emblem of union; and on the posterior part of the platform was a pedestal, on which was placed a Gothic chair for the hero of the day. He sat with his head uncovered, and his wounded limb rested on a purple cushion, while the other was sustained on a sort of imperial footstool, under which the monster, Corruption, was seen in an agonising attitude. On different parts of the Car were depicted wreaths of oak and laurel, the arms of the City of Westminster, and also the insignia of the United Kingdom. Ornamented draperies of crimson velvet and purple silk were distributed in various parts, and banners embroidered with gold gave to the whole a splendid effect. This equipage was drawn by four white horses, richly caparisoned and decorated with purple ribbons, but the horses were not four abreast, as was expected, but (by the particular desire of Sir Francis Burdett) were harnessed in pairs, and conducted by four persons leading them on foot." [1]

The concourse of people in all the streets was such as not to leave a foot of vacant ground. The carriages and coaches which lined the streets were covered with spectators. Every window was filled. In many places scaffoldings, erected in tiers, were crammed with people; even the roofs were crowded. The moment the Baronet became visible the air rang with cheers, in which, "had the King been in Town, he would have heard *the sense* of his people." Burdett's colours streamed everywhere, handkerchiefs waved, flowers and laurels were scattered as the car passed. Half a million of people are said to have joined in the celebration. The popular favour shown towards the Baronet exceeded all belief. No one since

[1] "Memoirs of the Life of Sir Francis Burdett," p. 39.

the days of the Great Commoner (Lord Chatham) had roused such enthusiasm among the people. And among all these dense crowds not a single accident, no disorder of any kind occurred.

Henry Hunt wrote : " Sir Francis Burdett was that day in sober earnest and in the honest sincerity of their hearts the pride of the people. It was no fiction, no joke, but in fact and in truth Sir F. Burdett was on that day ' Westminster's Pride and England's Glory.' All was peace and good order, every face beamed with good humour, and upon every brow sat a sort of conscious pride, as if each person felt that he had performed a duty by offering a tribute of devotion to the Baronet."

The procession reached the Crown and Anchor at 5 p.m., and no fewer than two thousand people attended the dinner to celebrate the occasion. The space was so crowded that many had to take their dinner standing. After dinner many toasts were given, among them :

(1) The King, the Constitution, the whole Constitution, and nothing but the Constitution.
(2) The People.
(3) Purity of Election; and may the electors of the whole kingdom take a lesson from Westminster School.
(4) That honest and incorruptible representative of the people, Sir Francis Burdett.
(5) May the ineffective of the *Regiment* be speedily disbanded, and the *Red Book* reduced to its proper dimensions.

In reply to the toast of his own health, Burdett said :

" Gentlemen, both parties laugh at the people; they despise the people; and those, who have robbed us most, have justly the most contempt for us. It is the common cant of both parties to deny that there is any such thing as *the People*, and I have been frequently asked insultingly where such a thing as the People is to be found in England. You, gentlemen, have furnished me with an answer to that question in Westminster, in the Metropolis of England."

Oddly enough, Lord Cochrane, the other Radical Member, returned for Westminster—about whom much must be said later—was not present at the dinner, nor was his health drunk. Lord Cochrane, who was a naval officer, had gone to sea in command of the *Impérieuse*. That explains his absence from the dinner. But why was his health not drunk ? The probable explanation is that given by Henry Hunt : " So little faith had Sir F. Burdett and his friends in the sincerity of Cochrane's principles that they never drank his health, or even mentioned his name. Cochrane had not yet been kicked by Government action into being a thorough patriot."

It is quite clear that Government had anticipated a riot, or at any rate considerable disorder on the occasion of the chairing, for we are told that the Guards about the Palace and about the Offices at Whitehall were doubled and supplied with ball-cartridge. The several regiments were drawn out in the morning and kept under arms. A great body of the Horse Artillery was kept harnessed in St. James's Park to draw the cannons, if necessary, to the scene of action. Volunteer Corps were mustered. But all these precautions proved unnecessary. Everything passed off quietly. Even those who refused to illuminate their houses at night, " remained undisturbed in the gloom of their discontent." And so the eventful day came to an end. For the rest of the summer Burdett remained at Wimbledon convalescing.

CHAPTER XI

THE YEARS 1808-1809

THE duel between England and Napoleonic France now entered on its penultimate phase. Napoleon, in despair of ever being able to conquer England at sea, determined to ruin her indirectly by destroying her trade and making her bankrupt. Though he had not a ship upon the seas, by the Decrees of Berlin and Milan he declared the British Isles in a state of blockade, forbade any neutral ship to touch at a British port on pain of confiscation, and declared all goods of British origin liable to seizure. England retaliated by Orders in Council (1807), proclaiming a blockade of the coasts of France and her allies, and declaring that every neutral ship must touch at England and pay dues before entering any port of the enemy.

Canning, having been informed by a confidential agent that Napoleon intended to seize the Danish fleet for use against England, determined to forestall his action, and in August 1807 despatched a British squadron to Copenhagen demanding that the Danish fleet should be surrendered to England—to be restored intact at the end of the war. On the Danish Government refusing the proposal, Copenhagen was bombarded and the Danish fleet captured (September 2).

The year 1808 is memorable in the history of Europe for the rising of the Spaniards against Napoleon and the beginning of the Peninsular War—the running ulcer that drained Napoleon of his strength. In June 1808 Sir Arthur Wellesley was despatched with an army to Portugal. Wellesley won the glorious victory of Vimiero, but concluded the inglorious Convention of Cintra, by which

Junot, with his defeated army of 26,000 men, was allowed to evacuate Portugal. The lenient terms of the Convention were bitterly attacked in England; a Court of Inquiry was held and Wellesley was exonerated from blame on the ground that on the arrival of Sir Hew Dalrymple as his superior in command he had been prevented from following up the victory at Vimiero, and that therefore he was justified in concluding the Convention, by which at any rate he secured the evacuation of Portugal. In April 1809 he was sent back to Portugal to take command of the British forces.

In the life of Burdett the year 1808 was comparatively uneventful. He had recovered from his wound and attended regularly the session of Parliament, which lasted from January 21 to July 4. During this session he put his finger on real grievances and brought them into the light of day.

On February 11 he attacked abuses in the disposal of moneys derived from the capture of enemy ships.

On February 29 he protested, but in vain, against a grant by Parliament from the public money to Lord Lake's [1] family, as adding unjustifiably to the burdens of the people. Was not this, he urged, a splendid opportunity for making use of the sinecures already at the disposal of the King. Why, then, come to Parliament for a special grant?

Ministers always pretended sinecures were necessary, that the Crown might be in a position to reward eminent services. What sort of eminent services were rewarded by sinecures, if not such services as those rendered by Lord Lake ? ! !

On March 14 he defended the interests of Army officers, and urged in vain that no officer should be dismissed the Service except by sentence of court martial.

---

[1] £2000 a year was voted to Lord Lake and the two next heirs male, the grant to be retrospective as from 1803 (the year of the Battle of Delhi).

On June 30 he defended the cause of the private soldier against unnecessary floggings,[1] and moved for a return—which Government refused—of all floggings in the Army during the last ten years.

It was a common practice for the Crown to grant a post with reversion on the holder's death to his son or some other specified person. On April 11 Burdett spoke in favour of a Bill by which the granting of administrative posts in reversion [2] was to be abolished.

Once again in February and March the abuses in Cold Bath Fields Prison were brought forward, this time by Sheridan, on a petition from the Sheriff of Middlesex and the gentleman who had been Foreman of the Grand Jury of Middlesex in 1807. Among other complaints was the story of a female prisoner who, it was alleged, had been debauched by Aris' son. Burdett delivered a fresh attack on Aris, and a new Royal Commission was appointed.

On May 12 Burdett spoke in favour of the claims of a certain Colonel Palmer to remuneration for the improvements he had effected in the post by the introduction of mail coaches. This was a curious case indeed. Till 1784 the post had been incredibly slow and ineffective, being dependent on pack-horses. Palmer, a prominent citizen of Bath, had devised a scheme for its improvement, and the younger Pitt had given Palmer an appointment in the Post Office as Controller of the Posts. An agreement was made that if, in consequence of Palmer's reforms, the Post Office revenue rose beyond a certain point, Palmer should receive $2\frac{1}{2}$ per cent. on such increase. Palmer's reforms succeeded beyond all expectation, but owing to certain disputes, which arose within the Post Office, Pitt dismissed Palmer and refused to carry out the agreement about the $2\frac{1}{2}$ per cent.

[1] In consequence of an active campaign by Reformers in the Press and elsewhere regulations were made in 1811 and 1812 to make flogging less frequent and less severe. (See Halévy, Vol. I, p. 69.)

[2] The granting of "Reversions" from this time fell into disuse though not abolished (Halévy, Vol. I, p. 18).

commission, only awarding him a pension of £3000 per annum (1799).   Pitt's action was endorsed by Parliament, but Palmer refused to withdraw his claim, and once more in 1808 brought it before Parliament.   Burdett supported his claims as based on justice.   He reminded the House that he himself had always opposed the squandering of public money, but there was such a thing as the sanctity of contracts and Palmer as a matter of simple justice was entitled to the covenanted remuneration.   The House of Commons on this occasion endorsed in principle Palmer's claim.   The matter was finally settled in 1813 by Lord Liverpool's Government, which awarded to Palmer, in addition to his pension of £3000, the sum of £50,000.

The year 1809 was to provide a much more exciting time within the walls of St. Stephens.

In January British spirits were depressed by the news of the retreat and death of Sir John Moore at Corunna.   But Moore's retreat, drawing like a magnet the French troops northwards, helped to save the Spanish insurgents from collapse, as did also the rising of the Austrians against Napoleon.

Military opinion in England was divided.   There were those who, like Canning, wanted to concentrate wholly on the liberation of Spain, but Castlereagh wished to create a diversion in aid of Austria by sending a large expedition to capture Antwerp, where France was building ships.   The result was that England's military strength was divided. Sir Arthur Wellesley, with a considerable force, was despatched to the Peninsula in April, but in July the largest force that had ever hitherto sailed from England—40,000 troops and a naval force to match—was sent under Lord Chatham and Sir R. Strachan upon the ill-starred Walcheren expedition.   Owing to delay, to incompetence, and misunderstanding between the two commanders the expedition ended in disaster amid the fever marshes of Walcheren.

" The Earl of Chatham with sword drawn
    Stood waiting for Sir Richard Strachan :
    Sir Richard longing to be at 'em
    Stood waiting for the Earl of Chatham."

But in England during the early part of the year attention
was almost monopolised by a terrible scandal affecting the
Commander-in-Chief, the Duke of York.

Rumours, that found their way into a pamphlet towards
the end of 1808, had been current about corrupt traffic in
Army promotions.   On January 27, 1809, Colonel Wardle,
a member for Okehampton, brought the matter before the
House of Commons.   He accused H.R.H. the Duke of
York, Commander-in-Chief, of corrupt connivance with
the action of his mistress, Mrs. Clarke, who had procured .
large sums of money from various people by using her
position with H.R.H. to secure promotions for them in the
Army.   Wardle moved for a Committee to investigate the
charges, and Burdett seconded the motion.

The charges were too specific and too serious for Ministers
to meet them with evasion.   Mr. Yorke might describe
them as " a product of Jacobinism," and a vile " conspiracy
against the illustrious house of Brunswick."   Lord Castlereagh might follow suit, and Canning could insinuate that,
if Wardle failed to prove his case, ignominy and infamy
would attend him.   All this cut no ice.   It was resolved
that the charges should be investigated by a Committee of
the whole House.

The inquiry opened on February 1, and for more than
three weeks the dirty linen of the Duke of York, Mrs.
Clarke, and others was washed in public.   It is no part of
my task to describe this investigation in detail, but only in
so far as it bears on the career of Sir Francis Burdett.   It
was incontrovertibly proved first that towards the end of
1803 the Duke of York had taken this married woman to
be his mistress.   He set her up in a magnificent establishment, which comprised some four or five female servants,

two or three male cooks, some five other male servants, eight horses and two carriages. He also gave her a house at Wimbledon. To keep up this whole establishment he only allowed her £1000 a year. Even this sum was not regularly paid, though it was admitted that during the three years' intimacy he may have given her in all some £5000. On May 11, 1806, the Duke of York cast her off for reasons unconnected with the matter under inquiry, but promised her, if her conduct were *correct*, an annuity of £400 a year. But he gave no bond, and as he judged her conduct *incorrect*, he failed to keep his promise about the annuity. And then she turned on him.

It was proved, secondly that Mrs. Clarke represented herself as possessing the power, through her influence with the Duke of York, of procuring military (and other) promotions, and in consequence received large sums of money from a number of officers and others, who regarded her as the means by which their promotions were actually obtained.

The only question at issue was whether the Duke of York had actively participated in or connived at this system of corruption. Mrs. Clarke asserted that he had; the Duke of York denied it " on the honour of a Prince."

Mrs. Clarke was a worthless, if clever, woman, whose word could not be accepted, unless it received corroboration. But her evidence *was* in many respects corroborated, among other things by letters of the Duke of York himself.

The hearing of the evidence closed on Wed. February 22. From March 8 to 20 the Report of the evidence was debated in the House of Commons. Wardle moved an Address to the Crown, calling attention to the corrupt practices that had been proved to exist, declaring that such abuses could not have existed without the knowledge of the Commander-in-Chief, and that the Duke of York ought to be deprived of the command of the Army.

Ministers defended the Duke of York, and gave it as their view that there was no proof of his having been party to the corruption. Finally, Wardle's motion was negatived (364 to 123), and Perceval, the Chancellor of the Exchequer on March 19 carried the resolution, " that it is opinion of the House that there is no ground to charge H.R.H. with personal corruption or connivance at the infamous practices disclosed in the evidence " (278 to 199).

On March 20 Perceval read to the House parts of a letter addressed by the Duke of York to the King, in which he tendered his resignation of the command of the Army. And the House then resolved that it did not think it necessary to consider further the evidence, as far as that evidence related to the Duke of York.

We have now to consider Burdett's attitude to the question. When Wardle originally moved for the investigation on January 27 Burdett seconded his proposal. But he was then struck down with a severe attack of gout, and during the whole of the taking of the evidence he was unable to attend the House. Though still suffering great bodily pain, he spoke in the debate that followed on March 10. He took a very decided line against the Duke. He expressed his astonishment that the Chancellor of the Exchequer, the officer of the public, and His Majesty's Attorney-General—the public accuser—and indeed all the Crown lawyers, whose duty it is to detect and punish public delinquents, have been upon this occasion arrayed upon the side of the party accused. They had acted as advocates, not as judges, and done their best to obstruct the Hon. Member in his honest attempt to extirpate abuses. He had been threatened with infamy, if he failed to prove his case. Let the House look at the conduct of the Duke of York himself. He had cast off Mrs. Clarke, left her in debt and distress, and threatened her, if she complained, with the pillory. It quite confounds the understanding that the Duke of York should leave to misery and want the woman to whom he had written the love-letters on the table. Where was the " honour of a Prince" ? The honour of Mrs.

Clarke induced her to offer to sacrifice her annuity, if the
Duke would pay the debts—*his* debts as much as *hers*, be it
observed—but this was refused. Where, then, was the
" honour of a Prince " ? The annuity was no mighty
settlement, considering the terms on which she had lived
with H.R.H.; it was not paid, and when required, the
answer was : " You have no legal bond," and there was
the " honour of a Prince." In short, H.R.H.'s honour rises
out of this discussion like Banquo's Ghost,

> " With twenty mortal gashes on his head,
>   To push us from our stools."

Burdett declared that in his opinion the charges against
the Duke of York were completely substantiated. It was
impossible that the Duke could retain the situation which
he held at the head of the Army.[1]

The corruption which had been proved in Mrs. Clarke's
case was but a single instance of the corruption that
saturated public life and threatened the country with ruin.
The acquittal of the Duke of York, in his opinion, reinforced the argument for the reform of the Lower House.
None but corrupt placemen could have returned such a
verdict on the evidence.

Addresses of thanks from cities and counties poured in,
congratulating Wardle on the manly part he had played,
and in these addresses votes of thanks were generally
included to Burdett, Folkestone, Whitbread and others
who had assisted him.

Wardle's popularity was short-lived. Lord Holland [2]
tells us he " was remarkable for nothing but the atrocities
he had perpetrated against the Irish insurgents in 1797."

---

[1] The exposure was a beautiful lesson in morality to the lower
classes. When the common people tossed up halfpence in the streets,
they cried " Duke and Darling " instead of " Heads and tails."
" Darling " was the title given to Mrs. Clarke in the Duke's love-
letters (" Lord Colchester's Diary," Vol. II, p. 174).
[2] " Further Memoirs of the Whig Party," p. 27.

It is impossible to touch pitch without being defiled. He had wormed himself into the confidence of this worthless woman Mrs. Clarke, and he had undertaken, in return for her vindictive exposure of the Duke of York, to furnish a house and settle an income upon her. But they soon fell out. An upholsterer named Wright had furnished Mrs. Clarke's house, and on July 3, 1809, he brought an action against Wardle for the cost of the furniture. He won his case. Wardle thereupon brought an action against Mrs. Clarke and the two Wright brothers for a conspiracy to make him responsible for the payment of goods supplied to Mrs. Clarke by the Wrights. It is with reference to this action that the following letters passed between Wardle and Burdett.

Colonel Wardle to Sir Francis Burdett.

James Street.
25 Nov. 1809.

DEAR BURDETT,

As far as we have gone, you have all before you, & I think I can divine your sentiments.

We expect the trial for the Conspiracy to come on on the 4th of Dec., Monday sennight. My Counsel hold the evidence you will be able to give as most material. *I mean—Mrs Clarke having put the letters into your hands, & being anxious that you should have brought on the business, without ground for expectation of any pecuniary recompense from you.*

This will go in direct opposition to the arguments they will urge & to false facts that they will endeavour to establish, & must infinitely serve the cause.

G. WARDLE.

Sir F. Burdett to Colonel Wardle.

Wimbledon.
Nov. 29, 1809.

DEAR WARDLE,

I greatly fear that both your Counsel & yourself

have made a mistaken conclusion, when you think that it
will be useful to you to summon me as a witness on your
approaching cause, & thus to expose me to a cross-examina-
tion by the Attorney-General. You say I have all before
me. I have nothing before me, except what all the world
knows of this business. You likewise add that you
" divine what my sentiments are," upon which divination
" your Counsel (for they can have no other intelligence) hold
my evidence, which I shall be able to give, as most
material." You & your Counsel think that to obtain from
my testimony a proof that from Mrs Clarke having asked no
money, nor security for money, from me, will enable your
Counsel to draw from thence an inference that she asked or
expected none from you. This will be a most useless &
ill-drawn inference indeed. For when they have got
possession of this new fact, I suppose that the Attorney-
General will not fail to ask me—" Why, Sir Francis, did
you forbear to take up this business yourself ? "   To which
I must answer, that I did not choose to have such an
associate as Mrs Clarke in any business, least of all in such a
business as this. The Attorney-General will not fail to ask
me, Whether I did not think that she would expect money
from me in the course of this transaction for her intelligence,
& that in the progress of it I should be in a manner at her
mercy for her correspondent testimony ?   I must certainly
answer that I did so think. Your inference, you see, is
nothing, & likewise my answer attended with disadvantage
to you.   However I suppose you are the best judges.   You
have a right to any testimony that I can give; & if you call
for it, I will obey your subpoena cheerfully & readily.   I
am, yours very sincerely,

                                        F. BURDETT.

    The action was tried on December 11, 1809.   We are
told by Mrs. Clarke that the Duke of York was on the bench.
Lord Ellenborough charged the jury in a sense very

unfavourable to Wardle, and the jury, after five minutes retirement, returned a verdict in favour of Mrs. Clarke and the Wrights.

Burdett had acted wisely in keeping clear of Mrs. Clarke as a person. The result was that when, in 1810, she published her scurrilous book " The Rival Princes," while she denounced Wardle in no measured terms as a mercenary adventurer, she expressed her admiration for the private worth and great ability of Burdett, who in the " *affaire York* " had only acted upon *public* principles. But, shrewdly enough, she adds the rider that he was " not very choice as to the character of his *political associates*." (Any way, he had kept clear of her.) " When Sir Francis possesses himself of a more perfect knowledge of Col. Wardle's character, I think he will be sorry that he has suffered such a man to *crawl up* his back."

Wardle's further history can soon be told. Cobbett and others stood up for him as a man who had been badly treated, and as one who had done yeoman service to the " popular " cause. Till the close of 1810 he retained a sort of popularity, and we shall meet with him again. By that time his financial position had become seriously involved. He therefore retired to the Continent and he died at Florence in 1833.

The " *affaire York* " had a two-fold effect on politics. The Reformers, having once tasted blood, were hot on the trail, that they might run to earth corruption in other quarters. And the movement for Reform, which had slumbered since 1797, was quickened into new life. Speaking to his constituents for the first time since his election on March 30, Burdett declared that none of this corruption was possible were it not for the state of the Parliamentary representation. It was impossible, he said, to get any delinquent punished, because the House of Commons was in the pay of the corrupters, and in no sense represented the people. " It is the only spot in all the world, where the people of England are spoken of with contempt." He rallied the nobility and gentry of England—its natural defenders—on giving up their time to agricultural pursuits,[1] fattening sheep and oxen, instead of taking the lead in rescuing their native land.

At the "Crown and Anchor" on May 1 Burdett explained that his remarks had been misunderstood. There were many gentlemen, *e.g.* Mr. Coke of Norfolk, whose liberal pursuits of agriculture were not more remarkable than the firmness and steadiness with which they came forward in the defence of the rights and liberties of the country. He had only meant that these pursuits ought not to be paramount. Such pursuits, *after* a gentleman had performed his public duties, were of the highest importance to the people.

This explanation was given when, on May 1, 1809, 1200 Friends of Reform dined at the Crown and Anchor, with Sir Francis as chairman, and passed resolutions for Reform, of which the substance was as follows :

(1) That the long duration of Parliament facilitated the corruption of Members, and removed them from the adequate control of their constituents.

(2) That in the year 1793 no fewer than 307 *English* M.P.'s were appointed by 154 individuals : that the situation was still worse in 1809 : that therefore the " people " were not represented, though they were taxed £70,000,000 a year.

(3) That by the Act of Settlement (1701) no minister, or placeman, or pensioner was to be capable of serving in the House of Commons.

(4) That seventy-eight of the present M.P.'s were in regular receipt from the Crown of £178,994 a year.

[1] Whitbread wrote to Creevey March 31 : "I cannot say how much I was surprised by Burdett's unprovoked attack upon the great agriculturists, who are almost without exception real friends of Liberty and Reform " (" Creevey Papers," p. 94).

(5) That in every department of the State scandalous abuses and corruptions had been detected.

(6) That the exclusion of the people from influence and the consequent corruption had caused the subjugation of the continental nations by Napoleon.

(7) That until the people were properly represented, corruption would increase, debts and taxes would accumulate, resources would be dissipated, the native energy of the people would be depressed, and the country deprived of its best defence against the enemy.

(8) That it was only necessary to recur to the principles handed down by our forefathers, and to restore the proper representation of the people in the House of Commons—a remedy equally necessary to the Throne and to the happiness of the country.

(9) That all towns and counties should apply to Parliament to adopt such measures as should secure to the nation the reality of representation.

Cobbett, who was no mean judge, declared that on this occasion " the speech of Sir Francis Burdett was the very best I have ever read. The *Whole* was good. I see not one word that I would wish to have left out. Full of sound constitutional principles, most aptly applied and ably illustrated." [1]

Burdett's contention that in the existing state of things it was impossible to punish delinquents was soon exemplified.

On May 11 Mr. Madocks, speaking from his seat in the House of Commons, made this deliberate charge : " I affirm that Mr Dick purchased a seat in this House for the Borough of Cashel through the agency of the Hon. Henry Wellesley, who acted for and on behalf of the Treasury; that upon a recent question of the last importance (*sc.* the

[1] "P. R.," May 6, 1809.

Duke of York's affair), when Mr Dick had determined to vote according to his conscience, the noble Lord (Castle-reagh) did intimate to that gentleman the necessity of either his voting with the Government or resigning his seat in that House : and that Mr Dick, sooner than vote against principle, did make choice of the latter alternative, and did vacate his seat accordingly. To this transaction I charge the Right Hon. Gentleman (Mr. Perceval) as being privy and having connived at it; this I will engage to prove by witnesses at the Bar, if the House will give me leave to call them."

The Chancellor of the Exchequer (Perceval) before retiring said, " This was to be a first step to general Reform . . . Whether *at such a time* it would be wise to warrant such species of charges as merely introductory to the agitation of the great question of Reform, he left it to the House to determine."

Most of the Whig leaders, with the notable exceptions of Whitbread and Folkestone, opposed the investigation.

Burdett, in the course of a speech supporting Madocks, said that if any Hon. Member were to contend that these practices formed part of the Constitution itself, then he must say that Bonaparte had a better ally within these walls than he had anywhere else.

Mr. Speaker Abbot says in his Diary [1] that Burdett was " hot and angry," and on his making this remark " a shout was raised from all parts of the House, so loud that the boats passing upon the river (it was about 7 p.m.) lay upon their oars with surprise at the sudden and violent burst of noise." (How did Mr. Speaker know this?) Burdett further said that if the House did not take action, it would only establish in the country a conviction that corruption was become so common with regard to seats in that House that it had ceased to be there regarded as an offence.

Ponsonby, who was supposed to be leader of the Whig

[1] Lord Colchester's " Diary," Vol. II, p. 186.

Opposition, said he would appeal to all who heard him, whether many seats were not sold, and that being notorious, he would never take such an advantage for the running down of a political adversary. For the practice of trafficking in seats had become as glaring as the noon-day sun.

Windham opposed Madocks' motion. He said that many things of the nature referred to were in fact coeval with the Constitution itself, and they had " grown with its growth, and strengthened with its strength." Never was a quotation—and that from the friend of Dr. Johnson—more unfortunate. In the neatest way possible, Burdett cornered Windham by asking : " What is it the poet speaks of when he says it ?

' Grows with our growth and strengthens with our strength '

Why, it is a state of disease, necessarily terminating in Death.

' The young *disease*, which must subdue at length, Grows with our growth and strengthens with our strength.' "

Madocks' motion for an inquiry was rejected by 310 to 85.

That the public conscience had to a certain extent been awakened was shown by a speech of the Speaker (June 1) on a Bill prohibiting the sale of seats, introduced by a Mr. Curwen. The Speaker characterised the question, Whether seats in that House shall be henceforth publicly saleable ? as " A proposition, at the sound of which our Ancestors would have startled with indignation; but a practice, which in these days and within these walls, in utter oblivion of every former maxim and feeling of Parliament, has been avowed and justified." He declared that the sale of seats " does indeed appear to me a great Political Evil and a great Public Grievance . . . and that it is a high Parliamentary offence, every page of our History, Statutes, and Journals appears to me to bear evidence."

Sir Francis Burdett had long been taunted with " wild

projects, visionary schemes, and not knowing what he
wanted." That taunt was no longer possible after
June 15, when he outlined to the House of Commons a
plan of Reform, and asked it to give an assurance that in
the following session it would take into consideration some
Reform in the state of the representation. It was the first
time since 1797 that Reform had been seriously brought
before Parliament.

He began by denying any desire for a Constitution based
on *a priori* speculations. What he desired was the ancient
constitution of England. He appealed to Tacitus and to
the history of the early Roman Empire to show that it was
no use to retain the *forms* of a free constitution, if the spirit
and essence had fled. The most cruel of all tyrannies was
that exercised under the *forms* of a free government. In
England, while the *forms* had been preserved, both the
Crown and the People had in *fact* fallen under the usurped
sovereignty of a Borough-Monger faction, using as its
agents the King's Ministers. The King ought to have his
Prerogative, and the People its shield against misgovern-
ment in a really representative House of Commons. It was
part of the ancient Prerogative of the Crown to issue writs
to such places as were judged from time to time most fit
to send representatives to Parliament. " If this Prerogative
had been maintained, can it be imagined that the posts
of Gatton or the stones of Midhurst would have been
required to send wise and discreet burgesses to assist with
their advice in the Great Council of the Nation ? " Since
1688 the Prerogative of the Crown had been increasingly
absorbed by the Borough-Mongers. The simple principle
that lay behind the ancient Constitution was this, that the
People cannot be legally taxed without their own consent.
But this principle is absolutely annihilated by the present
frame of Representation in this House, to which a
Petition on your table offers to prove that 157 individuals
have the power of returning a majority. So that the whole

property of the free subjects of this kingdom is at the disposal of 157 Borough-Mongers, or in other words 157 Borough-Mongers have usurped and hold as private property the Sovereignty of England.

" The position of the King himself is intolerable. His time is taken up in trying to keep his balance, in endeavouring to conciliate the support of such and such a Borough-Monger in order to obtain his permission to allow the Government to go on; so that he is more like a rope-dancer than a King, as they make it necessary for him to be perpetually on the alert to balance himself, whilst the utmost he can do is to keep his place.

" The People on the other hand suffer from an intolerable and unnecessary load of taxation, due to the corruption by which the whole system of Government is pervaded."

The plan of Reform suggested by Burdett was briefly this :

(1) Household franchise.
(2) The division of the counties into more or less equal electoral districts.
(3) All elections to be held and finished on one and the same day.
(4) The duration of Parliaments to be shortened.

Among other things, he claimed that all the scandals which disfigured the existing system of electoral contests would be got rid of.

Cobbett's comment in the " Political Register" on Burdett's scheme was, " Pass a Bill to this effect, and you need not fear Napoleon's gun-boats."

Burdett's speech gave a glimpse into the obvious, but the obvious was not obvious to his fellow-members, and his motion for Reform was rejected by 74 to 15.

Some other events in the year 1809 have still to be briefly mentioned.   Within the Cabinet antagonism existed between Canning, the Foreign Secretary, and Castlereagh, the Secretary for War. The ghastly failure in September of Castlereagh's pet scheme—the Walcheren Expedition—produced a crisis. Canning, in the early part of 1809, had intimated to the Prime Minister that he could no longer be a member of a Cabinet in which Castlereagh was included. Portland agreed to insist on Castlereagh's resignation, but wished that no action should be taken till the end of the session. The session ended on June 21, and that same day the Walcheren Expedition was resolved upon. It was decided by Portland that no further step should be taken till the issue of the Walcheren Expedition was seen. Shortly afterwards Portland fell dangerously ill and on September 6 he resigned office. He died on October 30, 1809.

Canning was throughout his life to many people an object of profound distrust, being suspect as a " climber." In the unhappy event which followed, Canning's friends asserted that the fault lay with the Duke of Portland for not having communicated to Castlereagh at an earlier date the decision that he must retire. But Canning's enemies took a severe view of his conduct. They said that he had organised an intrigue against his colleague, and, having obtained a promise of Castlereagh's dismissal, continued to sit in the same Cabinet, and left Castlereagh not only in the persuasion that he possessed his confidence and support, but also allowed him, in breach of every principle of good faith, both public and private, to originate and proceed in the execution of a new enterprise of the most important nature with his apparent concurrence and ostensible approbation. Such underhand and treacherous dealing was, they said, inexcusable.

When Castlereagh at last learnt the facts, on September 18, his fury knew no bounds, and the country was scandalised by a duel fought between the two Ministers on September 21, in which Castlereagh was untouched, but Canning was wounded, though not dangerously, in the thigh.

Mr. Perceval, the new Prime Minister, made overtures to the Whig leaders, Grey and Grenville, for an " extended Administration," but on their refusal he reconstructed the Ministry on a purely Tory basis, Lord Wellesley becoming Foreign, and Lord Liverpool Home Secretary. The only strength in Perceval's position lay in the fact that the Whig Opposition was also divided, the Moderates Grey and Grenville and Ponsonby being opposed to the " Mountain," with Whitbread and Folkestone as its leaders.

Here is a letter that must have amused Burdett, as he kept it in his family papers. The letter refers to Wellington's victory at Talavera on July 28, 1809. It was written by the Comte de Cely to Eliza, daughter of Lady Sullivan. The Comte de Cely was in the suite of the famous *émigré* leader, the Prince de Condé. Chicksands Priory, Bedfordshire, was the seat of Sir George Osborn, who married as his second wife Heneage, daughter of the eighth Earl of Winchelsea. Lady Essex Finch was Lady Osborn's sister.

Chicksands Priory
Sunday, 27 Aug. 1808 (till 10 Sept.
then I shall go at Lady Essex Finch)
(The date ought to be 1809).

DEAR ELIZA,

I am shameful to have not had the pleasure to entertain you since you have with disdain abandon London, but the respect which I am indebted to your Elder Sister had oblige me to think of her Ladyship first : i hope that you have better weather during your exertions on the Cart than we have here, for almost every day the tunder is rolling over our heads with noise that woud fright you, being so coward as a Turkey.

I am tranquilised on account of our English Armies in Spain by the wisely ordered retrait of Sir Arthur Wellesley, for it is very happy after the victory to Talavera by want of feed & of carriages he had not march on Madrid when the

Armies of Victor beated but not routed have taken a position during that Soult & Mortier crossing the Tagus where (sic) on the english Armies—if Wesley was so—generalissimo he woud have oblige Cuesta to combat what he have not done, for i have seen a letter to Sir George Osborne, which relate that the Spaniards except a few Corps have had a very cowardly conduct : if one have had not so clever a general as Sir A. Wesley i shoud have great anxiety for so brave armies, that God continue to preserve : be not surprized my dear Eliza that i write so perfectly well in english but since i live here i speak & hear speaking all day english & during my nights if some rats or mouses trouble me i say *go lon*, & they obey me understanding perfectly my english.

Sir George is suffering from a reumatism; Lady Heinage, who have the pretension to be a good phisician, but who is very ignorant, after that he have had a good breakfast yesterday has given him a Physic & after he have well dined she gave him another & made him take a walk au clair de la lune in place to be near a good fire, no a dog or a cat woud be mor prudent : before yesterday the bootler having eat & drink too much & being tormented with a strong indigestion my Lady gave him 8 grains of james Powder, the unhappy bootler was near to die & one was obliged to send for a phisician who arriving found him so weak that he judged it best to wait if the nature woud save him or not, but the unhappy bootler being of a strong nature he was restored.   Lady Heinage the best of Women is the worst phisician, she had killed some years ago a superbe ox with james powder, & on another occation having received 24 turkeys very fatigue to have walked to foot a too long journey she contrive to refresh them some huile de castor, but twelve of that number died & the rest did look melancholy so long as they did live : i have receive at this moment a letter from Lady Sullivan, i put my thanks at her feet, i have not time to write today, but i will comply soon with the liberty give me : be sure that i remember you in my prayers altho' not so good as i woud wish, believe the faithful friendship that i feel for you since you were no higher than my finger, write often & believe that i love a friendly letter better than a pursefull of guineas, yours,

LE COMTE DE CELY.

CHAPTER XII

BURDETT'S COMMITMENT TO THE TOWER AND THE BURDETT
RIOTS

IF incident is what a biographer wants, the biographer of Sir Francis Burdett finds a plethora of material for the year 1810. Sir Francis was indeed in this year a "Frantic Disturber" of "the borough-mongering faction" and of Governmental repose.

Public feeling had been deeply stirred by the disasters that attended the Walcheren Expedition. When the session of Parliament opened on January 23 this feeling was shown in the debate on the Address, Burdett, among others, attacking Ministers for their incompetence and accumulated failures.

On February 15 he called attention to the scandalous action of Captain the Hon. Warwick Lake in having landed a dishonest seaman, Richard Jeffery, on the uninhabited island of Sombrero in the West Indies and leaving him there to perish. Lake had been court-martialled and dismissed the service. But Burdett asked what further steps the Government intended to take.—As, however, it was not known whether Jeffery had perished or had been rescued (as proved to be the case), consideration of the matter was postponed.[1]

On February 16 Burdett opposed the grant of an annuity of £2000 to Sir Arthur Wellesley (now Lord Wellington) on the same ground as that on which he had opposed a grant in the preceding year to Lord Lake's family. Why

[1] See "Farington Diary," Vol. VI, p. 159. Jeffery was rescued by the American schooner *Adams*. He returned to England in October 1810, and was given compensation by the Lake family.

not provide Wellington, he asked, with such a sinecure as the Governorship of Portsmouth or the vacant Tellership of the Exchequer, without laying fresh burdens on an impoverished people ?

On February 8 and 9 petitions for a Reform of Parliament were presented from Middlesex and Westminster by the members for those constituencies. It had now become common form in these petitions to refer to the petition presented by Charles Grey in 1793. And the argument was reinforced in the Westminster petition by citing the charges of corruption brought against Castlereagh and Perceval in the session of 1809.

But the origin of the *émeute*, by which for some days the metropolis was plunged into confusion, arose from the discussion of the Walcheren disaster.

On January 26 Lord Porchester, by a majority of nine, carried against the Government a motion that an inquiry into the causes of the Walcheren failure should be held by a Committee of the whole House.

On February 2, when the House resolved itself into a Committee on the Scheldt Expedition, Charles Yorke, a member for Cambridgeshire, " spied strangers," and moved the application of the Standing Order for their exclusion. On February 6 Sheridan protested against this policy of secrecy. It would simply create in the country suspicion of their motives. He moved that the Standing Order should be modified in such a way that its application should depend not on the caprice of one individual, but on the vote of the whole House. Windham spoke in favour of retaining the order as it was. If the admission of strangers was claimed as a right, then we should no longer have a " Representative Government," but a " Democracy." Parliament would become subordinate to the " Press." In the course of his speech he referred disparagingly to the press-men.

Burdett scouted the idea of the inquiry being held in secret. The House, he said, was viewed by the country with grave suspicion.   He greatly feared that the reputation of the House had not a leg to stand upon.   For this remark he was called to order by the Speaker.

Sheridan's motion was rejected.   The inquiry was held in secret, and as a result on March 30 all the mismanagement and incompetence of Ministers was whitewashed by votes approving of their conduct.   But other events had meanwhile happened.

There was in Westminster a debating society called by the pretentious name of " The British Forum."   Its secretary was an apothecary named Gale Jones.   On February 19 the walls of Westminster were placarded with this advertisement :

" WINDHAM & YORKE.

" BRITISH FORUM, 33 Bedford Street, Covent Garden.

" Monday, Feb. 19, 1810.

" Question ;—Which was a greater outrage upon the public feeling, Mr Yorke's enforcement of the Standing Order to exclude strangers from the House of Commons, or Mr Windham's recent attack upon the liberty of the press ?   Last Monday, after an interesting discussion, it was unanimously decided, that the enforcement of the Standing Orders, by shutting out strangers from the gallery of the House of Commons, ought to be censured as an insidious & ill-timed attack upon the liberty of the Press, as tending to aggravate the discontents of the people, & to render their representatives objects of jealous suspicion.   The great anxiety manifested by the public at this critical period to become acquainted with the proceedings of the House of Commons, & to ascertain who were the authors & promoters of the late calamitous expedition to the Scheldt, together with the violent attacks made by Mr Windham on the newspaper reporters (whom he represents as 'bankrupts, lottery-office keepers, footmen, & decayed tradesmen') have stirred up the public feeling, & excited universal attention. The present question is therefore brought forward as a comparative enquiry, & may be justly expected to furnish a contested & interesting debate."

That same evening Charles Yorke called the attention of the House of Commons to the placard. He quoted the clause in the Bill of Rights (1689) : " That the freedom of speech, and debates or proceedings in Parliament ought not to be impeached or questioned in any court or place out of Parliament."

This, of course, was absurd, for the clause was intended to protect Members of Parliament from molestation by the King. It was never contemplated that it should be used to crush an apothecary ! To use the Bill of Rights for this purpose was like using a sledge-hammer to kill a fly. However it was good enough for the House of Commons. Gale Jones was haled before them on February 21, and though he expressed contrition for his offence, was committed by order of the House to Newgate. Burdett, owing to illness, was not present when this folly was perpetrated. But on March 12 he came down to the House and in a long speech moved that Gale Jones should be discharged from Newgate. He declared that the imprisonment of Gale Jones was an infringement of the law of the land. If the privileges of the House contravened the law, privileges must go. He drew a distinction between *privilege* and *power*.

" Privilege the House possessed for its own protection; Power was a right to be exercised over others. Privilege they were to exercise to prevent the Crown from molesting them in their proceedings. They were to use it as a shield for themselves, but they were not to allow it to change its character, to be converted into Power, and to use it for the destruction of others."

He then proceeded to illustrate the nature of the privileges of the House of Commons by a sketch of their history. Privilege in origin aimed at maintaining the personal freedom of Members from arrest; not one of them was contrary to law. Before the days of the Long Parliament (1640) there was no instance of the House of Commons taking justice into its own hand against a non-member. At the time of the Civil War, " from the peculiar circumstances of the Country, in order to resist the arbitrary encroachments of a despotic prince, the House of Commons found it absolutely necessary not only to extend their Privileges, but to assume Powers, the exercise of which abolished the House of Lords, brought the King to the block, and ultimately dissolved the whole frame of the Government. After the Restoration (1660) the House was unwilling to yield up its usurped power—submitted to in times of trouble and commotion, but incompatible with the return of order and the laws."

He illustrated the evils of privilege from the case of three judges, who, in consequence of a decision given by them in the King's Bench, were on a petition summoned before the House of Lords to account for their action. But the three judges refused to acknowledge the jurisdiction of the House of Lords. They appealed to Magna Charta and the law, and claimed their undoubted right as Englishmen to be tried by a jury of their equals, if they were accused of doing anything wrong. Suppose, they said, they were indicted elsewhere. If the House of Lords had acquitted them, they could not plead this in answer to the indictment; if the House of Lords had punished them, they might still be punished by the King's Bench a second time for the same offence. Now apply this, said Sir Francis, to the case of Gale Jones. Despite the action already taken by the House of Commons, there was nothing to stop Windham and Yorke from prosecuting Gale Jones for libel in the King's Bench, and therefore he might be punished twice for the same offence. If, however, the jury should find him not guilty, the House of Commons would have placed itself in the absurd position of having imprisoned him for an offence of which a jury had found him innocent.

Burdett then cited other cases, and proceeded : it was a doctrine laid down by Coke that no man could be fined or imprisoned but in a Court of Record.   But the House of Commons was not a Court of Record; it could not fine, therefore, *a fortiori*, it could not imprison.   Further, the Speaker's Warrant was in form illegal.   A legal warrant must conclude with the words " till the prisoner be delivered by due course of law."   The Speaker's warrant ends with the words " during the pleasure of the House."

The commitment, he said, was contrary to Magna Charta (of which Coke had said, " He is such a fellow that he will bear no sovereign ") and the law of the land.   The House of Commons could not administer an oath; there was no sworn evidence against Gale Jones.   The House of Commons had gathered into its own hands the rôles of the accuser, the Grand Jury, the Petty Jury, the Judge, the executioner.   This was contrary to all the principles of English law and English justice.   There can be no wrong without a remedy—that was the principle of English law— but where was the remedy for Gale Jones ?   He quoted the dictum of Sir Fletcher Norton, when Attorney-General, that he would pay no more attention to a mere resolution of the House of Commons than to that of a set of drunken porters at an ale-house.

Burdett in his speech had seemed to declare that the House had no jurisdiction over any persons but its own members, but in his reply he corrected this impression. He admitted that the House, when holding an inquiry, as the Grand Inquest of the nation, had the right to commit *anyone* for obstructing its proceedings.   But in this case there was no " obstruction."   How were the proceedings of the House " obstructed " by a libel subsequent in point of time ?

Burdett was answered by the Law Officers, who maintained that the right of commitment was an undoubted privilege of the House.

In the course of the debate Sheridan ridiculed the application of the clause in the Bill of Rights to the case of Gale Jones. If Yorke's interpretation of the clause was correct, it would " bar all public discussion, all consideration of politics outside the walls of Parliament." And he declared that " there was something so silly, so small, so ignominious, in the contest in which the House was involved that he could not think of it without pain, and therefore must feel anxious to rescue it from its warfare with the British Forum." He favoured the release of Gale Jones.

The motion was, however, rejected by a majority of 139. Burdett did not let the matter rest here. In the issue of Cobbett's " Register " on March 24 he published an open letter to his constituents, denying the power of the House of Commons to imprison the people of England.

In the letter Burdett accused the House of Commons— " a part of our fellow subjects, collected together by means which it is not necessary for me to describe "—of overriding the law of the land. If the House of Commons could arbitrarily imprison Gale Jones, any one of them might be treated in the same way. Arbitrary government under the name of Privilege was no better than the arbitrary government of the Stuarts, Charles I and James II, under the name of Prerogative. " Our Forefathers made sternvisaged Prerogative hide his head, and shall we their sons be afraid to enter the lists with undefined PRIVILEGE assuming the powers of PREROGATIVE ? " And why should the House of Commons stop short at imprisonment, if they were to be the sole judge of their own powers ? " Inflated with their high-blown fanciful ideas of Majesty they think Privilege and Protection beneath their dignity, assume the sword of Prerogative, and lord it equally over the King and the People." Well might Paine call the Bill of Rights the Bill of Wrongs, if it could thus be converted into an instrument to oppress and to destroy the liberties of the People.

Burdett by his exposure of abuses had long been a thorn in the side of Government, and Perceval, the Prime Minister, seems to have conceived for him a malignant hate.   Walking home from church with the Speaker on March 25, he laid the train that was to be fired by his puppet—a Mr. Lethbridge, member for Somerset—on the following day. On March 26, Lethbridge, seeing Sir Francis Burdett in his place, asked him whether he acknowledged the authorship of the letter that had appeared in the " Register." Burdett having acknowledged the authorship, Lethbridge gave notice that he would on the morrow move resolutions.

Accordingly on the 27th Lethbridge laid Burdett's " Letter and Argument " on the table of the House.   He said that he had marked certain passages, which he thought justified him in the charge he was about to make against Burdett.   The House decided that the whole document should be read, and its reading occupied one and a half hours.   Lethbridge then proceeded to point out the passages that seemed to him most offensive.

Sir Francis Burdett, on being asked by the Speaker whether he had anything to say, replied shortly that he had no idea that in his " Address, etc.," he was infringing any privilege of the House.   Was it to be supposed that the simple arguing on the powers of the Commons was a crime ?   Would not the House endure even an abstract doubt of their powers ?   He was willing to abide by the fact and argument of the paper.   He would stand the issue. He then withdrew.

The absurd man, Lethbridge, spoke of the embarrassment he felt at bringing such a charge, and several times apologised for his own incompetence.   But, he said, it was high time to put a stop to the practices of the Hon. Baronet. He had heard such things stated as made his hair stand on end !   (The House was convulsed with laughter.)   It was

perfectly true.   His hair *had* stood on end !   Burdett had
actually stated that the character of this House had not a
leg to stand on !   He then moved :

> (1) That the letter signed Francis Burdett, and the
> following paper, entitled Argument, contained in
> Cobbett's " Register " of the 24th March inst. are a
> libellous and scandalous paper, reflecting on the just
> rights and privileges of the House.
> (2) That Sir Francis Burdett, having acknowledged
> himself to be the author of the same, has violated those
> rights and privileges.

Ponsonby proposed that the debate should be adjourned
for a week, but Perceval moved as an amendment that the
matter be taken into consideration the very next day.

Whitbread retorted that Perceval's aim was simply to
withdraw attention from the examination of the Scheldt
fiasco.   Perceval's amendment was, however, carried.

On the next day there was a short debate, Mr. Brand
proposing a week's adjournment.   Perceval spoke strongly
on the other side, but in view of a speech delivered by the
Master of the Rolls against precipitate action, he finally
gave way and consented to a week's adjournment.

There was one amusing incident in the debate.   Charles
Yorke for his services (! !) had been given the sinecure
Tellership of the Exchequer, £2700 a year, together with
the post of First Lord of the Admiralty, but on offering
himself for re-election by Cambridgeshire he failed to
retain his seat (February 16).   Whitbread in his speech
had alluded to the " unfortunate legacy bequeathed to
the House by the Teller of the Exchequer and late member for Cambridgeshire " in bringing Gale Jones to the
bar of the House.   Nettled by this remark, Sir Joseph
Yorke, the brother of Charles Yorke, retorted that whatever legacy was bequeathed by the late member for
Cambridgeshire must be as good as any that proceeded

from a " brewer of bad porter." At this there was a loud outcry and demands for apology, and there was every prospect of an ugly scene. But Whitbread showed perfect good humour : " He could assure the House that he was in no other way affected than as a tradesman : the Hon. Gent. had no right to hold him out as a brewer of bad porter ! He would gladly give him a cask of his best porter, and all he should ask in return was that he would give it to the Electors of Cambridgeshire to drink the health of their late member ! "

The consideration of Sir Francis Burdett's " Letter " was resumed in the House of Commons on Thursday, April 5, and a long debate ensued. It would be wearisome to give the debate in detail, or enter into the legal technicalities of the cases cited as precedents. Suffice it to say that the chief speakers against Burdett were Sir J. Anstruther and Perceval; those in his favour Folkestone, Romilly, and Whitbread.

Folkestone moved as an amendment that the other Orders of the day be now read.

Sir S. Romilly, after an argument on the legal merits, said: Commitment for an alleged libel was contradictory to all principles of law, as it confounded the characters of judge and accuser, and the prisoner was not heard in his own defence. Let the House pause. It was proceeding against Burdett without having examined a single witness, without the power of examining on oath, without the possibility of any appeal.

The House was under no obligation—as a Court of Law was—to come to any conclusion. If it did, its decision might be very contrary to the feeling of the country.

Whitbread said Burdett's letter was not so strong in its reflections on the House as the address of the city of London to the King in the affair of Wilkes, or as Burke's " Thoughts upon the Present Discontents." In Burdett's letter he saw no libel whatever; in the " Argument " some exaggerations.   But a tendency to exaggerate was the constant error of the Honourable Baronet—an error common to sanguine men.   The House had much better get rid of its embarrassment by coming to no decision.

Canning regretted that the question had been raised at all, but as it had, he would vote for Lethbridge's resolutions. He had no feeling of unkindness towards Burdett.   On the contrary, he thought highly of his natural disposition, and in his opinion Burdett's talents were such as, properly directed, might render great service to the country.

Perceval thought the House ought to punish one of the grossest attacks ever made on its character and privileges.

The House then proceeded to divide.   Lord Folkestone's amendment was rejected by a majority of 191, and Lethbridge's motions were agreed to without a division.

Sir Robert Salusbury then moved that Sir Francis Burdett should be committed to the Tower.   A debate, from which strangers were excluded, then took place. Mr. Adam proposed an amendment that, instead, Sir Francis should be reprimanded in his place.   The numbers on the division were : for the amendment 152; for the original motion 189.   Majority for the commitment of Burdett to the Tower 37.

The House, having perpetrated this folly, rose at 7.30 a.m. on the morning of Friday, April 6.

The Speaker took the Serjeant-at-Arms to his house and immediately made out the warrant for Burdett's arrest. It was signed by 8.30 a.m.   It now hangs on one of the walls at Ramsbury and it is here reproduced in facsimile—

Warrant

Veneris 6 die Aprilis, 1810

" Whereas the House of Commons hath this day adjudged, that Sir F. Burdett bart., who has admitted that a letter signed ' Francis Burdett,' & a further part of a paper, intituled ' Argument,' in Cobbett's Weekly Register of

Veneris 6ᵒ *die Aprilis. 1810.*

Whereas the House of Commons hath this day adjudged, That Sir Francis Burdett, Baronet, who has admitted that a Letter signed "Francis Burdett", and a further part of a paper, intituled "Argument," in Cobbett's Weekly Register of March 24: 1810, ∴ was printed by his Authority (which Letter and Argument the said House has resolved to be a libellous and scandalous paper, reflecting on the just Rights and Privileges of the said House) – has been thereby guilty of a Breach of the Privileges of the said House:

And Whereas the House of Commons hath thereupon ordered, That the said Sir Francis Burdett be, for his said Offence, committed to His Majesty's Tower of London:

These are therefore to require you to take into your Custody the Body of the said Sir Francis Burdett, and then forthwith to deliver Him over into the custody of The Lieutenant of His Majesty's Tower of London:

And

And all Mayors, Bailiffs, Sheriffs, Under-Sheriffs
Constables, and Headboroughs, and every other
person or persons, are hereby required to be
aiding and assisting to you in the execution
hereof;

For which this shall be your sufficient Warrant.

Given under my Hand, the Sixth day of
April, 1810.

To The Serjeant at Arms
attending the House of Commons,
or his Deputy. ——

Chas Abbot
Speaker

March 24th 1810, was printed by his authority, (which
Letter & Argument the said House hath resolved to be a
libellous & scandalous paper, reflecting on the just rights
& privileges of the said House) has been thereby guilty
of a breach of the Privilege of the said House : And whereas
the House of Commons hath thereupon ordered, That the
said Sir F. Burdett be for his said offence committed to his
Majesty's Tower of London : These are therefore to require
you forthwith to take into your custody the body of the
said Sir F. Burdett; & then forthwith to deliver him over
into the custody of the Lieutenant of his Majesty's Tower
of London.—And all Mayors, bailiffs, sheriffs, under
sheriffs, constables & headboroughs, & every other
person or persons are hereby required to be aiding &
assisting to you in the execution hereof.   Given under my
hand, the sixth day of April 1810.

" CHA. ABBOT, Speaker.

" To the Serjeant-at-Arms attending the House of Commons or his Deputy."

The chief instigator to this act of folly had been Perceval,
the Prime Minister. We read in the " Farington Diary "
that, meeting Sir Robert Salusbury at dinner, he had said
to him : " Sir Francis ought to be committed to the Tower.
. . . You would be a proper person to move it; being a
country gentleman and not always voting with us, it could
not seem to arise from Ministerial influences."   Sir Robert
objected, saying, " he was not accustomed to speak in the
House." To this Mr. Perceval replied : " A few words
will be sufficient, as we shall support you."   Being urged
in this manner, Sir Robert, when Sheridan said : " Who
will be bold enough to move for Sir Francis being committed to the Tower ? " rose up and moved for his committal.

Sir Robert Salusbury had some reason seemingly to
regret his action; to avoid the mob that was roused by the

threatened arrest of Burdett, he had to withdraw to his brother's house in Hertfordshire. All the hotels in London refused to take him in from fear that their houses would be wrecked. Finally he had to retire to Wales. Even there he suffered. He was a partner in a bank at Newport and Abergavenny. A run was made upon these banks to ruin them. Their notes were industriously collected and brought in for payment. We are told that " Sir Robert was surprised to see a large quantity brought in by a person with whom he had lived on very good terms. On the man being asked why he proceeded thus against Sir Robert, he said, " He had no particular motive of his own, but that Mr.——, naming a Methodist preacher, had urged him and others to do it." [1]

Such were the consequences to him of attacking the most popular man in England.

When Diderot was once reproaching the Tsarina Catherine II for not giving actuality to her " enlightened " views, she replied : " It is all very well : your facile pen has only to run easily over smooth paper, and you can develop without hindrance enlightened views, but I, poor Empress, have to write on the ticklish texture of human skin. And that is nothing like so easy. *C'est une autre chose.*"

Similarly, the Speaker found it an easy matter to write out a warrant ; but when brought into collision with other human wills he was to find it nothing like so easy to get the warrant executed ; indeed, it required the marshalling of a whole army before the arrest of Sir Francis could be executed.

While Parliament was debating on his fate during the Thursday–Friday night (April 5–6), Sir Francis was at Wimbledon, but his brother, Jones Burdett, and Roger O'Connor were in attendance in one of the rooms of the House of Commons, and when the result was made known at 7.30 a.m. April 6, they set off in a post-chaise for Wimble-

1 "Farington Diary," Vol. VI, pp. 51, 88.

PROGRESS OF THE WARRANT

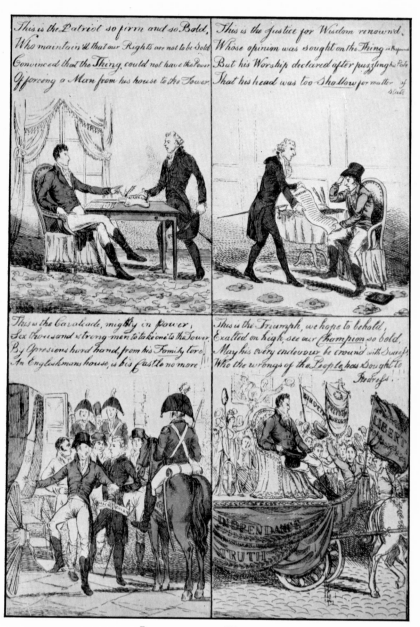

This is the Patriot so firm and so Bold,
Who maintain'd that our Rights are not to be Sold
Convinced that the Thing could not have the Power
Of forcing a Man from his house to the Tower

This is the Justice for Wisdom renown'd,
Whose opinion was sought on the Thing it Required
But his Worship declared after puzzling his Pate
That his head was too Shallow for matter of State

This is the Cavalcade, mighty in power,
Six thousand strong men to take one to the Tower
By Opressions hard hand, from his Family tore
An Englishmans house, is his Castle no more

This is the Triumph, we hope to behold,
Exalted on high, see our Champion so bold,
May his every endeavour be crowned with Success
Who the wrongs of the People has Sought to Redress!

PROGRESS OF THE WARRANT

don to acquaint Sir Francis with the news. Sir Francis mounted his horse, and returned to Town, arriving at 78 Piccadilly about twelve noon.

But already at 9 a.m. Mr. Colman, the Serjeant-at-Arms, and his Deputy, Mr. Clementson, had called at Burdett's house, and found that he was not at home. Having reported the fact to the Speaker (10 a.m.), Colman then wrote the following letter, which was taken by Clementson to Burdett's house. Clementson on arriving found some sixty or seventy persons collected near No. 78.

F. J. Colman to Sir F. Burdett.

6th April, 1810.
Sir,

Having received a warrant from the House of Commons & an order from the Speaker to wait on you to convey you to the Tower : I called at your house this morning at 9 o'clock & was informed that you were not at home. I shall be much obliged to you, to let me know when I can see you, that in doing my duty as Serjeant at Arms, I may not be deficient in paying every proper attention & respect to you. Wishing to consult your convenience as to the time & mode of your removal, I have etc. etc.

FRANCIS J. COLMAN.
Serj. at Arms.

This was the letter that Burdett found on his arrival from Wimbledon at twelve noon. He immediately wrote in answer :

Sir F. Burdett to F. J. Colman Esq.

Piccadilly,
April 6, 1810.
Sir,

I have just received your polite letter, & shall be at home to receive you at 12 o'clock tomorrow.

Yours etc.
FRANCIS BURDETT.

But Colman, before this letter had been delivered, paid a second visit to Burdett's house at 4 p.m.   Sir Francis in an interview told him that he had already replied, and would be ready to *receive* him the next morning at 11 a.m.   The Serjeant went away under the impression that Burdett would go with him quietly next morning.   (But Burdett had never *said* so; it is uncertain whether the determination to resist by force had already been taken, or was only taken after 4 p.m. on the advice of friends.)

In any case, the Serjeant said that in view of the large mob collected outside Burdett's door it would have been impossible for him to execute the warrant.   It was already obvious that, to effect the arrest, the Serjeant would need a considerable force.

Colman then visited the Speaker (5.30 p.m.), and met with a severe reprimand.   He was told that he must make the arrest immediately; but at the Secretary of State's office he found unwillingness to provide him with anything but a " civil " force.   If actual resistance took place, then, but only then, would troops be sent.

At 8 p.m. Colman, for the third time that day (April 6), visited 78 Piccadilly.   He told Burdett[1] that he had met with a severe reprimand from the Speaker for not executing the warrant in the morning; he hoped that Sir Francis would now submit to be his prisoner.   Sir Francis answered that he was sure the Speaker would not, upon consideration, think him to blame; for that it would not have been in his power to remain with him; as, without any personal offence to him, he (Sir Francis) would not have permitted him to remain.   The Serjeant then said, " I shall be obliged, sir, to resort to force, as it is my duty to execute the warrant."

Sir Francis observed, " If you bring an overwhelming force, I must submit; but I dare not, from my allegiance to the King, and my respect for his laws, yield a voluntary

[1] I follow the narrative of the Dublin *Correspondent* of April 13. Its information no doubt came from R. O'Connor.

submission to such a warrant; it is illegal. You must leave my house, but I have written a letter to the Speaker, which, if you please, you may take with you and deliver it. It contains my resolution as to your warrant."

The Serjeant begged leave to decline taking charge of any such letter; he said he had already incurred blame by not executing the warrant, and he should be considered as more criminal if he carried any letter in contradiction to it. He then withdrew.

Sir Francis therefore sent the letter to the Speaker by his own son Robert, a boy of fourteen, and his brother, Jones Burdett. It was delivered to the Speaker at 10 p.m.

The autograph copy of this letter in the Burdett Papers is in the handwriting of the Lady Susan North,[1] then a girl of thirteen. It would seem as though Sir Francis Burdett's nerve had been somewhat shaken by events, as the end of the letter, in contrast to the beginning, is very lame and halting.

To the Right Honourable the Speaker.

Piccadilly.
April 6th, 1810.

SIR,

When I was returned in due form by the Electors of Westminster, they imagined that they had chosen me as their trustee in the House of Commons to maintain the laws & liberties of the land; having accepted that trust I never will betray it.

I have also as a dutiful subject taken an oath of allegiance to the King to obey his laws, & I never will consent by any act of mine to obey any set of men, who contrary to those laws shall (under any pretence whatever) assume the power of the King.

[1] Lady Susan North was daughter of Lord and Lady Guilford and thus a grand-daughter of T. Coutts, and niece of Lady Burdett. After the death of her sisters, she became Baroness North in her own right and was the mother of the present Lord North (1930).

Power & Privilege are not the same things, & ought not to be confounded together. Privilege is an exemption from Power, & was by law secured to the third branch of the Legislature in order to protect them, that they might safely protect the people : not to give them power to destroy the people.

Your warrant, Sir, I believe you know to be illegal. I know it to be so. To superior force I must submit. But I will not, & dare not incur the danger of continuing voluntarily to make one of any set of men, who shall assume illegally the whole power of the realm; & who have no more right to take myself, or any of my constituents by force than I or they possess to take any one of those who are now guilty of this usurpation. And I would condescend to accept the meanest office, that would vacate my seat, being more desirous of getting out of my present association, than other men may be desirous of getting profitably into it.

Sir, this is not a letter in answer to a vote of thanks, it is in answer to a vote of a very different kind, I know not what to call it ; but since you have begun this correspondence with me, I must beg you to read this my answer to those under whose orders you have commenced it. I remain, Sir, your most obedient humble servant,

FRANCIS BURDETT.

Shortly before this letter had been received, Colman informed the Speaker that it was impossible, in view of the mob, to arrest Burdett that night. The magistrates said they had not sufficient force, and further arrangements must be made with the Lord Mayor to convey Burdett into and through the City from the confines of Middlesex.

Meanwhile the popular storm had risen. The river opposite the Tower was crowded with boats, and an immense assemblage had gathered near the Tower in hopes of seeing the prisoner. But it was chiefly in Piccadilly near

No. 78 that the crowd surged and swayed.   The mob filled the whole street and compelled everyone, whether on foot or on horseback or in coach, to cry " Burdett for ever " and to wave his hat.   Those who delayed or refused to pay homage were assailed with showers of mud.   The Earl of Westmoreland, among others, was covered with dirt from top to toe.   The crowd continually increased, and after nightfall bands of rioters scattered in all directions to attack the houses of those who had been prime movers of the Walcheren Expedition and of the attack upon Burdett.

Lethbridge's house in Berkeley Square had all its windows broken, before the mob discovered that it was in the possession of a Mr. Raikes, whose wife was lying dead within.   Lord Castlereagh's house suffered the same fate. The story ran [1] that, whilst the rioters were stoning his house, Castlereagh slipped on a greatcoat and joined the crowd.   Some one who knew him tapped him on the shoulder and asked him whether he saw a man being ducked in the fountain in the middle of St. James' Square.   Castlereagh took the hint and retired.   The house of Sir J. Anstruther was the object of peculiar vengeance.   Not a single pane of glass escaped : the window-frames and Venetian shutters were shattered; glasses, chandeliers, and other valuable furniture were destroyed.   Charles Yorke's house had a similar visitation.   Among other houses that suffered were those of Lord Chatham, Lord Dartmouth, and Perceval.   There was a general call for " illumination," and those who did not light up paid the penalty.   The Guards had to be called out for the protection of life and property.   And so the Friday closed in scenes of disorder.

On the morning of *Saturday April* 7 Burdett was up betimes.   For when the Serjeant called at 78 Piccadilly at 6.30 a.m., he was admitted to the house, but told that Sir Francis was not there.   Leaving Wright, a messenger, with

[1] Dublin *Correspondent* of April 11, 1810.

the warrant at No. 78, the Serjeant at 9.30 a.m. interviewed the Speaker, told him that he had drawn a " blank," but was now proceeding with officers to Wimbledon to effect the arrest. But the Serjeant went on a fool's errand, for Burdett had not gone to Wimbledon. He had taken breakfast with Roger O'Connor in Maddox Street. After breakfast the two walked to Half Moon Street, where Sir Francis mounted his horse and, accompanied by a groom, rode in the Park. On returning to his house at 12.30 p.m. he was told of the messenger's presence. On being shown up, the messenger said : " Sir, I am desired to serve this warrant upon you and to remain with you." The warrant was delivered to Sir Francis, who put it in his pocket.

Sir Francis : " My friend, this is not a sufficient warrant. You may return and inform the Speaker that I will not obey it."

The Messenger : " Sir, it is my orders to remain with you, and I must obey, unless I am forced to withdraw."

Sir Francis : " You must instantly withdraw."

He was accordingly shown downstairs (having parted with his warrant) by Roger O'Connor. The messenger wished force to be used. But O'Connor said : " There is the door open for you; you must go; but it is not my practice to be so uncivil as to lay violent hands on any one, and I hope you will not make it necessary now." The messenger bowed and retired.

At 1 p.m. the Serjeant returned from his fruitless errand to Wimbledon. Hearing that Sir Francis had been seen in the streets, he went about 5 p.m. to No. 78, but was refused admittance, the door being just a little opened, but held by a chain.

The Serjeant was truly deserving of pity. The Speaker had told him on Friday night that he really did not know whether the warrant justified the breaking open of doors. The magistrates, whom he met at the office of the Home Secretary (R. Ryder), were unwilling to give him anything but a civil force.   And there was a howling mob in Piccadilly.

It was all very well for the Speaker to write to the Prime Minister at 6 p.m., " The Serjeant's mismanagement of to-day exceeds, if possible, that of yesterday."   But what would " the little man with the big wig " have done himself in Colman's place ?   The only help that the Speaker gave was at 7 p.m. to issue a fresh warrant to replace that which Burdett had put in his pocket.

The scenes this Saturday in Piccadilly caused the utmost apprehension.   The shops were all closed, and riots worse than those of 1780 seemed imminent.   The town was in the grip of anger, curiosity, and alarm.   All kinds of wild rumours were current, such as, that Lord Moira, the Lieutenant of the Tower, had refused to receive Burdett; that the Lord Mayor had refused to allow a military force to enter the City; that the Foot Guards were at daggers drawn with the Life Guards and would help the " people "; that the Prince of Wales had gone to intercede with the King. Piccadilly in front of No. 78 was crowded with thousands of people, and in consequence Foot Guards and Horse Guards were summoned to save the situation.

We are told by Place that they rode upon the foot pavement and drove " the people before them, pressing on them in such a way, as to cause great terror, frequently doing some of them injury, and compelling them to injure one another, striking those who could not get out of the way fast enough with the flat of their swords." [1]

During a lull, he tells us, " there was a solemn stillness and a gloom half visible, which produced on me, as upon inquiry I afterwards found it had done on others, that peculiar sort of feeling, which has been represented as being felt by soldiers waiting for the dawn of day to commence a battle."

[1] Place Papers, 27,850 (184) and (186) as quoted by Graham Wallas in his " Life of Place."

Finally, the Foot Guards were stationed on the pavement close to the house,[1] and the cavalry on the opposite side of the street.

The scenes of the preceding day were re-enacted, those who refused to take off their hats and to shout " Burdett for ever " being pelted with mud.   The proclamation enjoined by the Riot Act was read about 1 p.m. by a magistrate, Mr. Read.   The Horse Guards charged down Piccadilly, the crowds retiring up the side streets and mocking at the heroes of " the Piccadilly Expedition."   On the Guards retiring, the crowd rallied.   The crowd between ten and eleven was prodigious, and cavalry were stationed at the end of every street leading into Piccadilly.

There was the same kind of mob around the Tower; the banks of the Thames were lined with spectators.   To avoid any surprise, the guns of the Tower were mounted, and the ditches surrounding it filled with water.

During the course of these days Burdett had been visited by many friends, including Coke of Norfolk, Lord Folkestone, Lord Thanet, Lord Cochrane, Madocks, Bosville, Cartwright, Curran, and Wardle. Coke and Whitbread are said to have now advised Burdett to give way, as having done sufficient to contest the right of arrest. But Burdett answered " No "; he had made up his mind, and would yield to nothing but force.

Indignant at all the " excursions and alarms " of the soldiers, he now played a further move, and wrote the following letter to the Sheriffs of Middlesex. (The autograph in the Burdett papers is again in the handwriting of the Lady Susan North.)

Piccadilly,

April 7, 1810.

Gentlemen,

In furtherance of an attempt to deprive me of my liberty under the authority of an instrument, which I know

---

[1] *i.e.* on the north side of Piccadilly.

to be illegal, viz. a warrant by the Speaker of the House of Commons, my house is at this moment beset by a military force.

As I am determined never to yield a voluntary obedience to an act contrary to the laws, I am resolved to resist the execution of such a warrant by all the legal means in my power; & as you are the Constitutional officer appointed to protect the inhabitants of your Bailiwick from violence & oppression, from whatever quarter they may come, I make this requisition to you, Gentlemen, to furnish me with your aid, with which the laws have provided you, either by calling out the Posse Comitatus, or such other as the case & circumstances may require.

It is for you to consider how far you may be liable, should I by any unlawful force, acting under an unlawful authority, be taken from my house.

I have the honour to be, Gentlemen,

your very obedient humble servant,

(*Signed*) FRANCIS BURDETT.

Matthew Wood Esq. & John Atkins Esq. Sheriffs of Middlesex.

Of these two Sheriffs, Wood was known to be a partisan of Burdett; Atkins was a waverer.

Meanwhile what were Ministers doing? The incompetence they showed was phenomenal. The only effective thing they did was to summon to the Metropolis all troops within 100 miles. They are said to have amassed in London an army of 50,000 men. Otherwise their conduct was imbecile. They were not prepared for the emergency, and their attitude at every point was marked by doubt and hesitation.

At 6 p.m. on Saturday the Speaker wrote a confidential letter to Perceval explaining that Burdett had pocketed the warrant for his arrest, and continued :

" I suppose I shall see the Serjeant himself this evening :

but he has now no warrant to justify touching him. Ought I not to give him a fresh warrant instead of that which he has sent to Sir Francis Burdett most unadvisedly? What think you? If I am prevented from hearing from you, I shall think it right to arm him with a fresh warrant.

"In the next place I hear (but on no authority) that Lord Moira has forbidden his Lieutenant to the Tower to take in Sir Francis Burdett, unless there comes an order by the Sign Manual for the purpose. If this is possible, the misunderstanding had better be cleared up. My warrant went with Crosby & Oliver to the Tower & was accepted.

Most truly yours,

C. ABBOT.

At 7 p.m. the Speaker gave the Serjeant a fresh warrant. At 9 p.m. he was visited by Sheriff Wood, who brought him Burdett's letter asking the Sheriff to protect him with the Posse Comitatus. The Speaker only said that he (the Speaker) had done his duty; the Sheriff was to do what he thought proper.

Perceval, the Prime Minister, showed equal doubt and hesitation.

Sp. Perceval to the Speaker.

7 April.

MY DEAR SIR,

Pray tell me whether the address to the Crown to issue a proclamation to take a person, against whom the Speaker's warrant is granted, is the course which has been pursued when the person could not be found, or only when, having been found, he had escaped.

yours most truly,

PERCEVAL.

Perceval, when asked by the Serjeant in the course of the Saturday afternoon whether his warrant authorised him to break open the doors of Burdett's house, said he did not know, and advised him to take a formal opinion from the Attorney-General.

Sp. Perceval to the Speaker.

(Sunday, April 8.)

My DEAR MR. SPEAKER,

. . . At 2 this morning a letter came from the Sheriffs enclosing a copy of Sir Francis Burdett's letter to them.

Ryder acknowledged the receipt of it, declined entering into Sir Francis Burdett's reasoning; but did not doubt that they would feel it their duty to give any assistance, which was required of them in aid of the warrant, instead of resistance to it. Mr Attorney-General has doubts whether the warrants will justify breaking open doors. Commitments for Contempt are so almost always *in praesentes* that the Common Law affords but very meagre authority or analogy.

Yours most truly,

Sp. PERCEVAL.

After church on Sunday morning the Chancellor (Lord Eldon), the Prime Minister, and the Speaker held a conference, in which Lord Eldon said he always felt there was an infirmity in the power delegated by a warrant from either House of Parliament.

The Attorney General, Sir Vicary Gibbs, was equally perplexed.

Sir Vicary Gibbs to the Speaker.

Sunday Morning,

My DEAR SIR,

The Serjeant has consulted me upon the question whether he may break into Sir Francis Burdett's house to serve the warrant. If you can furnish me with *any Parlia-*

mentary authority on the subject, I shall be much obliged to you. If the case be left upon reasoning from analogy, it will be a delicate thing to recommend an act upon which a question of murder may ensue.

Yours most truly,

V. GIBBS.

Sir Vicary Gibbs to S. Perceval.

April 8th.

DEAR PERCEVAL,

I agree with you as to the two warrants,[1] but I do not find that I can venture to recommend the breaking of the house, at the peril of what may ensue. I also doubt whether the warrant can be executed on a Sunday.

I do not think that what passed can be taken as an arrest. I will be with you this morning.

Yours ever,

V. GIBBS.

His formal opinion was brought to the Speaker at 9.30 p.m. on Sunday night by the Serjeant.   The gist of it was this : He could find no instance in which the outer door of a house had been broken open under the Speaker's warrant. He could therefore only reason from analogy from the powers that could be used in executing criminal process at the suit of the King.   If done, he thought the action could be defended; but, if viewed prospectively as an act yet undone, and in doing which force and resistance were to be expected and death might ensue, it was for the officer to judge whether, upon such an opinion, he would proceed. Everything would depend on whether the breaking of the door was held to be legal or illegal.   He could take any necessary force, civil or military; but it would be prudent

---

[1] *sc.* that the Sheriff should demand admittance by virtue of the first as well as the second warrant of the Speaker.

to take a civil magistrate in any case. The warrant ought
not to be executed at night.

Let us shift the scene to the Saturday afternoon and
Piccadilly. Sheriff Wood, having received from Burdett
the summons to his aid, went to consult his brother, Sheriff
Atkins, but found him out of town. At 7 p.m. he paid
the visit already described to the Speaker—the visit in which
the Speaker said he had no doubt the Sheriff would do his
duty. He then went to Burdett's house, in front of which
he found a strong military force, though there were then
but few persons in the street, and those by no means
indicating any disposition to riot.

Sir Francis requested him to spend the night in No. 78,
and on his consent, Lady Burdett said that she and her
family could now retire in tranquillity. At 10.30 p.m.
Wood went home to let his family know that he was staying
the night at Burdett's. He was just stepping into his
carriage to return to No. 78, when Sheriff Atkins arrived.
This caused a delay. The two Sheriffs wrote to the Secretary of State (Ryder), enclosing Burdett's letter requiring
their protection, and then went on to No. 78, where they
received the Home Secretary's reply already given.

Wood remained in Burdett's house till 2.30 a.m. on
Sunday morning, when he went home to make arrangements for the next morning. On Sunday at 7 a.m. the
Serjeant was again refused admission to Burdett's house.
At 9 a.m. the two Sheriffs went to Piccadilly, and found the
soldiers parading. From the disposition of the crowd no
riot or disturbance seemed likely, and so the officer in
command, at the request of the Sheriffs, removed the
troops for a hundred yards from No. 78 in both directions.
All people passing along Piccadilly were, as on the two
preceding days, forced to salute Burdett's house, and if
they did not were pelted with mud. The crowd, it would
seem, got more riotous, for at 3 p.m. the proclamation

prescribed by the Riot Act was read by a magistrate, Mr. Birnie, and the officer in command informed the Sheriffs that he had received written orders from the magistrates " to disperse the people and not allow any person to pass up or down the road." The Sheriffs warned him of the responsibility he would incur. Introduced by the commanding officer to the five magistrates in the Gloucester Coffee House, Sheriff Wood lodged his protest : " If any one shall be killed, you will be justly held responsible, and I shall certainly think it my duty to indict the parties offending." About 5 p.m. the Serjeant-at-Arms arrived; he was informed by the Sheriff that after a careful consideration he conceived the warrant was not a legal authority for breaking open an outer door, but that he was ready to give help in all other respects. The Serjeant, in answer to a question, admitted that he had not yet received the Attorney-General's opinion as to the lawfulness of breaking open the door. The Sheriffs remained at the coffee house till 11 p.m., and Wood on returning home found that all his apprehensions had been realised. Piccadilly had several times been cleared by the charges of the soldiers. Many people had been hurt and every street lamp had been smashed.

Near the eastern end of Piccadilly some houses were in process of being rebuilt, and were enclosed with boarding. After nightfall the mob pulled down the scaffolding to get bricks for throwing at the soldiers. They also adopted a stratagem. Abstracting a long ladder, they placed it shoulder high right across the street as a barricade. Then they provoked the Horse Guards to charge. Retreating under or round the ladder, they then showered missiles on the soldiers, but the horsemen seeing the barricade made a detour by St. James' Market and took the mob in rear, putting them all to a precipitate rout. Many people were wounded and perhaps a few killed.

On this Sunday Burdett held a " Council of War." It

was seemingly on the Sunday morning that (according to
Henry Hunt's account) [1] Lord Cochrane " called on the
Baronet in a coach, out of which a cask was handed into
the Baronet's house, and as a friend he was admitted by
old John the porter. . . . He very deliberately proposed to
undermine the foundation of the front wall, and deposit
there a cask of gunpowder, which he had brought for the
purpose, so that he might blow the invaders to the devil."
Sir Francis, we are told, demurred, and Cochrane " was
particularly requested to take away with him the cask of
gunpowder, which he did immediately."

Place's account of the " Council of War " is given in
Graham Wallas' " Life of Place." [2]   " On the Sunday
evening Burdett's brother came to call Place to a council
of war.   They were admitted into a house in Stratton St.
belonging to the Coutts family, and thence made their way
by cellar passages through guarded iron doors (the watchword for the evening being ' Place ') to the great house
in Piccadilly.   They found Burdett in consultation with
the semi-lunatic Roger O'Connor."   The story about
Cochrane is then given.   " Place saw clearly that this was
the kind of step, which should only be undertaken by men
who seriously contemplate the levying of Civil War.   ' It
will be easy enough,' he told the conspirators, ' to clear the
Hall of constables and soldiers, to drive them into the street
or to destroy them, but are you prepared to take the next
step and to go on ? '   This produced instant conviction of
the folly of attempting any such thing."

But it is difficult to regard this account as accurate, for
a number of reasons.   Place, as usual, exaggerated his own
importance.   The " great house " was the house in Stratton
Street, not that in Piccadilly.   If Hunt is correct, Cochrane's barrel of gunpowder had already been removed in
the morning !   And what was the need of bringing in all

[1] Hunt's " Memoirs," Vol. II, p. 391.
[2] Wallas, " Life of Place," p. 51.

this atmosphere of mystery and conspiracy? What was the need of a watchword, when all inside were friends? Why go " by cellar passages through guarded iron doors "? Apart from the fact that Thomas Coutts in 1802 had ordered the subterranean passage to be closed [1] (and I believe it was no longer in existence), why go by this mysterious route, when there was a simple door of communication between the two houses on the first floor?

However all that may be, Burdett determined to rely on the civil power for his protection.

Place, according to his own account, was under the Sheriff to organise the civil power and use it against the soldiers and government. Householders sworn in as special constables were to accompany the Sheriff. The Sheriff was to desire the officer commanding to withdraw his troops, and if he refused, to arrest him, or in the event of opposition, to serve him with a notice of an action at law. But the scheme ended in miserable fiasco. Place says that he himself was up to time on Monday morning, but fewer householders than had been expected turned up (only one hundred in all), and Sheriff Wood was late. Was he in earnest? On his way to the scene of action he was informed that Burdett had already been taken prisoner.

The Serjeant, unable to steer a clear course *between* Scylla (*i.e.* censure by the House of Commons) and Charybdis (*i.e.* a possible action for murder), had decided to avoid Scylla at all costs and risk Charybdis. He had at last been given adequate military support, and promised indemnity —so far as that was in their power—by the Government.

The family party at No. 78, including Sir Francis and Lady Burdett and their son Robert, Lady Guilford and her three daughters, Jones Burdett, Mr. and Mrs. Coutts, and Roger O'Connor, had just finished breakfast in the drawing-room on the first floor about 10 a.m. Mr. Coutts had retired, and Sir Francis—it can hardly have been a pre-arranged

[1] See p. 134.

tableau—was teaching his son to translate Magna Charta, when a constable's face was seen at the window. The constable had climbed a ladder. O'Connor ran forward. It would have been easy by giving the man a thrust to have precipitated him into the area twenty feet below, but Burdett called out, "Don't hurt him"; so O'Connor pressed the constable back and shut the window.

But already the "castle" had been taken by a postern gate. The soldiers had descended into the area and burst open the windows of a servant's room, by which they entered the house. The Serjeant-at-Arms, followed by a force of constables, entered the drawing-room and a dialogue ensued :

The Serjeant. "Sir Francis, you are my prisoner."

Sir Francis. "By what authority do you act, Mr. Serjeant? By what power, sir, have you broken into my house in violation of the laws of the land ? "

The Serjeant. "Sir Francis, I am authorised by the warrant of Mr. Speaker of the House of Commons."

Sir Francis. "I contest the authority of such a warrant. Exhibit to me the legal warrant upon which you have dared to violate my house. Where is the Sheriff? Where is the magistrate ? "

The Serjeant. "Sir Francis, my authority is in my hand. I will read it to you." (Here he read the warrant, with great trepidation.)

Sir Francis. "I repeat to you, that is no sufficient warrant. No, not to arrest my person in the open street— much less to break open my house, in violation of all law. If you have a warrant from His Majesty, or from a proper officer of the King, I will pay instant obedience to it; but I will not yield to an illegal order."

The Serjeant. "Sir Francis, I demand you to yield, in the name of the Commons House of Parliament, and I trust you will not compel me to use force. I entreat you to believe that I wish to show you every respect."

Sir Francis. " I tell you distinctly, that I will not voluntarily submit to an unlawful order; and I demand, in the
King's name and in the name of the laws, that you forthwith
retire from my house."

The Serjeant. " Then, sir, I must call in assistance and
force you to yield."

Thereupon the constables took hold of Sir Francis.
Jones Burdett and O'Connor immediately stepped up, and
each took him under an arm. The constables closed on
all three and drew them downstairs. Sir Francis then said :
" I protest in the King's name against this violation of my
person and of my house. It is superior force only that
hurries me out of it, and you do it at your peril."

In the early years of the nineteenth century it was common
form for ladies to faint on any trying occasion. So it is
not surprising that the Dublin *Correspondent* should state
that Lady Burdett was with difficulty kept from fainting.
But other authorities declare that the ladies behaved with
the utmost *sang-froid*.

A glass coach was waiting at the door, into which Sir
Francis stepped, being accompanied by his brother, the
Deputy-Serjeant and the Messenger. The Serjeant-at-
Arms rode ahead. The soldiers closed round the carriage,
and the cavalcade swept off at a rapid rate. In front were
four squadrons of the 15th Light Dragoons and of the Life
Guards; following the carriage were two troops of Life
Guards, and a squadron of the 15th Light Dragoons.
These were supported by two battalions of Foot Guards,
another troop of the 15th Dragoons forming the rear.
Westminster had to be avoided at all costs. So en route
to the Tower the cavalcade, with the exception of the two
battalions of Foot Guards, which took the direct road by
the Strand, made a long detour to the north, wheeling up
Albemarle Street, crossing Hanover Square, and proceeding
via Portland Road, the City Road, Moorfields, Aldgate
High Street, and the Minories.

THE RECEPTION OF SIR F. BURDETT AT THE TOWER BY LORD MOIRA.

From a coloured drawing in the possession of the Lord North.

The arrest had been made so early in the morning that it was not realised by the people till the carriage had passed up Albemarle Street. Then a cry was raised, " They have taken him, they have dragged him out of his house," and the streets were soon in an uproar. The immense crowd followed, shouting and hulloaing and insulting the troops with abusive language. The Minories and all the district near the Tower were blocked with people.

The Foot Guards, who had gone by the direct route, arrived at the Tower just before twelve noon—a moving mass of scarlet. They drew up three deep in a line from the Tower gates covering the entrance. The main cavalcade of Dragoons and Horse Guards arrived at 12.15. And we are told that, " as the procession entered by the further side of the Trinity House, it came on Tower Hill in a serpentine form, and the military spectacle was very grand."

Closed in by the escort of soldiers was the carriage with Sir Francis, its windows all down. Sir Francis sat on the right behind. He leaned forward and was well seen. The squadrons of the Light Dragoons opened right and left and cleared the ground in all directions, forming a circle two deep round the entrance from the Tower. Through this circle the carriage passed amid loud cries of " Burdett for ever ! " Sir Francis alighted; he passed over the bridge within the gate, and was received by Lord Moira, the Constable of the Tower. A gun was fired to announce the reception of the prisoner. There had been some pelting of the troops, and many of the crowd had been forced into the shallow water of the Tower ditch, but so far no material damage had been done. During the retirement of the troops there was more serious rioting; mud and stones were showered on the soldiers, who in return at various places charged the mob, firing their carbines and pistols. Several people were killed and many wounded. At the suggestion of the City Marshal, to prevent any further disturbance in the city, the officers commanding led the troops over London Bridge to the Surrey side of the river, and by this route the troops returned to the "Horse Guards." Regiments and artillery were stationed at all strategic points in London, but torrents of rain cleared the streets. For many months to come the Life Guards were known as the "Piccadilly Butchers."

The Speaker in his Diary states that "Sir Francis, whilst carrying to the Tower, was apparently in low spirits and said little." But perhaps the wish was father to the Speaker's thought.

Mrs. Spencer Stanhope, wife of Spencer Stanhope, M.P., wrote to her son on April 10 : "I hear he (sc. Burdett) looked very much frightened as he got out of his carriage at the Tower." It would probably have been nearer the truth if the Speaker and Mrs. Stanhope had said that he looked very much bored.

Within the Tower he was assigned a comfortable house near that of the Governor—the house in which Lord Thanet had been formerly imprisoned—and on giving his parole not to pass the gate, he was allowed the whole range of the Tower precincts. That same afternoon he wrote a note to Lady Burdett, announcing his safe arrival, and another to Samuel Brooks, chairman of the Westminster Committee.

Sir F. Burdett to S. Brooks Esq.

Tower.
Apr. 9.

Dear Sir,
    I am arrived safe, & no mischief I hope & believe has been done to anyone. The Soldiers, Magistrates, & Messengers broke into my house & took me away by force. I receive every attention from Lord Moira, who met me here,

yours truly,
F. Burdett.

In the evening he was visited by Lady Burdett, his son, and Lady Guilford.   The following letters from Lady Burdett to her daughter Sophia illustrate the excitement of the day.

Lady Burdett to Sophia Burdett (afterwards Mrs Otway-Cave) at Wimbledon.

April 9. 1810.

MY DEAREST SOPHIA,

In great haste & *flurry* I write to tell you yr Papa was taken from His House this morning between eleven & twelve.   A troop of Horse & Magistrates were sent to force the doors, which yr Papa had order'd to be shut & secured, but *thank God He* is quite safe, tho' in the Tower. I need not say (tho' I know him to be *safe*) how much this has agitated me, tho' the conviction of his *safety* helps most powerfully to quiet my poor nerves.   I send off this line in *great haste* to catch the Post, that you may be sure of a letter this Evening, as I cannot spare the Coachman, not knowing *at present* whether I am to go to the Tower or no this Evening, & must wait for some further notice. My little Clara being so much better has acted like *opium* upon my nerves, as my anxiety for Her had kept them in perpetual agitation—that load being off my spirits has been a great help to me.   God bless you all.   Kiss each other tenderly for yr ever affectionate Mama.

I cannot just now say *when* I shall be at Wimbledon, but as soon as I possibly can I shall.

Thank you, sweet Sophia, for yr kind little note.   I assure you I have often thought of you & hope we shall soon see you.   No harm can happen to yr Papa, & I hope all will be well.

SOPHIA B.

[Endorsed by the daughter.]

April 9, 1810.   Papa forced from his house & taken by

a military force to the Tower. *He* is *safe*, but *thinking* will drive me *mad*. *What a day.*

(Tuesday, April 10, 1810)

MY DEAREST SOPHIA,

I was so harrass'd & busy this morning it was impossible for me to write, so I sent a verbal message by Jones that you might know I was as well as could be expected, better indeed. I was obliged to lie in bed till past 12 to-day, having undergone so much fatigue yesterday. The going to the Tower five miles over the rough stones is no little fatigue to *me* in itself, & the agitation, mobs, etc., very overpowering. Yr Papa has very comfortable appartments & is perfectly well. *That last is the great comfort*, so I hope all is well that ends well, or at least will be well. I am very happy the dear little Girls are not disturbed by knowing what they could not understand, & that dear Susan is so good a girl.

Ever yr affectionate,

MAMA.

(On the back in the young Sophia's handwriting)

> " Let all the ends thou aim'st at be thy Country's
> Thy God's, & Truth's, then, if thou fall'st
> Thou fall'st a blessed martyr."

When the House of Commons met on Monday, April 9, the Speaker read the letter he had received from Burdett, and the Serjeant having given his report, the debate on the letter was adjourned till the next day. In the course of the Tuesday's debate the general tendency was for Ministers to throw all the blame on the Serjeant-at-Arms. But many members held that the Serjeant was blameless, and that Ministers, owing to their lack of foresight and resolution, were wholly responsible for events. However, no one had a good word to say for Burdett. Members were only restrained from voting his expulsion from the House of

Commons by the well-grounded fear of a new Westminster election, when the military would have to be withdrawn, and his re-election would be a foregone conclusion. Finally the House voted, " That it is the opinion of this House that the said letter is a high and flagrant breach of the privileges of the House; but it appears from the report of the Serjeant-at-Arms . . . that as the warrant of the Speaker for the commitment of Sir Francis Burdett to the Tower has been executed, this House will not at this time proceed further on the said letter."

The Whig leaders in the House of Commons did not attempt to justify Burdett's letter to the Speaker, but took the line that Burdett had proceeded too far in his resistance. For this they were severely trounced by Cobbett in the " Register." In his opinion, they showed that all the contests in the House of Commons were simply a game between the " ins " and the " outs." Both Whigs and Tories were part of the same " system."

On the other hand, Burdett by his resistance had done the utmost service to the popular cause. A dozen of constables would have sufficed to take any other man to the Tower. To put Burdett in the Tower an army of 50,000 men had been necessary. This bare circumstance spoke more than whole volumes. It was undeniable proof that " the people " were with him, as against their misrepresentatives in the House of Commons. " Burdett has been raised to a height of popular favour, which perhaps no man before him ever attained."

Burdett did not take his imprisonment lying down. He served the Speaker and the Serjeant and Lord Moira with notice of actions-at-law for trespass and false imprisonment. When the Speaker informed the House of Commons of the threatened actions, the more ardent spirits wanted the House to imprison the solicitor employed by Burdett. It was pointed out that, if the Speaker pleaded to the action in the King's Bench, the privileges of the House of Commons might on appeal be brought before the House of Lords to determine.   But more prudent counsels prevailed; the matter was referred to a Committee of the House, and on its report it was resolved :

(1) That the Speaker and Serjeant be allowed to appear and plead to the action in the King's Bench.

(2) That the Attorney-General be instructed to defend the Speaker and Serjeant against the said action.

The mills of the law ground slowly, and it was only on May 17, 1811, that the action of Burdett *v.* the Speaker was tried before the King's Bench.[1]   L. C. J. Ellenborough and the other judges decided :

(1) That the House of Commons' power of commitment was established by prescription, Parliamentary recognition, and numerous precedents.

(2) That the Speaker's warrant was properly made out.

(3) That the forcing of the door of Burdett's house was lawful.

On June 19 it was decided by a jury in the King's Bench that the Serjeant had not used unnecessary force in breaking open the door.   Burdett's action against Lord Moira was then dropped.

But, whatever the law-courts might decide, the " man in the street " thought that, even if the House of Commons had the *legal* right, the exercise of that right had been unnecessary and inconsiderate.   That, too, was the opinion of Lord Holland, who in 1818 described the action of the

---

[1] The case went on appeal to the House of Lords, and was only finally decided on July 7, 1817, in favour of the Speaker. So the final decision on the privileges of the Commons went before the House of Lords ! (Colchester's " Diary," Vol. III, p. 13).

House of Commons as an "ill-timed execution of an arbitrary power." For "the Privileges of the Commons are intended as a means of defence against power, not as weapons of offence against liberty."

The prisoner's stay in the Tower was one long series of ovations. Addresses of thanks and congratulations poured in from every quarter of the country—from places as far apart as Middlesex, Westminster, the city on the one hand, and Liverpool, Berwick-on-Tweed, Carmarthen, Berkshire, Reading, Sheffield, Nottingham, Coventry, on the other. Jones Burdett was kept so busy in answering them that it gave him a regular aversion to the sight of pen and ink.

Corresponding petitions and protests from all kinds of places, asking for the release of Burdett, citing the proved corruption of Perceval and Castlereagh, and demanding Reform, were presented to the House of Commons.

The petition from Westminster, as coming from Burdett's constituency, was allowed to lie on the table, but most of the protests, including those from Middlesex and the Livery of the city, were rejected by the House of Commons as insulting.

It would be tedious to give all these addresses in detail, and more than tedious to give the address from Middlesex, which was composed by Major Cartwright. Let us confine our attention to Westminster and the City of London. Most of the addresses followed the common form laid down by them.

A monster meeting of Westminster electors, convened by the High Bailiff, was held on Tuesday April 17, in Palace Yard. Hustings had to be erected. "The meeting," Cobbett says, "far surpassed in point of numbers anything ever before seen." He puts the number at 40,000. The whole line of the houses opposite was crowded with spectators, ladies, Members of Parliament, and other gentlemen appearing in groups in the balconies and windows.

Many resolutions were unanimously voted approving of all that Burdett had done, and the following address to the House of Commons was adopted with enthusiasm :

" We, the Inhabitant-Householders, Electors of the City & Liberties of Westminster, feel most sensibly the indignity offered to this City in the person of our beloved Representative, whose letter to us has fallen under the censure of your Honourable House, but which, so far from deserving that censure, ought in our opinion to have led your Honourable House to reconsider the subject which he had so ably, legally, & constitutionally discussed. We are convinced that no one ought to be prosecutor & juror, judge & executioner, in his own cause, much less to assume, accumulate, & exercise all these offices, in his own person.

" We are also convinced that the refusal of your Honourable House to inquire into the conduct of Lord Castlereagh & Mr Perceval, (then two of his Majesty's Ministers) when distinctly charged with the sale of a seat in your Honourable House, evidence of which was offered at the bar by a member of your Honourable House ; & the avowal in your Honourable House ' that such practices were as notorious as the sun at noon day ' ; practices, at the bare mention of which the Speaker of your Honourable House declared ' that our ancestors would have started with indignation ' ; & the committal of Sir Francis Burdett to prison, enforced by military power ; are circumstances which render evident the imperious necessity of an immediate Reform in the Representation of the People.

" We therefore most earnestly call upon your Honourable House to restore to us our Representative, &, according to the notice he has given, to take the state of the Representation of the People into your serious consideration ; a reform in which is, in our opinion, the only means of preserving the country from military despotism."

BURDETT IN THE TOWER.

The following letter to Sir Francis Burdett was then unanimously voted by the meeting :

To Sir Francis Burdett Bart., now a prisoner in the Tower of London.

SIR,

We nominated you to be our Representative without your Knowledge, & we elected you without your interference. We were confident that you would perform the duties of a Representative in Parliament with ability & fidelity. In every respect you have not only fulfilled but exceeded our expectation. We derive satisfaction from having pointed out to the Nation the way to be fairly represented. Had it been possible that our example could have been followed, & a proper Representation thereby produced, the scenes we have lately witnessed, would not have disgraced our Country.

We understood the nobleness of your mind, & were confident you would not descend to barter your trust for a place under Government, nor be the partisan or leader of those, who support or reject measures, just as they happen to be proposed on this or on that side of the House.

We feel the indignity that has been offered to you, but we are not surprised to find that, when every excuse is made for public delinquents, the utmost rigour is exercised against him who pleads for the ancient & constitutional rights of the people.

You nobly stepped forward in defence of a fellow-subject unjustly imprisoned, & you questioned with great ability & knowledge of the law the warrant issued on that occasion ; the House of Commons have answered your argument by breaking into your house with a military force, seizing your person, & conveying you by a large body of troops to the Tower.

Your distinction between Privilege & Power remains

unaltered; the Privileges of the House of Commons are for the protection, not the destruction of the people.

We have resolved to remonstrate with the House of Commons on the outrages committed under their orders, & to call upon them to restore you to your seat in Parliament, which the present state of the country renders more than ever necessary for the furtherance of your & our object, a reform in the representation in that House.

While so many members are collected together by means which it is not necessary for us to describe; we cannot but entertain the greatest apprehensions for the remainder of our liberties; & the employment of a military force against one of their own body is but a sad presage of what may be expected by those who like you have the courage to stand forward in defence of the rights of the people.

When we reflect on your generous exertions to destroy the horrors of *secret & solitary confinement*—to mitigate the *severity of punishment in the army*—to prevent the cashiering of *officers without cause assigned*—to restore for the comfort of the *worn out soldier* the public property conveyed by a job to a private individual—to prevent the *extension of the barrack system*, the obvious effect of which is to *separate the soldier from the citizen*—to prevent the *introduction of foreign troops*—to bring to light an atrocious act of tyranny, by which a British sailor *was left to perish on a barren rock*—& above all, your unremitted exertions to obtain *a full, fair, & free representation of the people in Parliament*—when we reflect on the firmness, the unshaken constancy, which you have invariably shewn in evil report & good report; We are eager to impress the sentiments of gratitude & attachment to you, with which we are impressed, & we are convinced that those sentiments are not only felt by the inhabitants of this city, but by every person through out the land who is not interested in the continuance of public abuses.

(Signed at the request & in the name of the Meeting)
ARTHUR MORRIS. (High Bailiff)

The petition and remonstrance was carried straight from the meeting into the House of Commons.   It was presented by Lord Cochrane, and after a short debate allowed to lie on the table.

The letter from the Westminster electors was presented by the High Bailiff to Sir Francis in the Tower, and he returned an answer, equally magnanimous and high sounding, dated from the Tower on April 20, 1810.   The practical part of it lay in the concluding paragraph.

The People of England must speak out—they must do more—they must act; & if, following the example of the Electors of Westminster, they do act in a firm & regular manner upon a concerted plan—ever keeping the Law & Constitution in view—they must finally succeed in recovering that to which they are legally entitled—the appointment of their own guardians & trustees for the protection of their own liberty & property.   They must either do this, or they must inevitably fall a sacrifice to the one or the other of the most contemptible factions that ever disgraced this or any other country.

The question is now at issue; it must now be ultimately determined whether we are henceforth to be slaves, or be free.   Hold to the Laws, this great country may recover; forsake them, & it will certainly perish.

I am, Gentlemen,
your most obedient humble servant,
FRANCIS BURDETT.

On April 26 the freeholders of Middlesex drew up their petition and remonstrance to the House of Commons and passed a number of resolutions, including an address and vote of thanks to Burdett.   At the mention of his name there was a tremendous outburst of applause, many voices crying out, " There is not his equal in the world."   When the petition was presented to the House of Commons

(May 2) it was described by Perceval as a " deliberate and unparalleled insult " and it was rejected by a majority of 81.

The address was presented to Burdett at the Tower on May 5 by Sheriff Wood and Mr. Byng, and Burdett made a suitable reply.

On May 8 it was the turn of the " Livery of the City." When the remonstrance of the Livery was presented to the House of Commons, it too was described by Perceval as " presented for the express purpose of insult," and the House by a majority of 92 declined to receive it.

The following day a procession of the Livery, headed by Sheriff Wood, delivered the resolutions of the Livery and their vote of thanks to Burdett on the Esplanade of the Tower. Burdett, in his reply thanking them, bore witness to the kindness of Lord Moira, referred with praise to a speech that Lord Erskine had delivered in the House of Lords on May 7, and declared that " the nation had been crucified between two thieves "—*i.e.* the Whig and Tory factions, and that the Reform of the House of Commons was imperative.

It must not be supposed that Sir Francis spent the whole of his time at the Tower receiving and replying to addresses. For one thing he took an interest in the antiquities of the place, as is shown by a letter from Henry Clifford to Samuel Lysons [1] (Keeper of the Tower Records) asking that Burdett should have an opportunity of seeing some of the old records.

And he had his lighter moments; witness this :

Tower,
May 10, 1810.

DEAR CREVEY,

When will (you) come again to dinner ?   You shall have *two* bottles of claret next time, & as good fish.

yours,
F. BURDETT.

---

[1] Samuel Lysons, 1763 to 1819.   Appointed Keeper of the Tower Records December 1803.

He was generally allowed the free run of the Tower, but this privilege was for a time, at any rate, curtailed because he had been witness to the flogging of some soldiers.

Sir Francis Burdett to Lady Burdett.

Tower.
Sunday Morning (6 May, 1810).

MY DEAR SOPHIA,

I have no linen; you have enough to do, but I wish you would send my linen every Saturday & take the other back. I am not sorry you did not come yesterday; I was so uncomfortable, I had witnessed a most shocking sight, the flogging of some soldiers; it seems it got rumoured about that there was no flogging, because I was here : so they, I suppose, determined that should no longer be said. They were however, I think, not a little embarrassed by my presence, & a young man, who has a place here in the Ordnance office, a nephew of Mr Frend,[1] who happened to call upon me with Mr Frend, & who walked out from the house with me when these executions were going on, got thereby into a scrape, & had a complaint lodged against him by the Major, that old man who came with Lord Moira on his visit.

Among those whom we know to have visited Sir Francis in the Tower, apart from those already mentioned, were Mr. Bickersteth (afterwards Lord Langdale), Henry Hunt (who, though in the King's Bench for an assault, had the " run of the key "), the Duke of Sussex, and Lady Oxford ; [2] we are told that the Princess of Wales was very anxious to visit him, but whether she did is not actually stated.

With the prorogation of Parliament at 3.30 p.m. on

[1] Mr. Frend was an advanced Reformer.
[2] " Farington Diary," Vol. VI, p. 44.   " Lady Oxford now visits Sir Francis Burdett in the Tower; the Princess is very desirous to see him.   Lady Oxford brought to her a message from Sir Francis that the most injudicious thing the Princess could now do would be again to run into debt."

June 21 Burdett's imprisonment automatically came to an end.   Some days previously a committee of his friends had resolved to give him a triumphal progress—such as had never been seen before—from the Tower to his home.

The following description of the scene is taken from the Memoir of Burdett's friend, Henry Bickersteth.

" Soon after break of day the populace was in motion, and the sound of music was heard in every street.   At 9 a.m. a multitude consisting chiefly of persons from the parish of St. Ann's Soho proceeded to the Tower as a guard of honour : and by 10 a.m. all the places of rendezvous pointed out by the committee were filled with the partisans of Sir Francis.   Towards the afternoon the whole line of the streets from the Tower to Stratton Street was thickly planted with people.   Every window and elevated station was occupied; in Piccadilly scaffoldings were erected and the sides of all the streets were lined with waggons teams and carts, filled with men, women, and children, every eye eagerly turned to the quarter whence the spectacle so much desired was expected to come.

" In the meantime measures of precaution had been taken by the civil magistrates by a proper disposition of military assembled in and about the metropolis.

" The different bodies of men that were to form the procession wore blue cockades.   This badge was also everywhere to be seen among the multitude that lined the streets.   Most of the ladies wore the garter-blue ribbon. From many houses were suspended wands with ribbons of the same colour.   Numerous bodies of the Westminster Electors began to repair to the Tower about 1 p.m. preceded by bands of music and with blue silk colours flying, on which were inscribed various devices such as, ' The Constitution,' ' Trial by Jury,' ' Magna Charta,' ' Burdett for ever.'   The North and West side of Tower Hill were immensely crowded with people of every description.   About 300

men on horseback arrived at Tower Hill about 2 p.m.
Among whom was Major Cartwright and Col. Hanger [1]
mounted on a white horse with a large oak stick in his
hand. They all wore blue cockades. . . . After a long and
anxious expectation of the appearance of Sir F. Burdett,
a soldier in the Tower called out several times to the
populace through a speaking trumpet, ' He is gone by
water,' but no one seemed to credit what he said. A little
afterwards one of the constables, posted on Tower Hill,
assured the people that Sir Francis Burdett had really gone
by water.

" It is extremely difficult to banish ardent hope and
expectation. The constable was not credited for his
assertion any more than the soldier. At 4.30 p.m. however
3 placards were suspended over the gates of the Tower with
the following inscription : ' Sir Francis Burdett left the
Tower by water at half past three o'clock.' That he was
enabled to do so, though it was within a few minutes only
after the prorogation of Parliament was pronounced, was
by means of a sort of telegraphic communication established
between the Parliament House and the Tower. The news
of Sir Francis having gone from the Tower by water
excited not only surprise but indignation in many. For
some time considerable confusion prevailed, and discontent
appeared in every countenance. After a short consultation,
the Westminster Committee resolved to conduct the procession to Sir Francis Burdett's house in Piccadilly ; but it
was near half an hour before they could communicate their
intentions to the whole of those who were to form it.
The order of procession being fixed, Col. Hanger followed
by Major Cartwright led the van. Immediately at their
heels were gentlemen from the country on horseback four
abreast, and after these a long column of the Electors of
Westminster on foot, six abreast, and an immense number
of carriages, in some of which were several members of

[1] Afterwards fourth Baron Coleraine. See " D.N.B."

the Common Council and many Liverymen of London. Next came Sir Francis Burdett's phaeton, the horses of which were led by several attendants on each side. A great part of those who had originally intended to take part in the procession left Tower Hill and the Minories, when it was ascertained that Sir Francis had gone by water, but many others joined it in its progress.

" The procession was preceded by horsemen with trumpets and a long line of people on foot, with blue sashes and ribbons, decorated with appropriate mottoes and emblems. A close coach appeared in the cavalcade, drawn by the populace, preceded and followed by an immense line of hats with blue ribbons, as deep as the passage of the street would permit, and surmounted by a number of persons wearing the same livery. This was a hackney-coach with Mr (Gale) Jones [1] the cause of all the tumult. When he arrived at Piccadilly, he mounted the roof and harangued the populace; but such were the confusion and noise that not a word was heard of what he said.

" The grand procession, as it was called, reached Piccadilly about 8 o'clock. By the efforts of the Sheriffs and constables Piccadilly was nearly cleared by 10 o'clock; but parties went off in various directions exclaiming, ' Light up.' The summons was instantly obeyed and the town in a short time displayed a general illumination."

What had happened was simply this. Burdett had arranged with his friend Henry Bickersteth to have a boat waiting for him at the water-gate of the Tower. Burdett stepped into the boat, and was rowed across to the Surrey side of the river, where he found his brother and horses waiting, and they all sped away to Burdett's house at Wimbledon.

That this move caused real annoyance to many of Burdett's Radical friends is perfectly true. Here are the naïve words

---

[1] Gale Jones is described by Place as " a poor emaciated, crazy-looking creature."

of one of the crowd :[1] " I looked forward to a glorious day. . . . I filled my pocket with stones for the evening's business, and went to my club at 9 a.m. We found a large basket of blue ribbands sent us anonymously. We drank confusion to the Ministers and sallied forth. I waited patiently till I had nearly dropped with fatigue, having been appointed standard-bearer to the party, and after having lugged about a large blue flag upon a pole till my arms ached, I heard that you were gone by water. I confess I was angry, I swore a little, and might have said it was a shabby trick."—We can pity the poor fellow on a hot June day. Hunt says that many of the people dubbed Burdett " Sir Francis *Sly-Go*," and declares that the people never placed implicit faith in him again.

Two members of the Westminster Committee waited on him for an explanation. Sir Francis said his action was deliberate; his enemies had been base enough to charge him with the blood shed, when he was taken to the Tower, and had he, by gratifying his personal vanity, been the cause of similar bloodshed, he should have reflected upon it with pain for the rest of his life. And that, I think, is the simple explanation of the part he played as shown by his own letters.

None the less other interpretations were put on it at the time and later, not unnaturally, for Burdett, by disappointing his supporters of their " day," had made them look absurd, and his action was resented in many quarters. The explanation given by Francis Place was that Burdett was a " damned coward and poltroon." [2] That answer is more plain than true. It does not harmonise with the intrepid courage shown on many occasions by Burdett. It is, however, more or less endorsed by Graham Wallas in his " Life of Place," and by M. Halévy in his " History

---

[1] " Adultery and Patriotism," p. 14.
[2] Hunt's " Memoirs," Vol. II, p. 423.

of the English People in 1815 "; " Only the timidity of
Sir Francis, who avoided the manifestations, in his honour,
deprived the popular triumph of its final crown."[1]
Burdett's motive is misconceived by both these writers.
Graham Wallas suggests a strange motive for this "timidity."
He asserts that Burdett in the Tower had " half per-
suaded himself that Place might arrange with the Govern-
ment to have him shot as he rode in the triumphal car."[2]

It is quite true that Burdett in the Tower had come to
regard Place with profound distrust.   He believed that the
delay of the civil power to come to his assistance on the
morning of his arrest was due to Place's treachery.   But
there was another reason why Place had recently fallen under
the grave suspicion of the democrats.   On the night of May
30, 1810, the Duke of Cumberland—the King's son—was
seriously wounded in St. James' Palace, and in an adjoining
chamber his valet, an Italian named Sellis, was found with
his throat cut.   The current rumour was—but the Duke
was very unpopular—that Sellis had met his death at the
Duke's hands.   Now at the inquest held in the Palace Place
was the foreman of the jury that returned a verdict of
suicide.   The evidence adduced at the trial certainly tended
to show that Sellis, jealous of a fellow-servant, had accused
him of peculation, and on failing to gain his point with the
Duke, had first attacked the Duke and then committed
suicide.   None the less it was said that where exalted
persons are concerned, matters can be easily hushed up.
The following letter from Frend, a Reformer friend
of Burdett, to Tate, a clergyman to whom Burdett was
sending his son Robert for instruction, would seem to
suggest that the Duke had made improper overtures to
Sellis' wife.

[1] Halévy, " History," Vol. I, p. 144.
[2] Wallas, " Life of Place," p. 55.

Rev. W. Frend to Rev. J. Tate.

1st June, 1810.

DEAR SIR,

. . . You will have heard by the Herald of the strange attempt against the Duke's life. English husbands would not have been so terribly violent. It is remarkable that the regrets excited by the catastrophe were not so strongly expressed as might have been expected. I called at the Duke's at 11 last night & found that he had been removed to Carlton House, & at both places heard a favourable account.

Ever yours,

W. FREND.

Whatever the rights or wrongs of this case may have been, it was thought by the Radicals that Place had been bribed by the Court to screen the Duke of Cumberland. " Since that period," says Hunt, " Place has been a *very rich* man, but before it he was a *poor, very poor democrat.*"

Burdett was full of suspicions, and for nine years he did not speak to Place. He told James Mill at Oxford in 1813 that Place on the morning of his arrest had betrayed him. In 1814 he wrote to the committee of the West London Lancastrian Association (this was a body formed for the purpose of educating the " lower " classes) demanding the expulsion of Place from the committee as a Government spy.

This, then, is probably what was behind the statement that " Burdett thought that Place might arrange with Government to have him shot." But as an explanation of Burdett's leaving the Tower by water it is absurd. Not less absurd is the statement made in an anonymous pamphlet that Burdett was ashamed to ride with Gale Jones through the city.

On July 31 Burdett was given a public dinner by his constituents at the " Crown and Anchor " to celebrate his

liberation from the Tower. In an after-dinner speech he
reiterated his views on the constitutional question. The
people had nothing to fear from the King. Their enemy
was the borough-monger faction, which had usurped
sovereignty. He criticised a speech which the Whig leader,
Lord Grey, had delivered in the House of Lords towards
the end of the session. Lord Grey had stated that it was
the fashion of the times to vilify and defame all public
men. Burdett invited him to descend to particulars. Who
had been calumniated and in what had they been calumniated ? Lord Grey had gone back on Reform. (This was
perfectly true. Lord Grey's advocacy of Reform reached
its nadir in 1810. The Charles Grey of 1793–7 and the
Lord Grey of 1830–2 were very different from the Lord
Grey of 1810.)

Grey had stated that he had somewhat changed the
opinions which he had pressed with ardour in his youth
that experience had made him wiser. Burdett then in
commenting on Grey's explanation, expressed sentiments
which many years later, in 1837, when he had joined the
Tory Party, were quoted rather unfairly against him.

" If this is the case, if the principles of men can change
as they advance in years—if no man can be pledged for the
consistency of his opinions—if it is to be a sufficient answer
for every man who thinks proper to change his political
opinions to say that ' to-day I am older than I was, when I
pledged myself to a different opinion,' then I say that such
men do cut up and destroy all confidence. We ought to
ask whether such men could ever have been actuated by
any principle at all. A principle once formed remains for
ever the same : it does not alter by time : the man professing it may grow older, perhaps he may not grow wiser
or honester, but the principle he has professed continues
one and the same, and when a man once pledges himself to
certain principles, he has stamped on himself the character
which he intends shall belong to him : and if he departs

from those principles, it is impossible for any reasonable man ever after to put trust in him."

Lord Grey in his speech had protested " against men, who under pretence to Reform would drive us into extravagant theories, but I have always been a friend to moderate Reform." Burdett declared that the Reform he demanded was moderate. Grey had declared that there must be no yielding to popular clamour. But when Grey went out of office in 1807, the excuse he offered for not having granted Reform was that the people did not ask for it. Yet now, when people did ask for it, their asking for it was described as " popular clamour " that must be resisted. Grey had talked a great deal about " wild theory and speculation " and described him (Burdett) as a " misguided man lending himself to doctrines to the tendency of which he was blind." Burdett replied that " practice " without " vision " would lead to disaster. He alluded with indignation to the punishment of Cobbett for expressing his views on the flogging of Englishmen under the supervision of German soldiers, and concluded with a reference to the sufferings of Ireland.

This was solid meat for an after-dinner speech, but it contained sound political sense.

A postscript, by anticipation, may concern itself with the later fortunes and opinions of the Radical apothecary, for opposition to whose imprisonment Burdett had been sent to the Tower. With considerable impudence, Gale Jones opposed the Burdett party in the Westminster elections of 1818 and 1819. But later on he was content to receive pecuniary assistance from Sir Francis, and to congratulate him on returning to Parliament as a Tory member.

John Gale Jones to Sir F. Burdett.

21 Crossier St.

Brunswick Square.

Oct. 30, 1837.

SIR,

I have receiv'd your second favor for which I again beg leave to return my grateful acknowledgments as well as for the kind expressions with which they were accompanied. That delicacy that has ever distinguished all your actions led you, Sir, to appretiate justly my feelings when you supposed that I should prefer receiving pecuniary aid from yourself to any other channel. . . . I am at once flatter'd & honor'd by the distinction.

Permit me, Sir, to seize this opportunity of thanking you in the name of every real & constitutional reformer for the noble stand you have made in support of our liberties both civil & religious & of declaring my unfeigned satisfaction that you are again seated in the Senate of your Country by the independant (sic) & intelligant (sic) yeomanry of Wiltshire from your own paternal (! !) mansion, & in the bosom of a grateful tenantry by whom you have long been deservedly esteemed & belov'd. I am, Sir,

yours most respectfully,

JOHN GALE JONES

Surgeon etc.

CHAPTER XIII

FAMILY AFFAIRS. LADY OXFORD

SIR FRANCIS BURDETT's fortune was much exaggerated by his contemporaries. According to the "Farington Diary"[1] he was said to have an income of £14,000 a year. Now the truth was this. The estates he had inherited from his Burdett forbears brought in a gross income of £7400 a year (after deduction of the land tax); those he had inherited from his mother's side brought in (after deduction of the land tax) £5500 gross. Therefore the gross total income from his estates (after deduction of the land tax) was £12,900. The land tax he paid was £1138. But the charges on these estates for relations, mortgagees, etc., amounted to £5400. So his net income after payment of the land tax was in the year 1802 about £7500. This was, of course, apart from anything his wife had from her father.

By 1807 his monetary position had greatly changed for the worse. In that year he drew up a financial statement, which showed that the gross income from his estates (presumably after the deduction of the land tax) was between £10,000 and £11,000, and that the charges on his estates were £6800. He calculated that his net revenue was only £4200. This serious reduction in his income was no doubt mainly due to his Middlesex elections. It is difficult to estimate their total cost, particularly as various subscriptions were opened in aid of the expenses incurred. Thus, for example, the Bank books of Coutts & Co. show that a subscription of more than £7000 was raised to cover

[1] "Farington Diary," Vol. II, p. 273.

the expenses of the election petition against the younger
Mainwaring in 1804.   But the main expense of the
elections fell on Burdett.

According to the financial statement drawn up by him
in 1807, while his ancestors had left a capital sum of incum-
brances on the estates amounting to £35,670, he had himself
diminished the capital value of his property by £78,000 in
six years, together with a liability to pay annuities amounting
to £1434 per annum.   The Middlesex elections had proved
a costly affair.

What Thomas Coutts gave his daughter, and what he
gave Sir Francis, and how the expenses of the common
house (1 Stratton Street and 78 Piccadilly) were arranged,
there is no evidence to show.

It is difficult to understand Bank ledgers and cross
accounts of monies paid by Coutts to Burdett and by
Burdett to Coutts.   Coutts on the day of Burdett's wedding
to his daughter (August 5, 1793) put £5000 to the account
of Burdett.   Then there is a mysterious mortgage of
£20,000 on the Marquess of Lansdowne's property in
Middlesex—mysterious, because it is constantly being
tossed from Coutts to Burdett and from Burdett to Coutts.

Coutts had advanced this sum to Lord Lansdowne in
April 1791.   On June 3, 1794, this mortgage of £20,000
was assigned by Coutts to Burdett and became Burdett's
property.   Coutts advanced the sum of £4000 to purchase
for Burdett the seat at Boroughbridge (1796–7), and thereupon Burdett deposited the Lansdowne mortgage with
Coutts as security for the £4000 which Coutts had paid to
the Duke of Newcastle's representatives.   In August 1802
it would seem that Coutts had already advanced £10,000
on the security of the Lansdowne mortgage, which was
then re-transferred to him, the balance being paid into
Burdett's account.

What is clear is that by 1807 Burdett's income was greatly
reduced, and he was seriously alarmed.   It was no wonder

that he refused to squander any more of his capital on election contests.

By 1811 he was the father of five children, one son and four daughters : Sophia, *b.* 1794; Robert, *b.* 1796; Susan, *b.* 1800; Joanna, *b.* 1804; Clara, *b.* 1805. Robert had already become a source of anxiety to his parents. While Sir Francis was in the Tower, Robert was taken away from Eton, but the experiment of sending him to a tutor in Yorkshire proved a failure. After eight weeks the tutor refused to keep him any longer and he was sent home.

The relations of Sir Francis with Lady Burdett had become much easier. He was temperamental by nature, and his love for his wife at times seemed very real. Very few letters from husband to wife during the years 1802 to 1812 have been preserved, presumably because they were mostly together, and few were written.

But the relations of husband and wife were strained by the intrigue of Sir Francis with Lady Oxford. The whole truth about this will never be revealed, though possibly some further information might be gleaned from unpublished Oxford papers.[1] Those who knew the facts kept their mouths sealed—namely, Charles Warren the lawyer, Horne Tooke, J. Bellenden Ker.

Sir Francis had long ceased to be a lover of Lady Oxford, though he still had much of her society in the circle of the unfortunate Princess of Wales, when the scandal of his former relations with her was brought before the Scotch Court of Session at Edinburgh, on July 11, 1811. Why the case was brought before a Scotch instead of an English tribunal is itself mysterious; for the defendant, William Scott, Lady Oxford's brother, was a Serjeant at Law and a

---

[1] The last Earl of Oxford of this creation died in 1853 without issue. Most of his property passed to his two daughters, Lady Jane Langdale and Lady Charlotte Bacon. These two sisters did not see eye to eye, and Lady Jane Langdale left all she could, including many family papers, to a distant (if any) connection—a Mr. Harley of Brampton Bryan.

member of the Inner Temple. I will first give an account of the action, based on the report of the *London Courier* of July 16, and then the hitherto unpublished letter written by Sir Francis to Lady Burdett on the day after the trial (July 12).

"*Court of Session.   Edinburgh.   July* 11, 1811.   *Before Lord Meadowbank.*

"*Sir F. Burdett* v. *W. Scott.*

  "Counsel for Plaintiff—Mr. Jeffrey.
  "Counsel for Defendant—Mr. Clerk.

  "*Mr Jeffrey* for the pursuer (*i.e.* plaintiff) stated that Sir Francis Burdett sued Mr. Scott upon a bond for £5000 of borrowed money : that Mr. Scott had put in long and special defences, every syllable of which was denied by Sir F. Burdett : but besides this general denial Sir Francis positively denied that any trust of any sort was ever reposed in Mr Scott.

  "The defence put forward by William Scott was this :
  "'A lady, whose name it is unnecessary to mention, having been debauched by Sir F. Burdett, became pregnant by him, and the parties were reduced to a state of the greatest distress and embarrassment. It became the duty of the defender (*i.e.* defendant) to protect this female and her child, and to obtain from Sir Francis some provision for the latter, to be used as future exigencies might require. In spring 1801 Sir Francis granted his bond, in the English form, to the defender for £40,000, defeasible upon payment of £20,000 within six months from the date thereof. It was understood that the defender was to use this bond for the purpose already alluded to.

  "'Soon after the bond granted, Sir Francis agreed to pay to the defender the sum of £10,000 in part of the bond; but not having the whole of that sum at his command he

THE PATRIOT PUZZLED, or the trusty SCOT producing his Vouchers.

paid £5000 only, and the defender indorsed the said payment
of £5000 upon the bond.

" ' Sir Francis as well as the lady had apprehended an
immediate public disclosure and disgrace, but as this very
luckily for them did not follow, the defender in the exercise
of his discretion and under the circumstances of the case
did not think it necessary to call upon Sir Francis for any
further payments upon his bond, but he thought it proper
to retain the bond in his custody.   And to provide against
any bad consequences, that might happen in case of his
own death, he made a will, by which he bequeathed the
£5000 he had received from Sir Francis as a legacy to the
child : and by this will he appointed as his executor, with
the same powers over Sir Francis' bond that he himself
had, Charles Warren Esq., barrister at law, who was well
acquainted with all the circumstances of the transaction,
and he shewed the will to Mr. Warren, and informed him
of his motives for making it.

" ' During the autumn of 1805 and the spring of 1806
the pursuer and the defender had some differences with
respect to the pursuer's bond, and the payment of £5000,
which the pursuer for reasons best known to himself
demanded back from the defender; but the defender
positively insisted upon retaining the £5000 for the benefit
of the said child, and the pursuer was at last obliged to
desist from his demands, and either was or pretended to be
perfectly satisfied with the defender's conduct in the
business.

" ' At this time however the defender was informed by
the said Charles Warren that the pursuer felt extremely
uneasy that his bond for £20,000 was standing out against
him; that if the defender thought under the circumstances
of the case the £5000 already paid was enough, Sir Francis
requested that the £20,000 bond might be discharged.
Upon which the defender informed Mr. Warren that he
had no objection whatever to discharge the pursuer of the

£15,000 remaining due upon the bond. And besides doing this, the defender offered of himself to execute a bond for the £5000 payable in 5 years to be deposited in the hands of Mr. Warren as the defender's obligation for the money to Sir Francis and so be delivered to Sir Francis in case the child should die. But if the child should be alive at the end of the five years, then the pursuer was to discharge the defender's bond in the same manner that the defender was to discharge the pursuer's bond. The defender was afterwards informed by Mr. Warren that the pursuer had agreed to these terms.

" ' Thereafter the defender shewed Mr. Warren that he had disposed of part of the interest of the £5000 to the mother of the child, and that the remainder not so disposed of had accumulated in his hand to the amount of £750 : therefore he executed a bond for £5750, which he delivered to Mr. Warren along with a letter referring to the conditions on which he had executed the bond : but, in order to avoid mentioning the child's name in writing, he alluded to the condition—that the bond for £5750 should be discharged, if the child should live—in these words " if circumstances should require it." It will be proved that at this time the defender held the bond of the pursuer undischarged; and therefore, unless the conditions upon which he executed his own bond are complied with, the consequence will be that it was granted without any consideration whatever.

" ' Warren afterwards called upon the defender and informed him that the pursuer had seen what the defender had done, and had agreed to all the conditions upon which the defender had granted his own bond and proposed to discharge the bond of the pursuer. And Mr. Warren then advised the defender, instead of entering a discharge upon the bond and keeping it as evidence of the transaction, to return it cancelled to the pursuer, whereby the defender would have no power over it as evidence : and this Mr. Warren advised for the purpose of removing any apprehen-

sion that might be in the pursuer's mind respecting the
defender's intention. At the same time Mr. Warren
assured the defender that he might rely on the pursuer's
honour that the transaction should never be misrepresented :
he stated that the pursuer was under too much obligation to
the defender ever to attempt any violation of the condition
upon which the pursuer's bond was returned.

"'Ultimately the transaction was concluded by defender
giving up the pursuer's bond to be cancelled and returned
to him, he having already deposited with Mr. Warren the
bond now in question upon the conditions mentioned.

"'It would appear that the pursuer was successful in
obtaining the bond from Mr. Warren even before the
expiry of the five years, during which Mr. Warren was to
have retained it in his custody, and although the said child
is yet alive, and the defender is bound to keep the money
received from Sir Francis for the benefit of the said child,
Sir Francis has thought proper to raise the present action
for payment of the bond, in doing which he seems to have
totally forgotten every circumstance relating to the transaction, its meaning and object, and the terms agreed upon
by the parties.

"'The defence against the present action therefore is
that the defender is not liable to pay the contents of the said
bond, and that he ought to be assoilzied with full expences.'

"*Mr. Jeffrey* stated that the whole of the defence was
false and calumnious; that Sir Francis denied that he ever
had a child except by his own wife; and the defence was
irrelevant.

"*Lord Meadowbank* stated that he was quite clear that
the defence was relevant. The facts must be investigated.
Mr. Warren should be examined.

"*Mr. Scott* (in the absence of his counsel) said, that
although Sir Francis Burdett had come forward with a
positive denial of every syllable of these defences, yet it

was in his power to prove the falsehood of this denial under Sir Francis Burdett's own hand, and by a variety of evidence, which he insisted upon being allowed to produce, that he might be able to keep himself right and safe in this infamous business.

" *Mr. Clerk* (having returned) observed that Sir Francis Burdett brought this action against his client without any notice whatever and had recourse to the most rigid and outrageous proceedings against him. That Mr. Scott came forward immediately with his defences. The cause was inrolled, and his Counsel came ready to debate it about 6 weeks ago. What course did Sir Francis then take? He told his Lordship that he was not then prepared to meet the defence and craved a delay. It was his duty to mark this proceeding, and although he might have insisted on an ' absolvitur,' he did not oppose Sir Francis being allowed a reasonable time to prepare. The cause was not inrolled again by Sir Francis till the last day of this Session, and now he came forward with an objection to the relevancy of the defence.

" *Lord Meadowbank* said ' and a denial also of the facts stated in it.'

" *Mr. Clerk* continued that he would avoid as much as possible mentioning names, or saying anything that might be unpleasant to the feelings of any party. That Sir Francis had got himself into a situation of great difficulty and embarrassment, could this be denied?

" *Lord Meadowbank* again said all was denied and declared to be absolutely false.

" *Mr. Clerk* stated that as mentioned in the defences Sir Francis had granted his bond to Mr. Scott for £20,000. Was that fact denied? He called upon his learned brother to admit or deny that most important feature in this case.

" *Mr. Jeffrey* answered that they denied all the scandalous and calumnious part of the defence.

" *Lord Meadowbank* observed that they had denied the

whole, positively denied every fact, and that Mr. Scott offered to meet the denial by real evidence.

" *Mr. Jeffrey* answered that he would not deny the £20,000 bond, but he denied that it was granted for any such purpose as that stated in the defence.

" *Mr. Clerk* begged to put his learned friends upon their guard as to the question he was going to put.   He averred that, after Sir Francis Burdett had executed and delivered this bond to his client, he engaged to pay £10,000 upon that bond : that Sir Francis afterwards excused himself and said it was not in his power, and in fact he only paid £5000. Mr. Clerk asked, Was this true or false ?

" The other Counsel not answering, he said the Counsel for Sir Francis ought to be prepared either to admit or deny every fact stated in defence.   That Mr. Scott under the circumstances of the case and in the exercise of his discretion was content with the £5000, and did not call upon Sir Francis for further payment.   That he always insisted in every stage of this business that he would retain this money for a certain infant, and that no other person but that infant should have it.   That this would be proved by the most satisfactory evidence; that Mr. Scott, to satisfy his own honour and that this money should not by any accident become his own private property, executed his bond for it at a time when he held Sir Francis Burdett's bond to the extent of £15,000 undischarged.   Mr. Scott delivered this bond to a respectable gentleman, to be retained by him for a certain time, and if the infant should be then dead, Sir Francis was to have the bond delivered to him; if not, it was to be discharged and not delivered to him.

" *Lord Meadowbank* passed the following decree, July 11th, 1811 :

" ' Having heard parties procurators on the grounds of the Libel and defence, before Answer appoints the Defender to give in a Condescendence of the facts which he avers and offers to prove by way of defence, and of the mode in which he means to instruct or prove the same, and that against the Box day [1] in the ensuing vacation : allows the pursuer to see the same and to give in answers against the second Box day, and the Defender to reply against the first Sederunt [2] day in November next.' "

Sir Francis dropped the action and the case looked black against him; but it was not so black against him as it looked. He gave his own explanation in a letter to his wife.

Sir Francis to Lady Burdett.

MY DEAR SOPHIA,

I can assure you with the utmost truth that you never were under a greater mistake in your life than in supposing that I had at any time even for a moment given a preference to Lady O. over yourself, whom, I declare, as sincerely as man can speak, I ever greatly preferred to Lady O. loved and esteemed. It would ill become me to say anything more about Lady O., and you would think me a base person, more than what relates to myself. As to the *want* of *confidence* in which we have lived, I do not think that is the correct term to express the situation, it should rather be called *want* of *intercourse* because I have ever felt the most complete confidence in you, but something or other in our manners, I pretend not to say whose fault it is, has barred our conversation, but I know not the thing which I should fear to trust to you. As to the confidence you suppose

[1] Two days are appointed by the Court in each vacation, and one in the Christmas recess for " the boxing of papers," *i.e.* the lodging of papers in the judges' boxes. These days are known as Box Days. It is a device to prevent the Vacation from interrupting the progress of an action. Thus, although the Court is not sitting, a summons may be called, or defences lodged on any Box Day.

[2] First Sederunt day means the next occasion on which the Court is sitting.

denied to you & which you say you saw given to one of
your own Family, I really know not which of your own
Family particularly you allude to, nor am I aware that I
have more confidence in one than in another, for I really
have the greatest confidence in them all, & would trust
all or any of them, with anything—anything I mean not dishonourable in me to trust—but whatever it was, I should
not have the slightest fear from so trusting.

I cannot imagine how our children can have grown up
in a believe (sic) that I have no affection for you, in the
first place because it is not the fact, in the next because they
must always have seen you principally considered in all
domestick arrangements . . . As to your merit truth &
integrity, Should anyone say they surpassed you I should
think they never deserved to be believed again—No new
trials are, I hope in store for you, nor shall you be compelled, here let me speak proudly, to withdraw your esteem
from me, nor is there anything in the act, which now causes
this renewal of uneasiness, which can have that effect.   For
what is that act ?   I having been informed by W. Scott
that I had been the cause, however unintentionally, of
Ld. Ox determination to separate from Lady Ox., and she
having no provision in that case made for her, (for W.
SCOTT had at this very time perswaded her to relinquish
her marriage settlement in order, as he said, to enable Lord
O. to discharge some very pressing debts) thought myself
bound to secure Lady Ox. in case of such separation, from
being left destitute, I deposited therefore money in the
hands of W. Scott with direction to lay it out in the American
Funds for that purpose.   As soon as Lady Ox. was
acquainted with the money having been deposited she
desired it might be restored & on finding that it was not
begg'd of me to insist on having it back, there never in
truth having been any reason for the deposit, & the whole
story of the intended separation having been made by
W. Scott to get the money which he has applied to his own

purposes. I therefore desired it back, which he refused; in consequence I arrested him, he then confessed he had misapplied the money, could not pay it, but would give a bond for it, which he did, & I withdrew the arrest. This bond became payable the other day when he refused to pay it pretending that it was in trust for a child, which is all false, & as this was transacted by Mr Warren he will attest the falsehood, & if Scott still swears to it, convict him of perjury. This is a plain statement of the transaction which all originated in a lie of Scott about Ld & Lady O. intended separation on my account & which Lord Ox. has since assured me there was no truth in.

F. BURDETT

July 12, 1811.

This account given by Sir Francis Burdett to his wife plainly contradicts the statements made by William Scott. Now Burdett was sometimes careless and inattentive, and he may have given himself the benefit of the doubt; and I am not concerned to deny that he had immoral relations with Lady Oxford. But he was not a liar. In contradistinction from Cobbett, for example, not one lie can be brought home to him in the whole of his public career. He was, if anything, too honest and outspoken. He lived in the " Temple of Truth." And I do not believe that on this occasion he told a lie to his wife. In plain English, the charge brought by W. Scott was that Sir Francis was the father of the young Lord Harley born January 20, 1800. But which of the two was the better deserving of belief, Sir Francis Burdett, or W. Scott?

Comparatively little is known about William Scott, but what is known is not to his credit. Born in 1773, he matriculated at St. Mary Hall, Oxford, in May 1792 and joined the Inner Temple. Later on he became a Serjeantat-Law. Some information can be gleaned from an action brought by Scott against his sister, Lady Oxford, and Lord

Oxford for libel at the Hereford Assizes on August 12, 1808. From the account of this action it would appear that some years after their marriage Lord and Lady Oxford, being in a state of financial embarrassment, went abroad (? 1801), making over their estates to W. Scott and a certain Hugh Smith as trustees.   The Oxford returned in 1804, and in 1805 Lady Oxford wrote letters to Lord Oxford's steward and to her brother, the Rev. James Scott, accusing W. Scott of having swindled Lord Oxford out of thousands of pounds.   Hence the action.   Counsel for the defence dwelt on the ingratitude.   Lord Oxford, he said, had lent to Hobbes Scott [1] a sum of £20,000 in 1798, but was not himself concerned in this action except as husband of his wife.   " Where is the imperious necessity to bring a sister forward to answer publicly for private letters ? "   The jury awarded W. Scott the immense sum of £20 as damages !

It follows that after 1805 Lady Oxford was at daggers drawn with her brother, W. Scott.   It was therefore sheer hypocrisy when he pretended in the action brought by Burdett that it was to protect an injured sister that he refused to pay the £5000.   We can only conclude that he was a blackmailer.

This was obviously the view taken by Charles Kirkpatrick Sharpe, when he wrote to Lady Charlotte Campbell in 1811 :

" I have written so much that I can find no room for Lady Oxford's adventure with that rogue her brother. . . .

" You flatter me greatly by desiring a second number of the gazette extraordinary, which I hasten to transmit, albeit the adventures of Lady Oxford & her brother are now what is termed in Scotland Piper's news. . . . Lady Oxford, poor Lady Oxford, knows the rules of prudence, I fear me, as imperfectly as she doth those of the Greek & Latin grammars; or she hath let her brother, who is a sad

[1] A brother of W. Scott.

swine, become master of her secrets, & then contrived to quarrel with him. You would see the outline of the melange in the newspapers, but not the report that Mr Scott is about to publish a Pamphlet, as an addition to the Harleian Tracts, setting forth the amatory adventures of his sister. We shall break our necks in haste to buy it, of course crying ' shameful ' all the while; & it is said Lady Oxford is to be cut, which I cannot entirely believe. Let her tell two or three old women about town that they are young & handsome, & give some well-timed parties, & she may still keep the society which she hath been used to. The times are not so hard as they once were."

Lady Charlotte Campbell also wrote in her diary :

" Sir F. Burdett has been pursuing Mr Scott, Lady Oxford's brother, for £5000 paid for the maintenance of a child, & which he now repents to have given, & denies it was for that purpose. One would suppose a public man's character was of more value to him than £5000. Will Lord & Lady Oxford go on as usual, & take no notice ? "

That is all very well. Sir Francis might have let the £5000 go, but he was one of those, who refuse to yield to blackmail. He preferred to face the ordeal.

My own belief is that Sir Francis was not the father of Lord Harley, but he could only have shown up W. Scott as a blackmailer by putting Lady Oxford into the witness box, & that for obvious reasons he was unwilling to do.

Burdett's intimacy with the Oxfords was not broken by the trial : for one year later we read in Lord Broughton's " Recollections " that he and Burdett dined together, with the Oxford family (July 23, 1812). But Lady Oxford had then become infatuated with Lord Byron. Lady Oxford, Byron, and Burdett in these years were all members of the circle which gathered round the Princess of Wales. In

1813 the Oxfords went abroad to Italy, and passed out of Burdett's life. Such is the disagreeable story, of which we shall once more hear an echo in 1817. Even if Sir Francis was not the father of Lord Harley, it must have been very unpleasant for Lady Burdett to read—if she did read them—such squibs as those which follow in the papers that collected the scandals of the day.

ADVERTISEMENT EXTRAORDINARY.

" LATELY was published an additional volume of the ' HARL-EAAN MISCELLANY ' carefully edited by Sir F. B. Baronet, and imprinted nearly eleven years ago at the Oxford Press. This beautiful work was arranged by the Editor during a trip to France in 1801, and the proof sheets were delivered at Paris. On his return to England, both this work and his baggage were bonded, which has occasioned the extraordinary delay in the publication.

" *N.B.* Another volume by a different Editor is in great forward-ness, having been some months in the Oxford Press, and will in a short time be ready for delivery ! "

"PATRIOTIC GENEROSITY.

" That Frank each selfish action scorns,
      I'll swear on Holy Book—
He gave his friends a pair of HORNS,
      Himself but one HORN TOOK."

" Sir Francis Burdett is a subscriber to the Oxford Produce stakes. There is no truth in the report of the Baronet's having withdrawn his support from this race."

The only serious attack on Burdett for his conduct was made in an anonymous pamphlet called " Adultery and Patriotism," dated two days after the trial (July 13, 1811). The writer professed to be an elector of Westminster, whose trust in Burdett as a public man had been based on belief in the private virtue of Burdett as husband, father, friend. Taunts about the insincerity of so-called patriots, he tells us, taunts about Burdett's friendship with O'Connor and Despard, and his treatment of Paull had failed to shake his loyalty to Burdett. He had admired Burdett for the attack, which, despite the pain it gave him, he had made on

the Duke of York in 1809.   What other line, he replied to
maligners, could an exemplary husband, shocked at
conjugal infidelity, have taken ?

His faith in Burdett had only suffered shipwreck when he
discovered at the trial that Burdett had " A CHILD LIVING,
BORN OF ANOTHER MAN'S WIFE SINCE HER MARRIAGE
AND YOURS."

Was there, he asked Burdett, such a child in existence ?
If there was, how could Burdett have had the effrontery to
stand up and revile the son of his King and say the Duke
of York's affair with Mrs. Clarke " shewed a picture of
hypocrisy & profligacy truly revolting to propriety &
decency," while he himself was the father of an illegitimate
child by a married woman ?

The writer then taunted Burdett for his meanness in
demanding back the £5000 from Scott.   Speaking of the
way in which the Duke of York had treated Mrs. Clarke,
Burdett had said : " Such conduct makes a man's blood
run cold : the annuity was refused by the Duke, though
formerly promised, and on what grounds was it refused ?
Because, though a BOND HAD BEEN PROMISED, yet no BOND
HAD BEEN GIVEN."   Burdett had literally furnished the
words that now could be turned against himself.   If his
private virtue was a sham, what guarantee was there that
his public virtue was not also a sham ?   " Go, teach your
son to write Latin : be detected clasping Lady Burdett to
your heart—do, Hypocrite—Do you suppose you can ever
deceive us again ? "

Sir Francis' Counsel in the course of the trial seems to
have said that Sir Francis did not recollect all the circumstances of the case.

In a postscript to the second edition of the pamphlet [1]
Burdett was mocked for his " want of Memory," just as in

---

[1] Only two or three copies of this pamphlet are said to be in
existence.   I have been told that the whole issue was bought up by
the daughter of Sir Francis, Lady Burdett-Coutts.

1820 the Italian witnesses against Queen Caroline were mocked for the answer " *non mi recordo.*"

" Might I venture to ask," he writes, " *why* you lent Mr Scott Five Thousand Pounds ? (that is, if you recollect)."

If it had been mere charity, Burdett would certainly have puffed it. The writer then tried to refresh Burdett's memory, and made mysterious allusions to a certain hotel in Dover Street, where Burdett had forgotten to draw curtains and shut doors.   This might lead him to remember where his bond to Scott had got to.

The pamphlet seems to have attracted no interest. Whether it was that the men of that age were indifferent to sexual morality—and certainly the standard among public men was very low—and acquitted Burdett of the charge of meanness, and regarded Scott as the blackmailer he was, there is no evidence to show.   Anyway at the General Election of 1812 there was no mention made of the scandal, and Burdett was unanimously re-elected for Westminster.

CHAPTER XIV

1810–1814

APART from the Oxford scandal, the life of Burdett after his release from the Tower (May 1810) till the end of 1813 was comparatively uneventful.

At the close of 1810 it became necessary to provide for the exercise of the Royal Power. The wavering balance of George III's mind was upset by the illness and then the death (November 1810) of his favourite daughter Amelia. From this date he fell into hopeless insanity, and it was necessary to appoint a Regent.

The Prince of Wales was created Regent under certain restrictions, most of which were to last for one year only; the care of the King's person was given to the Queen, assisted by a Council.

On December 19 the six Princes of the Blood Royal addressed to the Prime Minister, Perceval, a letter of protest against the restrictions, but in vain. The Regency Bill became law on February 5, 1811.

Surely the time of the Whigs had at last come. The Prince Regent would dismiss the Tories and call the Whigs to power. The Whig leaders were busily engaged in intrigues for the distribution of offices. But they counted their chickens before they were hatched. They were not the first nor the last to find that the Prince of Wales was a broken reed, whereon if a man leaned, it would go into his hand and pierce it.

On February 4 he informed Perceval that he had decided for the time being not to remove the present Ministers, as such removal might retard the King's recovery. That was a good enough excuse for the nonce. The Whig leaders had not yet realised that the Whig leanings of the Prince had been a mere veneer to cover opposition to his father. Nor did the Whig leaders show to advantage. It is true that Grey and Grenville frowned on the proposal—said to be near to the Regent's heart—that his brother, the Duke of York, should be reappointed to the command of the Army. But, on the other hand, Grenville was determined to combine once more the two incompatible offices of First Lord of the Treasury and Auditor of the Exchequer. Perceval had meanwhile insinuated himself into the good graces of the Prince Regent by consenting to the reappointment of the Duke of York as Commander-in-Chief (May 1811).

The Session of Parliament (January 15 to July 24) provided no sensations, but Burdett, as usual, put his finger on the real grievances of the day. The procedure in prosecutions for libel was a scandal. On March 28 Lord Folkestone moved for an examination into the practice of ex-officio informations filed by the Attorney General in cases of libel. The number of these ex-officio informations had greatly increased. From 1801 to 1807, only fourteen of them had been filed. From 1808 to 1811, forty-two had been filed. Only in sixteen out of the forty-two cases was the defendant brought to trial. Burdett, supporting the motion in a well-reasoned speech, dwelt on the oppressive nature of this method of proceeding. The charge did not need to be endorsed by a Grand Jury. Everything depended upon the caprice of the Attorney General; having preferred the charge, he need not proceed with it until whatever time he chose, but might keep it hanging over the defendant's head; he could hold the defendant to bail or imprisonment; if the defendant was complaisant, the Attorney General could enter a *nolle prosequi*; if he prosecuted and secured a verdict, he need not call the defendant up for judgment, but again might keep the charge indefinitely hanging over his head. In any case,

the defendant was involved in large legal costs.   Burdett
further criticised the way in which special juries were
appointed in such libel cases.   The list was arbitrarily
chosen by the Master of the Crown office.   From his own
knowledge he certified that to be a special juryman
was a source of income and a means of livelihood.   Special
jurymen were in some shape or other always connected
with " Government."   Under all these circumstances he
stated that the so-called liberty of the Press was simply a
farce.   It did not exist.

There was one cause which Burdett and Cobbett had
made peculiarly their own, and that was the abolition of
flogging in the Army.   Cobbett was then in Newgate for
having criticised the flogging of militia men at Ely carried
out by Hessian troops.

Burdett's efforts in Parliament were now to secure some
mitigation of the cruelty.   On June 18, 1811, he raised the
whole question in the House of Commons.   He cited
horrible cases of cruelty.   He himself, when in the Tower,
had seen the flogging of an old man of seventy, who had
served thirty years in the Army and received no fewer than
seventeen honourable wounds in service.   He could not
have had any idea of the severity and the cruelty of the
punishment, if he had not seen it himself.   The system was
brutalising to all concerned.   It did not contribute to
efficiency; for the most efficient regiments were those in
which flogging was not used as a punishment.   He concluded by moving an address to the Prince Regent that
" he would give orders to Commanding Officers that
would restrain and finally lead to the abolition of this
cruel, and unnecessary, and ignominious mode of
punishment."

The motion was rejected by a majority of 84.   Cobbett's
comment in the " Register " was : " This will not be the
first instance in which Sir Francis Burdett has taken the lead

in bringing forward that which all men have finally agreed in regarding as greatly beneficial to the Country." [1]

As a matter of fact, Burdett's efforts were not without immediate effect. A clause was introduced into the Mutiny Act of 1811, which, while it did not alter the law, gave a hint to courts martial that other punishments, if this did not involve danger to the Army, should be substituted for flogging. And on March 25, 1812, the Duke of York issued a circular to commanding officers with recommendations against the frequent use of flogging. " The Commander-in-Chief has no hesitation in declaring that the maintaining of strict discipline *without severity of punishment* etc. are the criterions by which His Royal Highness will be very much guided in forming his opinion of the merit of officers."

But Burdett could not secure the total abolition of flogging. His motion on March 13, 1812, for its total abolition was rejected by 6 to 79.

The final session of the Parliament elected in 1807 was opened on January 7, 1812. Burdett by a *ruse de guerre* on this opening day created a sensation. It had been arranged that Lord Jocelyn should move the Address in reply to the Prince Regent's speech, but no sooner had the Speaker read the speech to the House of Commons than Burdett got up. The Speaker, under the impression that Burdett had risen on a point of order, was taken by surprise. But Burdett was undoubtedly " in possession of the House." He made a long speech, ending off with an address to the Regent that he proposed for the acceptance of the House. Lord Jocelyn's address had therefore to be moved as an " amendment " to Burdett's proposal, and was of course carried by a large majority. Burdett's speech was described

[1] Cp. the tribute paid by Lord Holland to Burdett for the part he played in the matter of flogging (" Further Memoirs of the Whig Party," p. 102).

by Speaker Abbot in his Diary as "very wicked and very foolish"; by the *Morning Post* as "a *prepared and studied* satire, such as might become a seditious tavern meeting, upon the whole of His Majesty's long and venerated reign." However that might be, a reprint of the speech went through fifteen editions before the beginning of March, and 30,000 copies of it were sold.

The speech and address passed in review the great evils of the time. The war was fought, not in defence of freedom, but on behalf of despotism. It was a failure. "Our allies had been compelled either to abdicate their thrones, or to content themselves with scanty pittances of the dominions they had once possessed." Burdett then called attention to economic distress at home, the introduction of foreign troops into England, the dressing of our own troops in "German" style, the flogging of soldiers, the destruction of the liberty of the Press by ex-officio informations. And all these evils he traced to their prime original—that is, to the absence of a real representation of the people in the House of Commons.

In February 1812 the restrictions on the power of the Regent came to an end, and the Whigs hoped that their day of triumph had at last arrived. They did not yet know the Regent. On February 13 he expressed the gratification he would feel "if some of those persons, with whom the early habits of my public life were formed," would join the Government. Grey and Grenville refused the overture, chiefly on the ground that they would not consent to defer the removal of Roman Catholic disabilities. The Prince Regent was only too glad to fall back on Perceval.

Cobbett in an "Open Letter" told the fortune of the Whigs. They would never, he informed them, be brought into power by the Court. They had a great opportunity to become once more the leaders of "the people," but from their recent record—their attitude towards Madocks' resolution in 1809, and towards Burdett's imprisonment in 1810, etc.—he anticipated that they would not seize the opportunity, but would simply remain " sulky spectators. And there they may stand till they turn to stone."

The spring and summer of 1812 were a time of great distress. The harvest of 1811 had been poor, and the price of bread was consequently high. The policy of the Orders in Council and the retaliatory steps taken by France and America made it impossible for manufacturers to sell their goods, and therefore there was much unemployment. In various parts of the country the so-called Luddite Riots aimed at the destruction of machinery (which, by displacing hand labour, was supposed to be the cause of the unemployment). The rioters were put down by the soldiery, and " frame-breaking " was made a capital offence.[1] Later in the year the chief rioters were tried by a Special Commission, and many of them were executed. Disaffection was for the time silenced, but was not subdued.

On May 1 there was a " breeze " in the House of Commons over an " estimate " for building barracks, especially a barrack in the " Regent's Park " for the Horse Guards. The quartering of soldiers in barracks had always been a sore point with the Radicals as withdrawing soldiers from intercourse and sympathy with the " people." Burdett and others attacked the proposal not merely on the ground of expense—that was a minor matter—but on the constitutional side. The barrack in Regent's Park was intended as " a Praetorian Camp to overawe the City." For we had now come to Government by the sword. The magistrates were not justified in letting the soldiery loose upon the people. The Riot Act only contemplated the use of the civil arm.

Perceval sprang up and accused Burdett of having taken under his protection " rioters and incendiaries." These forsooth were the " people." He taunted Burdett with

[1] Lord Byron made his maiden speech in Parliament on this question

the tumults he had raised in London in 1810 to resist what he (Perceval) might now confidently describe—for it had been settled by a jury—as the law of the land.   He described Burdett's speech as " declamatory nonsense." As a matter of fact, Burdett had not expressed any approval of the rioters, but he was sensible enough to see that force by itself was no remedy.   There was genuine distress, and the Government ought to have been sympathetic to the sufferers.   Perceval never argued the points raised by Burdett.   It was almost the last speech he made in the House of Commons.   On May 11 he was assassinated by Bellingham.

For a month after Perceval's death there was an interregnum in the Government, though on May 21 an address to the Regent was carried by two votes in the House of Commons requesting the formation of a strong and efficient administration.   The Regent played with parties and statesmen.   There were the remaining members of Perceval's Ministry.   Of these Lord Liverpool was the chief.   There were the Whig leaders, Grey and Grenville. There was Lord Wellesley, who had resigned from the Perceval Ministry in the preceding February because (1) he thought the war in the Peninsula was not adequately supported, (2) he wanted something done for the Roman Catholics, (3) he regarded Perceval as unequal to the position of Prime Minister.   Wellesley was closely united with Canning.   Canning was a follower of the Pitt tradition. He was a convinced opponent of Reform, but an advocate of Catholic relief.   On the other hand, he was viewed with profound distrust by Grey, because in 1807 he had joined the Portland administration, though it was based on the principle of Catholic exclusion.   In 1809 he had fought a duel with his colleague Castlereagh, and since that year had been out of office, whereas Castlereagh had succeeded Wellesley as Foreign Minister in February 1812.

Lord Moira was, or rather had been, a personal friend of the Prince Regent.

Negotiations proceeded between the Prince, Lord
Wellesley, Lord Grey, and Lord Moira, for the formation
of an Opposition Government.   It is significant that in
these negotiations the question of REFORM was not even
raised by Lord Grey.   Grey finally refused to take office,
because the Prince Regent would not undertake to change
the " Gentlemen of the Household."   Since it was impossible to form a Government out of all this discordant
material, the Prince Regent fell back on Lord Liverpool,
who was appointed Prime Minister on June 8, 1812.   The
Tories were to be in the ascendant for another seventeen
years.   Canning refused to join the Ministry, because
Castlereagh was to be the leader in the House of Commons.

On June 22 a motion made by Canning to take into consideration the Catholic question early in the next Parliament
was carried in the House of Commons by a large majority
(235 to 106).

On July 28, two days before the end of the Session
Burdett, in the course of a long speech, declared that the
payment of sinecures amounted to more than £1,000,000 a
year, and that expenditure could be reduced by £9,000,000
per annum without affecting the efficiency of the public
service.   He ended by moving an address to the Regent
similar to that proposed by him at the beginning of the
session, but including a proposal that the Princess Charlotte
should become Regent in the event of the Prince predeceas-
ing his father, in order that the borough-monger faction
might not in such an event do what they had done at the
end of 1810, *i.e.* " suspend the Kingly part of the Constitution."   The address found no supporter.

Burdett had always maintained that the " borough-
monger faction " had encroached on the rights of the
Crown no less than on those of the people.   And he had
protested against the restrictions placed on the Regent in
the Regency Bill of 1811, as they seemed to indicate that
the prerogative of the Crown was regarded by Ministers as
a superfluity.

Parliament was prorogued on July 30, and dissolved on September 29, 1812.

Meanwhile what had happened to Cobbett? Having attacked Government for the flogging of English soldiers at Ely under the auspices of German cavalry, in the Political Register (July 1, 1809) he had been prosecuted by the Attorney General and sentenced on July 9, 1810, to two years' imprisonment, and a fine of £1000. Financially he had been almost ruined. Apart from the fine, the costs of his trial had amounted to £5000. This was not all. His dealings with his London agent, Wright, had got into an inextricable muddle. They had both been very un-business-like, but Cobbett roundly accused Wright of having embezzled thousands of pounds. That may or may not have been the case, but it is certainly true that Cobbett would have been made a bankrupt had not Burdett and others advanced him large sums of money. Whether Burdett's advance was a gift or a loan became in after years a subject of sharp dispute.

On July 9 Cobbett, having paid his fine and having entered into recognisances, was liberated from Newgate. His release was celebrated by a large dinner, over which Sir Francis Burdett presided, at the "Crown and Anchor." But Cobbett's enemies were not behindhand. The "bloody *Times*" had on this very morning stated that Cobbett in 1810 had offered to discontinue the "Register" if Government would not call him up for judgment. Leaflets had been struck off, and as each of the 600 diners entered the "Crown and Anchor" the leaflet was presented to him; and a waiter had been bribed to put under the plate of each guest the views that Cobbett had expressed about Burdett in 1802 : "I LOATHE, I DETEST Sir Francis Burdett." This latter passed off as a joke. But Cobbett in the course of an after-dinner speech denied that he had ever in 1810 made, directly or indirectly, any overtures to Government for dropping the " Register." Not content with this, in the " Register " of July 18, 1812, he declared that the allegation was FALSE—wholly destitute of truth. Now the evidence that such overtures were made through Wright and John Reeves is incontrovertible. Cobbett could not have forgotten the circumstances, and therefore must be convicted of having told a deliberate lie.

In October 1812 the elections for the new Parliament took place. The supporters of the Liverpool Government were returned by a big majority, but in Westminster the Radicals, Sir Francis Burdett and Lord Cochrane, were returned without opposition. It was at this election that, according to family tradition, the little Clara Burdett, a child rising seven years old, being asked her name, replied, " Clara Burdett for ever, sir." Once again Burdett did not seek the electors, the electors sought him. I have before me his election address, printed with beautiful distinctness by the Clarendon Press on a white silk handkerchief. These handkerchiefs were, I suppose, distributed among the ladies of Westminster. Parts of the address will suggest the temper of the time :

GENTLEMEN,

In addressing so enlightened a portion of the community as the electors of the great metropolitan city of Westminster, it would ill become me to adopt the hacknied style of congratulation & profession usual on occasions like the present. I cannot congratulate the people on the opportunity afforded them for redressing their manifold grievances, by a due exercise of their constitutional right to appoint their representatives in Parliament, well knowing, & that too they know full well who cause this cheating appearance of an election to take place, that no such opportunity is in point of fact or is intended to be afforded the people. You, Gentlemen, are too well informed of the real condition of your country not to regard such language as deceptions, & to treat it with merited contempt. Neither can I with truth profess that I shall be highly, or at all, gratified by being returned a member of an assembly, where corruption is acknowledged to be as " notorious as the sun at noonday," & where " practices, which would have made our forefathers startle with indignation, in utter oblivion of every former maxim & feeling of Parliament," have been impudently avowed & shamelessly justified. This has brought us into a situation almost impossible, within the limits of an advertisement, to depict. Nine Hundred millions of debt; inland fortresses under the name of barracks; an army of German & other foreign mercenaries; an army of spies & informers; of tax & excise agents; an inquisition of private property; a phantom for a king; a degraded aristocracy; an oppressed people; a confiding Parliament; irresponsible ministers; a corrupt & intimidated press; pensioned justices; packed juries; vague & sanguinary laws, sometimes shamefully relaxed, at other times violently stretched beyond their tone; which, together with a host of failures of foreign expeditions, & the present crushing burthen of taxation, are some of the bitter fruits of corruption in the House of Commons. A House of Commons, the members of which did, agreeably to a return laid before it in 1808, put into their own pockets £178,994 a year [1] in sinecures, salaries, & pensions, besides their staff appointments & their commissions, & besides the money received by their wives & their relations. In fact the whole of the evil arises here. Those who vote the money are some way or other interested in the expenditure of it. The small number of independent men have no weight at all.

Gentlemen, it is often affirmed, that the savings in our power to make from sinecures & pensions would afford no relief to the people : let us take a few out of numerous

[1] The House of Commons of to-day puts a considerable larger sum into the pockets of its members ! !

instances. The House of Commons itself, in sheer places & pensions, swallows as much as would give 50/ a year to 71,224 families. Would this be nothing? Would it not be felt by the people? Lord Arden brother to the late Minister,[1] with reversion to the late Minister himself, receives from his sinecures £38,574 a year. This is the exact sum stated. But it is said that he has immense sums arising from interest. Here is support all the year round, at 12/ a week for more than a thousand families. The same may be said for the family of Grenville. The Duke of Grafton's sinecures & pensions would maintain half as many; & in short it is in this way the nation is impoverished & reduced to misery. The Lord Chief Justice Ellenborough, besides his salary, receives in sinecures £8933 a year; besides having offices to sell, & participating in the emoluments of his own gaoler. The sinecures of the Chief Justice would keep 300 families. Mr Garnier, the Apothecary-General has a clear £12,000 a year, according to his own acknowledgment; besides, the sums given to the princes out of the droits of admiralty, the King's private property in the Funds exempted from the income tax, & Mr Addington (the maker & the breaker of the treaty of Amiens) in 1801, misapplying upwards of £50,000 pounds (voted for the Civil List) as a loan to the Duke of York, only a small part of which has been repaid & that without interest. What noble examples they set us of making sacrifices, & for reconciling the people to their sufferings from the weight of the taxes & the distresses of the times!

Gentlemen, there was formerly a law for putting a badge of distinction on every pauper receiving alms from his parish; but what BADGES OF INFAMY do those men deserve, who thus extort alms from every poor man in every parish of England? who embezzle, in unmerited pensions & sinecure places, & divert into private purses the public resources of their country?

[1] Spencer Perceval.

Gentlemen, our usurping oligarchy assumes a power of making our most innocent actions misdemeanours; of determining points of law without appeal; & of imprisoning our persons without trial; of breaking open our houses with the standing Army; & murdering the people in the streets by soldiers paid by the people themselves for their defence. . . . The House of Commons instituted to redress our grievances is become the GREATEST OF ALL GRIEVANCES, itself the ready instrument of all our oppressors; a two-edged sword to destroy, instead of a shield to protect us. Gentlemen, the people of England are entitled by several positive laws, as well as by that which is superior to all law, reason & common sense & common good to ANNUAL PARLIAMENTS & free elections. These are the vital principles of the constitution; the only means of ensuring JUSTICE, PEACE, & SECURITY to the community at large.

In 1813 a considerable portion of Parliament's time was taken up by the unlovely story of the Prince Regent's relations with his wife and daughter. In order to secure the payment of his debts, the Prince of Wales in 1795 had married his unfortunate cousin, Caroline of Brunswick. His treatment of her can only be described as disgusting. He spent his wedding night in a hopeless state of intoxication. He forced his latest mistress, the Countess of Jersey, on his consort as her first lady-in-waiting. After the birth of their own child, the Princess Charlotte (January 7, 1796), the Prince and Princess of Wales finally separated. The Prince remained at Carlton House, and in 1801 the Princess settled at Montague House, Blackheath. By her indiscretions she played into the hands of her horrible husband. In consequence of a story spread by a Lady Douglas that the Princess had been delivered of an illegitimate son, the King in 1806 appointed a small Committee of Lord Erskine (the Lord Chancellor), Lord Ellenborough (the Lord Chief Justice), Lords Grenville and

Spencer, to conduct a " delicate investigation " [1] into the affair.

The " delicate investigators " completely cleared the Princess of the main charge, but censured her for the levity of conduct she had shown on various occasions. The old King, however, consented to receive her again at Court, and rooms were assigned to her in Kensington Palace.

When George III became permanently insane and the Prince of Wales was made Regent, restrictions were placed by him on intercourse between the Princess of Wales and her daughter Princess Charlotte. Matters came to a crisis in 1813.

On January 14, 1813, the Princess wrote a letter of remonstrance [2] to the Regent. This letter was returned unopened. On January 19 the Princess sent the letter to the Prime Minister, Lord Liverpool, for communication to the Regent. Lord Liverpool replied that there was no answer.[3] The Princess then, acting on the advice of Brougham, on February 10 published the said letter in the *Morning Chronicle*. The matter was referred by the Regent to a Committee of twenty-three Privy Councillors, who reported on February 27 affirming " the propriety of regulation and restriction on the intercourse between the Princess of Wales and the Princess Charlotte."

On March 1 the Princess of Wales wrote a letter to the Speaker [4] for communication to the House of Commons, throwing herself on the House of Commons for the protection of her honour.

In the debates that ensued Ministers admitted the complete innocence of the Princess. (Perceval, as a matter of fact, had been the Counsel of the Princess in 1806, and

---

[1] A full account of the " delicate investigation " is to be found in Cobbett's " Political Register " (1813).

[2] The letter is to be found in " P.R." of February 20, 1813.

[3] Lord Liverpool's reply is given in " Creevey Papers," ch. IX.

[4] For the letter to the Speaker, see " Colchester Diary," Vol. II, p. 429.

had been ready to issue as a " Book " the whole of the case laid before the " delicate investigators " of 1806, and the defence of the Princess.)

On March 23, 1813, the Duchess of Brunswick, the sister of George III and mother of the Princess of Wales, died. The next day Lord Castlereagh in the House of Commons moved an address of condolence to the Regent. Burdett, who was at this time living in the entourage of the Princess,[1] suggested that either the Princess should be associated with the Prince Regent in the address, or else that a separate address should be presented to the Princess. In the absence of precedents, this idea was discouraged. But if Parliament declined to address the Princess on the occasion of her mother's death, this was not the line adopted by the City of London or by Westminster. The City of London presented a formal address to the Princess at Kensington Palace.

On April 15 a monster meeting was held in Westminster. Sir Francis, who was suffering from gout, was unable to attend, but he wrote a letter in support of it, making this pointed reflection : " Is it not curious to observe that those persons, whose sensibility was so alive to the misfortunes of the Queen of France, who thought all England & all the world should draw the sword to avenge her injuries, have no sensibility alive, no commiseration awake, to the injuries of the innocent & calumniated Princess of Wales ? "

Resolutions were passed denouncing the introduction of " tribunals unknown to the Constitution," and congratulating Her Royal Highness on her triumph over her enemies. An address was voted declaring Westminster's indignation at the foul conspiracy against Her Royal Highness and expressing their devotion to her cause.

At the end of 1813 the Princess of Wales moved into a

---

[1] Lady Charlotte Campbell wrote in her Diary on February 11, 1813 : " The circle of the Princess's acquaintance grows smaller every day. . . . The Oxford & Burdett party prevail."

house in Connaught Place, and was only on rare occasions allowed to see her daughter. All parties were acting at cross purposes. The Prince tried to strike at his wife through the Princess Charlotte, but the Princess Charlotte took the side of her mother. Brougham and Whitbread were using the Princess of Wales and the Princess Charlotte as pawns in the game of embarrassing the Prince Regent, in retaliation of his betrayal of the Whigs.

Meanwhile, Napoleon had been at last vanquished. He abdicated in April 1814. In June the victorious allied Sovereigns, the Tsar of Russia, the King of Prussia, etc., paid a state visit to England. This state visit gave the Prince Regent a fresh opportunity to affront his wife. She was not allowed to appear at the receptions, and the Sovereigns were requested not to visit her.

The Princess Charlotte was for a short time affianced to the Hereditary Prince of Orange, but not to mention the fact that he was physically distasteful to her—" I think him so ugly," she said to her mother, " that I am sometimes obliged to turn my head away in disgust when he is speaking to me "—she disliked the marriage on other grounds, because the Prince of Orange had taken the side of her father against her mother, nor did she want to reside out of England, over which it was probable that she would one day reign as Sovereign. But her father, the Prince Regent, was furious. He broke up her establishment at Warwick House, and ordered her immediately to return to Carlton House. The young Princess, goaded to fury, escaped (July 12, 1814) in a hackney carriage to her mother's house in Connaught Place, and it required a deputation of the Archbishop of Canterbury, the Prime Minister, the Lord Chancellor and the Duke of York to induce her to return to her father's house. In August 1814 the Princess of Wales, wearied out by indignities, went abroad.

Both in 1812 and 1813 the Burdetts seem to have gone

to Oxford as a health resort.   Sir Francis suffered on and off from gout, and Lady Burdett was receiving there what we should now call a massage treatment.   In those days it was called a " rubbing."   It was probably at this time that Burdett formed a friendship with Dr. Routh, the President of Magdalen, with whom he corresponded often in later days.

Robert Burdett matriculated at Brasenose College on June 23, 1813, but he was not proving a very satisfactory son, as appears from this letter :

Lady Burdett to T. Coutts for his birthday :

18 Sep. 1812.
Oxford

Thanks, my dear love, for your kind thought in regard to *Robert*, which no doubt will be highly gratifying to him hereafter, when he will be at liberty to enjoy the *Theatricals*. You are always kind & considerate, & it only grieves me that the poor dear Fellow should not be *quite deserving* of your kindness—that drinking turn frightens me so, 'tis sad. When he comes *here*, I hope he may lose it, as drinking is not at all the *Fashion* amongst the young men, I understand : in which case, the *sooner* he comes here, the better I think, & he is now quite old enough—but I do not think Burdett seems desirous of his coming here, which I wonder at almost, for everybody tells us the young men are particularly quiet, not having so much of that wildness amongst them as they used to have in his (Burdett's) own time. Robert is going for 17 & I believe the young men come here about that age.

This is the 18th of September.   Many, many, happy ones I trust will return to you, my dearest Papa.   'Tis lovely weather, & we had a charming day at the Forest Fair, 'twas a most lovely sight.   It is called *Gypsying* here, every one carries their dinner, & you see parties of all descriptions,

LORD COCHRANE

Défenseur des Grecs.

Lith. de Ducarme.

Galerie Universelle.   Publiée par Blaisot.

some under Tents, some in the open air, dining al Fresco, dancing etc., & all this in the most *beautiful* scenery—Forest Scenery—you can possibly imagine—2000 people there, but I must conclude. God bless you all.

Ever your affectionate SOPHIA.

A case intimately affecting Burdett was brought before the Court of King's Bench in 1814. That year was full of exciting events. Napoleon, after his disastrous retreat from Moscow and his defeat in " The Battle of the Nations " at Leipsic, had returned to France and stood at bay. The vicissitudes of the struggle, as fortune veered this way and that, were eagerly watched in England and were reflected on the Stock Exchange in the rise and fall of prices. It was in these circumstances that in the early hours of February 21, 1814 (1.15 a.m.), an officer roused the inmates of the Ship Inn at Dover, announcing that he was Colonel du Bourg, aide-de-camp to Lord Cathcart. He had just landed, he said, and was the bearer of glorious news. He was dressed in a grey military overcoat, with a scarlet uniform underneath, a star on his breast, and a medallion suspended on his bosom. He wore a military cap with gold fringe. He demanded a post-chaise, with four horses, to take him to London, and while these were preparing, he penned a letter to Admiral Foley at Deal announcing that the allies had obtained a final victory, and that Napoleon had been torn in pieces by Cossacks. The Admiral received the letter at 3 a.m., and had it not been for the mistiness of the atmosphere, the semaphore telegraph, connected with the Admiralty, would have very quickly taken the news to London. Meanwhile " Colonel du Bourg " had got his chaise and posted to London via Canterbury, Rochester, and Dartford, announcing at places en route the victory of the allies and the slaughter of Napoleon. " The Cossacks had fought for shares of his body as if it had been gold." From Dartford " the Colonel " was driven to the

Marsh Gate at Lambeth, and thence he went by a hackney coach to Lord Cochrane's house at 13 Green Street, Grosvenor Square. A number of people, including the landlord of the Rochester inn, the postillion who drove the chaise from Rochester to Dartford, and Crane, the driver of the hackney coach from Lambeth to 13 Green Street, agreed with slight variations as to the character of " Colonel du Bourg's " dress—the grey overcoat, the scarlet uniform underneath, the red star, the medallion.

The great news had reached London ahead of " du Bourg," it is not explained how. When the Stock Exchange opened, Government securities, such as Consols, rapidly rose, but when no confirmation of the news arrived, prices began to sag; presently it was announced that French royalist officers had driven through the city in a post chaise decked with laurels, and once more Consols rose. It was only when Government failed to confirm the news that securities fell to their original level. As a result of the hoax those who sold Consols at the higher price made a considerable profit, and those who bought at the higher price suffered considerable loss.

The hoax roused a storm of indignation, and the Stock Exchange appointed a Committee of Inquiry. On March 7 the Committee reported, tracing the movements of " du Bourg " from Dover to Lord Cochrane's house in London, and informing the Stock Exchange that Lord Cochrane, his uncle Andrew Cochrane Johnstone, M.P., and a Mr. Butt had made enormous sales of Consols, etc., on February 21, and by so doing had made the following profits : Lord Cochrane £2470, Cochrane Johnstone £4931, Butt £3048. The Committee also offered a reward of £250 for the identification of " Colonel du Bourg."

Lord Cochrane (b. 1775), the eldest son of the ninth Earl of Dundonald, had entered the Navy at an early age, and in command of the *Speedy*, the *Pallas*, and the *Impérieuse* had gained great distinction as a seaman, capturing innumerable prizes. Though he never had supreme command in any general engagement, his fertility of resource was such that it is probably no exaggeration to place him among the greatest of our Admirals. But he never " suffered fools gladly," always spoke his mind, blurted out what he thought to be the truth, and told his superiors his opinion of them. Thus in 1801, when his request to Lord St. Vincent for the promotion of his lieutenant was refused on the ground that the small number of people killed on board the *Speedy* did not warrant the application, he was tactless enough to point out that still fewer people had been killed on Lord St. Vincent's ship in the action which had won for Lord St. Vincent a peerage. And in 1809, after the destruction of French ships in the Basque Roads—an action in which Cochrane had played the most prominent part—when our Government proposed that a vote of thanks should be passed by both houses of Parliament to Lord Gambier, the Admiral in command, Lord Cochrane, as member for Westminster (where he had been elected as Burdett's colleague in 1807) opposed the vote on the grounds that Lord Gambier had done everything within his power to frustrate the success of the operation. He was supported by his colleague Burdett, who said that Lord Gambier's plan seemed to be to preserve his own fleet, Lord Cochrane's to destroy that of the enemy. The friendship between the two members for Westminster was long continued.

It was not only that Cochrane as M.P. exposed abuses in the naval administration—the hardships endured by the sailors, the inadequate nature of their pay and pensions, the fees exacted on their discharge, the scandals of the prize-courts, the system by which preferment in the Service was often given by Parliamentary influence—but he had also joined the ranks of the Radicals led by Burdett. He had attended meetings, in which the relations of the Duke of York with Mrs. Clarke had been severely handled and the borough-monger faction had been painted as involving the country in perpetual misfortune, etc. In 1809 he had supported Madocks' motion charging Ministers with the sale of seats. He had denounced the action of the House of Commons in sending Burdett to the Tower. He had seconded Burdett's proposed address to the Regent at the opening of the session of 1812. He had denounced the whole system of sinecures and pensions. Lord Cochrane was therefore a marked man, unpopular with the Government and the Admiralty. Rightly or wrongly, he regarded J. W. Croker, the secretary to "My Lords of the Admiralty," as his particular enemy.

In 1814 Sir Alexander Cochrane (Lord Cochrane's uncle) had been appointed to the command of the North American Fleet. He had nominated Lord Cochrane to the command of the *Tonnant*, which was intended to be his flagship. But as the *Tonnant* was not yet ready, Lord Cochrane was left behind to bring her out when fitted, and thus chanced to be in London on February 21.

Having been informed of the report of the Stock Exchange Committee, Lord Cochrane got leave of absence from Chatham and came to town. On March 11 he made a sworn affidavit, revealing *inter alia* that the officer who had visited him on February 21 was a certain Captain de Berenger, who was dressed on the occasion in a "*grey greatcoat, a green uniform and a military cap*." The Stock Exchange Committee afterwards said that from information already supplied to them they had been led to believe that "Colonel du Bourg" was really Captain de Berenger. However that may be, Lord Cochrane could not have known it. It is a great point in favour of his innocence that he was the *first* person to give information publicly that led to the identification of "Colonel du Bourg."

On March 22 Cochrane's servants also deposed in affidavit that the officer who visited him on February 21 wore a grey greatcoat, and that his undercoat had a *green* collar.

On March 23 a fisherman, when dredging, hauled up from the bottom of the Thames " du Bourg's " uniform— a scarlet uniform with silver star, badge, etc.

Cochrane's own account of his movements on February 21 was this. He had breakfasted with his uncle, Cochrane Johnstone, and Mr. Butt, and had left them to visit the manufactory of a Mr. King, who was making to his specification a special kind of lamp that he intended to patent. While he was at Mr. King's, he was brought a note by his servant, Dewman, requesting him to come to 13 Green Street. He could not decipher the signature to the note, but on hearing that his visitor at Green Street was an army officer, he thought that it must be someone bringing news of a brother, who was seriously ill in Spain. He went home, and there, to his surprise, found Captain de Berenger.

This de Berenger was by his own tale descended from the ancient Lombard Kings. However that may have been, he was a Prussian subject, who had come to England, and had gained introductions to Lord Cochrane's uncles. Lord Cochrane had on several occasions met him at their houses. He had acted as adjutant to the Duke of Cumberland's Sharp-shooters, commanded by Lord Yarmouth. He was a skilled instructor in drill and an expert on the subject that was Lord Cochrane's special interest, pyrotechnics—fireships, explosives, etc. There had been negotiations between Sir Alexander Cochrane and de Berenger about his going with Sir Alexander to North America, but the chief obstacle had been de Berenger's nationality; and, in the meantime, de Berenger—one of those inventors who are always in financial difficulties—had, owing to his debts, got within the rules of the King's Bench, a form of modified imprisonment.

This was the man whom Cochrane found at his house on his return. Cochrane was positive that de Berenger was dressed in a *grey overcoat and green uniform underneath*. de Berenger then opened up the question of going with

Lord Cochrane in the *Tonnant*. Cochrane replied that without the consent of the Admiralty it was impossible, but that if he got a recommendation, *e.g.* from Lord Yarmouth, he might possibly be allowed to join the *Tonnant* at Portsmouth. de Berenger then asked him for a change of clothes. He said he could not go to Lord Yarmouth in the dress he had on, nor return to his lodgings (*i.e.* within the rules of the King's Bench), where it would excite suspicion. Cochrane having his clothes lying about, preparatory to his departure, gave him a change of clothes. Such was Lord Cochrane's account of events on February 21.

On April 27 the Grand Jury returned a true bill against de Berenger, Lord Cochrane, the hon. A. Cochrane Johnstone, Mr. Butt, and three others for conspiracy to defraud. The case was tried before L. C. J. Ellenborough on June 8 to 9, and ended in a verdict of guilty against all the defendants.

All the other defendants were undoubtedly guilty, but I believe that in the conviction of Lord Cochrane there was a grave miscarriage of justice. Having been unjustly—as I believe—convicted, Lord Cochrane, like a wounded animal at bay, turned with fury and made altogether unjustifiable attacks on judge, jury, and Government.

First let us consider the attack on Lord Ellenborough.

(1) The statement in the "Autobiography of a Seaman"[1] that Lord Ellenborough as a Cabinet Minister was a party to the prosecution, and then as Lord Chief Justice presided at the trial, is a ludicrous mistake. Lord Chief Justice Ellenborough was—*pessimo exemplo* it is true—a member of the short-lived "Cabinet of all the Talents," 1806 to 1807, but he was not a member of Lord Liverpool's Cabinet in 1814.

[1] Published by Lord Dundonald (Cochrane) himself (1860), shortly before his death.

(2) It was said that he had acted rather as Counsel for the prosecution than as a judge. It is true that his summing up was strongly against the defendants. But that, I conceive, is the function of a judge, if the evidence, in his opinion, strongly points that way.

(3) Lord Ellenborough was blamed for having called on Counsel for the defendants to open the defence late at night (10.30 p.m. on June 8), when both Counsel and jury were exhausted—for the Court had sat since 9 a.m.—and for having separated the speeches of Counsel for the defence from the evidence of the defence's witnesses. (The speeches for the defence lasted till 3 a.m. on June 9, and the Court then adjourned till 10 a.m.) As a matter of fact, such prolonged hours seem to have been not unusual in those days, and there were other reasons, which it is unnecessary to detail, why Lord Ellenborough should wish to get on with the case.

(4) A great point was made by Cochrane and Burdett of the difference between Lord Ellenborough's summing up, as reported in the *Times* and his summing up as given by the shorthand reporter of the trial. In the *Times* the judge is reported as saying: " He pulled his scarlet uniform off there (*sc.* in Cochrane's house), and if the circumstance of its not being green did not excite Lord Cochrane's suspicion, what did he think of the star and medal ? . . . He came before Lord Cochrane fully blazoned in the costume of his crime."

In the shorthand report of the trial Lord Ellenborough is only represented as stating hypothetically this fact of the " scarlet " uniform. " If he actually appeared to Lord Cochrane stripped of his greatcoat and with that star and order, he appeared before him rather in the habit of a mountebank than in his proper uniform of a ' Sharp-

shooter.' "   It was even suggested that Lord Ellenborough
had " cooked " his own summing up, and had altered the
words he had actually used in addressing the jury.

This aspersion on Lord Ellenborough's character was
groundless, and, as we shall presently see, the difference
between the two accounts was of no importance.

But if Lord Cochrane was innocent, as I believe he was,
who was responsible for the miscarriage of justice in his
conviction ?   I believe, first, that much of the mismanagement of the case was due to his own fault, especially his
carelessness; secondly, that he was badly served by his
solicitors and counsel.   That, it seems to me, is the only
conclusion to which anyone can come who believes in his
innocence.

There was an all-important difference between Cochrane's affidavit of March 11, in which he swore that de
Berenger appeared at his house in a *green* uniform, and the
brief given by his solicitors to his Counsel, in which it
was admitted that the uniform was *scarlet*.   The brief had
been submitted by the solicitors to Cochrane, but they
had not called his attention to the difference.

Sir Francis Burdett, speaking in the House of Commons
on July 19, 1814, said : " From my knowledge of Lord
Cochrane I am sure that, if he read over the brief, his head
was scheming or dreaming over plans which drew his
attention from it."

Cochrane consistently asserted that he had not noticed
the difference between the brief and his own affidavit as
to the colour of de Berenger's uniform.

Cochrane ought not to be judged by an ordinary standard.
At sea and in inventions he was all there—full of resource
and versatility.   But in ordinary life he was eccentric,
scatter-brained, and careless.   Conscious, as I believe, of
his innocence, he did not make adequate preparation for his
defence.

Then as to the lawyers for the defence.   They were a

goodly array, including Scarlett (afterwards Lord Abinger), Brougham (afterwards Lord Chancellor), Best (afterwards Chief Justice and Lord Wynford). But despite this imposing list of names, I think that Lord Cochrane suffered from their mismanagement in two vital respects.

They decided on a joint defence of *all* the defendants. Now there is no question that all the rest of the defendants were guilty, and Lord Cochrane, not being separately defended, suffered from having his defence joined to that of the guilty, and to the general discredit attaching to the attempted proof of an alibi for Berenger by perjured witnesses.

Counsel, following the brief given them by the solicitors, made what was, so far as Cochrane was concerned, the fatal admission that de Berenger, when he visited Cochrane, was in scarlet uniform. Best in his opening speech tried to explain away the statement, made by Cochrane in his affidavit of March 11 that the uniform was green, by saying that Cochrane had made a slip because green was the colour in which he had been accustomed to see de Berenger on other occasions. But Lord Cochrane always declared that de Berenger's costume was green, and this he maintained till the day of his death.

It is necessary to stress the evidence on this point. Let me repeat it. Lord Cochrane in his affidavit of March 11 swore that the uniform of de Berenger was *green*. Dewman, the servant of Cochrane, in his affidavit of March 22 swore that de Berenger " wore a grey regimental coat buttoned up. I saw a green collar underneath. I never saw any person dressed as described by Crane the hackney coachman."

Mary Turpin, one of Cochrane's servants, swore on March 22 : " The said officer had on a grey greatcoat, and his undercoat or his greatcoat had a green collar to it."

Lord Yarmouth in his evidence at the trial on June 9 declared that the uniform of his corps was a *green* waist-

coat with a *crimson* collar : the greatcoat had black fur
round it, and no crimson collar.   (It would therefore follow
that if Lord Cochrane's account was correct, de Berenger
cannot have been dressed in the full uniform of the Sharp-
shooters.   But who would be able to give a perfectly
accurate description of another person's dress a month
later ?)   The defendants' lawyers, in view of the evidence
given by those who had seen de Berenger on various stages
of his journey from Dover to Lord Cochrane's house in
London, deliberately decided not to dispute the fact that
de Berenger beneath his overcoat had a scarlet uniform.
Mr. Atlay[1] says their decision was well grounded, but, so
far as Lord Cochrane was concerned, I must beg to differ
from him.   They could not have made a decision more
fatal to Lord Cochrane's interest.

Lord Cochrane and his co-defendants were found guilty
on June 9.   But, in accordance with the usual procedure,
judgment was not pronounced, as it was possible for the
defendants to move for a new trial up to four days after
the opening of the next term.

Lord Cochrane, with characteristic carelessness, had not
been present at the original trial, but on June 14 he appeared
in person before the full court of King's Bench, and moved
for a new trial.   But his request was refused on the ground
that it was an established rule of Court that in such a case
no such application could be entertained unless it was
made by *all* the defendants.   This was impossible, as
Cochrane Johnstone and Butt had already fled the country.

On June 20, before a full court of the King's Bench,
the prosecution moved for judgment.   Serjeant Best, on
behalf of Butt, moved for arrest of judgment.   Cochrane
refused to join in the request.   And Lord Ellenborough
said, " We will afterwards hear as a distinct thing whatever may occur to you as fit to be presented to the Court
to induce them to grant a new trial."   (But it is by no

[1] "Lord Cochrane's Trial," by J. B. Atlay.

means clear to me that the Court did not feel itself bound by the rule that *all* the defendants must join in the application.)

After Lord Ellenborough had read through the evidence of the trial, Lord Cochrane made a lengthy speech :

He had been implicated in the guilt of others, with whom all his transactions had been blameless. He knew nothing of the under-plotters (the men who had driven through the city in the guise of French officers). His relations with de Berenger had been solely concerned with de Berenger's proposal that he should be taken out in the *Tonnant* as an instructor in drill and pyrotechnics. Had he really been in the conspiracy, it would have been madness for him to allow de Berenger to come to his house. It was he who had first revealed the identity of " du Bourg " with de Berenger. He repeated his declaration that de Berenger had appeared before him in a *green* uniform; de Berenger might have changed his red uniform in the hackney coach before his arrival, and stowed it away in the portmanteau that, according to the evidence of Crane, the hackney coachman, he carried with him. He admitted that he gave de Berenger a change of clothes (his clothes were lying about in preparation for his departure on the *Tonnant*) that he might call on Lord Yarmouth. " Does any volunteer officer go out of a morning to make calls in his regimentals ? "

He had gone back to his house from the lamp-maker, because on February 18 he had received news of his brother's illness abroad, and thought that the writer of the note had brought him news of his brother. The signature of the note was illegible.

He then read an affidavit sworn in court on June 14, in which he repeated most of the above statement, and swore that the sale of the stock owned by him on February 21 was due to a general order given by him on February 14 that the stock was to be sold whenever it rose 1 per cent.

The Court refused a new trial, and sentence was pronounced on June 21. Lord Cochrane, with whom alone we are concerned, was sentenced to a fine of £1000, and twelve months' imprisonment; also at some time during his imprisonment he was to stand in the pillory near the Royal Exchange for one hour. The extent of Cochrane's punishment did not end with the actual sentence. For he was immediately dismissed from the Navy and degraded from the Order of the Bath.

On July 5 his case was brought before the House of Commons, Cochrane having been fetched from prison and attending by order of the House. Cochrane made a speech sufficiently impressive to convince the Whig leaders, Ponsonby and Whitbread, that there was need for further inquiry; but Cochrane spoiled his speech by the reckless violence with which he attacked the Stock Exchange, the Government, Lord Ellenborough, his own solicitors and Counsel. He was several times stopped by the Speaker, and Castlereagh warned the reporters that they would publish out of doors at their own peril any of the slanders uttered by Lord Cochrane in his speech. Cochrane ended by asserting in the presence of Almighty God his entire innocence. He was then ordered to withdraw. A motion, seconded by Sir Francis Burdett, that all the papers relating to the case should be referred to a Select Committee of the House was rejected, and Lord Cochrane was expelled from the House of Commons by a majority of 140 to 44.

Sir Francis Burdett was throughout a believer in the innocence of Lord Cochrane. Here is a letter written by him to T. Coutts just after the publication of the report of the Stock Exchange Committee, and three months before the trial.

F. Burdett to T. Coutts.

I shall be quite grieved if Lord Cochraine, for whom I have a great regard, should be found to have had any hand in the disgraceful & dishonest cheat practised on the Stock Exchange, & I am perswaded it cannot be the case. I shall also be sorry, should that be the case with C Johnstone or Mr Butt, about whom however I am neither so confident nor feel the same interest. The mere fact of their having sold stock on that day will not surely be deemed sufficient to convict them of such an atrocious fraud. I am certainly glad it so happened, that nothing on that day was done for me, & yet it might very easily have happened otherwise & I have been equally blameless, & so it may be, for anything that at present appears, with them.

Another believer in the innocence of Cochrane was Dr. Routh, the well-known head of Magdalen College, Oxford :

Sir F. Burdett to Dr Routh.

6 Aug. 1814.

MY DEAR DR. ROUTH,

. . . It is a great confirmation of my opinion respecting Lord Cochraine to know that a person so discriminating & so out of reach of all possible bias as yourself should be of the same way of thinking. I did or endeavoured to do what I felt my duty to a cruelly injured man. . . .

yours very sincerely,

F. BURDETT.

Henry Brougham was one of the Counsel for the defence at the trial, and it is interesting to note his belief in Cochrane's innocence as given at a later date. In his " States-

men of George III," Vol. III, p. 220, he wrote (1843) :
" I must be distinctly understood deeply to lament the
verdict of guilty. . . . I take it upon me to assert that
Lord Cochrane's conviction was mainly owing to the
extreme repugnance which he felt to giving up his uncle,
or taking those precautions for his own safety which would
have operated against that near relation."

On March 29, 1844, he wrote to Lord Dundonald [1]
himself : " Your Counsel was clearly of opinion that the
verdict *as concerned you was erroneous*, & I always concluded
that you had sacrificed yourself out of delicacy to your
uncle, the person really guilty."

It should be remarked that Brougham was Lord Chancellor in the Government which advised William IV to give
Lord Dundonald a free pardon in 1832.

Brougham was one of the queerest public men in the
nineteenth century, always tortuous in his courses.   In
1814 he was without a seat in the House of Commons,
and when Lord Cochrane was expelled from the House,
he started a rather indelicate intrigue to get himself elected
to the seat vacated at Westminster. But it was not to be.
Burdett stood manfully by Cochrane.

At a meeting (July 11) convened by the High Bailiff of
Westminster to consider nominations for the vacant seat,
Sir Francis Burdett, amidst the loudest applause, said :
The question was whether an innocent individual should
be destroyed by the machinations of corruption and power.
Alluding to the defence that Lord Cochrane had made in
the House of Commons on July 5, he said that Lord
Castlereagh, the nose-leader of that illustrious and august
body, not having the power to gag Cochrane in the House
of Commons, knowing the effect that Cochrane's speech
would produce outside the House, rose in all the blushing
honours of his blue ribbon to impose silence upon the

[1] Lord Cochrane by the death of his father became Earl of Dundonald, July 1, 1831.

corrupt and degraded Press that is still suffered to exist. He (Burdett) found no fault with the verdict of the jury on the evidence put before them—evidence which had been so feebly met by the lawyers for the defence. He criticised the Rule of Court [1] which caused the rejection of Cochrane's application for a new trial as contrary to law— for the Law never demands impossibilities.

It remained for the electors of Westminster to vindicate his illustrious friend. If Lord Cochrane was to stand in the pillory, he should feel it his duty to attend also, and it would be the end of the pillory as a punishment.

The meeting then passed two resolutions :

(1) That in the opinion of this meeting Lord Cochrane is perfectly innocent of the offence for which he has been sentenced to an infamous punishment.

(2) That it is therefore the opinion of this meeting that Lord Cochrane is a proper person to represent the City of Westminster in Parliament, and that he be put in nomination at the ensuing election.

Burdett was indeed one of those whose motto is : " Stick to your friends and disregard your enemies."

The day of the election came, July 16, 1814.

Sir Francis Burdett came forward on the hustings and proposed Lord Cochrane, who was unanimously re-elected for Westminster.

In reply to a letter of congratulations from the Committee, Cochrane wrote from King's Bench Prison on July 18.

" With regard to the Case . . . only let it be said of me—The *Stock Exchange* have accused; *Lord Ellenborough* has charged for guilty; the *Special Jury* have found that guilt; the *Court* have sentenced to the pillory; the *House of Commons* have expelled; & the *Citizens of Westminster*

---

[1] Ponsonby in the debate in the House of Commons on July 5 had also criticised the " Rule " as repugnant to all equity and reason.

HAVE RE-ELECTED. Only let this be the record placed against my name, & I shall be proud to stand in the Calendar of Criminals all the days of my life. . . ."

On July 19 Lord Ebrington moved in the House of Commons for an address to the Crown praying that the "pillory" part of Lord Cochrane's sentence might be remitted. But he began his speech by reading a letter from Cochrane saying that he did not wish his past services to be prostituted to such a purpose. "If I am guilty, I richly merit the whole of the sentence which has been passed upon me, and if innocent, one penalty cannot be inflicted with more justice than another."

Lord Castlereagh informed the House that the Crown had already determined to remit the "pillory" part of the sentence. But it was popularly supposed that this determination had been reached by two other considerations than mere mercy.

(1) Sir Francis Burdett—the most popular man in England—had announced his intention of standing by Cochrane's side.

(2) The temper of the London populace was rather nasty. Just a week before, the Princess Charlotte had fled from Warwick House to her mother, and had been forced by Government pressure to return. The Government was very unpopular.

Sir Francis, in the course of this debate, manfully stood up for Cochrane. The report of the Stock Exchange Committee, he said, had thoroughly prejudiced the popular mind, and created an atmosphere unfavourable to Cochrane, or ever the trial began. Even Cochrane's Counsel seemed to have been affected by it.

If the degradation of the pillory was remitted, not so the ceremony of August 11, in which the King at Arms removed Cochrane's banner from Henry VII's Chapel in Westminster Abbey and kicked it down the steps.

On March 6, 1815, Cochrane, by an ingenious noose, which he threw from the roof of the prison over its outer wall, escaped from the prison, and on March 20 unexpectedly reappeared in the House of Commons—only to be dragged from its precincts by the officers of the Marshal of the King's Bench. No notice was taken by the House of *this* glaring breach of its privileges. Cochrane was now closely confined in a " strong room," and not released before he paid the £1000 fine (July 3, 1815).

He paid the fine by a £1000 Bank of England note, which he endorsed with these words : " My health having suffered by long and close confinement, and my oppressors being resolved to deprive me of property or life, I submit to robbery to protect myself from murder in the hope that I shall live to bring the delinquents to justice."

On April 30, 1816, Cochrane in the House of Commons moved that thirteen charges, which he brought against Lord Ellenborough, should be referred to a Committee of the whole House. This step was intended as preparatory to an impeachment. But no one except Burdett was found to support the proposal. This was creditable to Burdett's heart, if not to his head. There was really no case against the Lord Chief Justice. He had summed up strongly against Cochrane, but the evidence, as presented, seemed to point that way. Certainly there was no matter for impeachment. Cochrane's proposal was negatived by 89 to 0.

Cochrane had meanwhile adopted the complete programme of the advanced Radicals. We shall hear something of these " advanced " politics later. But one of the meetings Cochrane attended must be specially mentioned. It met at the City of London Tavern on July 29, 1816, under the auspices of the " Association for Relief of the Manufacturing and Labouring Poor," at a time of great economic distress. The Duke of York took the chair, and was supported by the Royal Princes, the Duke of Kent and the Duke of Cambridge. The Duke of Kent moved the first resolution, " That the transition from a state of extensive warfare to a system of peace has occasioned a stagnation of employment and a revolution of trade deeply affecting the situation of many parts of the community and producing many instances of great local distress."

Lord Cochrane then sprang up and said the resolution was founded on a gross fallacy. The existing distress was not primarily due to the transition from war to peace, but was due to the prodigious burden of taxation and to profligate expenditure. A large part of this expenditure was on compliant placemen, *e.g.* the Duke of Rutland, whom he saw present, had £9000 a year. He concluded by moving an amendment, " That the enormous load of the National Debt together with the large military establishment and the profuse expenditure of public money was the real cause of the present public distress." Commotion followed, and the Royal Dukes were put in a position of considerable difficulty. Finally the Duke of Kent recast his motion to a form which did not specify the *cause* of the public distress, and in this shape it was unanimously carried.

Lord Cochrane once more addressed the meeting. Parliament and the Government, he said, were alone competent to alleviate the distress. The only persons who could really assist the poor were the placemen, the sinecurists, the fund-holders, who must give up at least half of their ill-gotten gains. The gist of his remarks was that they were war-profiteers, and that shallow charity such as that recommended was mere humbug. The meeting broke up in disorder.

The Government were determined once more to get their knife into Cochrane. He was prosecuted at the Guildford Assizes on August 17, 1816, for having escaped

from prison, and he was accompanied to the trial by Burdett. The jury had no alternative—for the fact was
admitted—but to bring in a verdict of guilty; they added
a recommendation to mercy on the ground that he had
already suffered adequate punishment. Cochrane was
sentenced to pay a fine of £100 and on his refusal to pay
he was again (November 21) taken into custody. A
subscription was immediately opened, and no less than
£1100 is said to have been collected in pennies. Cochrane
was finally released on December 7, 1816. He had naturally become more Radical than ever. The last speech he
made in the House of Commons was in favour of Burdett's
motion for Reform (June 2, 1818).

At this time the Spanish colonies in South America
were in armed revolt against their mother country, trying
to secure their independence. In August 1818 Cochrane,
at the invitation of the Government of Chili, sailed to
South America to reorganise the Chilian fleet. It is no
part of my task to describe in detail his wonderful naval
achievements first as Admiral of Chili (1818–1823), and
then as Admiral of Brazil (1823–1825). With overpowering odds against him, he swept from the seas the
ships of Spain and Portugal. The independence of Chili
from Spain, of Brazil from Portugal, was secured. But
in both countries his work was largely nullified by the
selfish folly and mean treachery of those he helped. In
1825 he returned to England with large disputed claims
against the Governments of Chili and Brazil.

A new proposition was opened to him. Would he go
as Admiral to help the Greeks? That race, which for
centuries had knelt to Turkey on the necks of the other
Balkan races, was now in revolt against the Sultan. They
had more than half persuaded the nations of Western
Europe that they were the descendants of the heroes of
Marathon and Salamis. Greek Committees had been
formed in every Western capital. Needless to say, Bur-

dett, as the constant friend of the oppressed, was on the Greek Committee in London.

"Lord Cochrane is looking very well," wrote Burdett on August 20, 1825, "after eight years of harassing and ungrateful service, and I trust will be the Liberator of Greece. What a glorious title ! "

Cochrane anticipated, but did not perhaps realise to the full extent, the incompetence, the jealousies, the intrigues, amid which the Greek Liberation movement was conducted. But he was willing to give his services *on conditions*. I have before me the following memorandum in his handwriting—

" *Required.*

" Six Steam Vessels having each two guns in the bow & perhaps two in the stern not less than 68 pounder long guns; because if mounted with Carronades as now intended the steam apparatus will be knocked to pieces by the Turks.

" The bottoms of two old 74 gun ships, upper decks cut off, & *heavy* cannon mounted on the lower deck.

" These vessels well manned appear to be sufficient to destroy the whole Turkish Naval power.

" Lord Cochrane will give any advice relative to details that may be required to further the interests of Greece, so far as regards naval matters. But he cannot consistently subject his family to the loss of half of all he is entitled to for seven years' service in South America, by offering his services as an Officer. Nor would he under any circumstances engage in the service of Greece as a Naval Commander of their present inefficient naval force.

" Should the Greeks however deem Lord Cochrane's services of importance to them, he will accept two thirds of what he can shew to be due to him in South America, & never require the remainder until the Greek funds shall be at the contract price or par.

" And further he will serve without pay, or other recompense save the proceeds of Captures made from the Enemy as is customary in such cases amongst all civilised nations."

Finally a Greek loan for £2,000,000 was floated in London. Out of this sum £37,000 was to be given Lord Cochrane on starting, and a further sum of £20,000 was to be paid him on the completion of his services. £150,000 was to be spent on building six steamships in England, and another £150,000 on building two 60-gun frigates in America.

Cochrane, having ground for fearing that he was to be prosecuted by the Government under the Foreign Enlistment Act, left London for Boulogne in November 1825, and subsequently (December 28) moved to Brussels. He was half-minded, in view of all the difficulties, to resign the Greek enterprise. But Burdett encouraged him to persevere.

Sir F. Burdett to Lord Cochrane.

18 Nov. 1825.

DEAR LORD COCHRANE,

I have taken four & twenty hours to consider your last letter, & have not one moment varied in my first opinion as to the propriety of your persevering in your glorious career. According to Brougham's opinion, you cannot be put in a worse situation,—that is, more in peril of Government here,—by continuing foreign service in the Greek cause than you already stand in by having served the Emperor of the Brazils. In my opinion you will be in a great deal less; for, the greater your renown, the less power will your enemies have, whatever may be their inclination, to meddle with you. Perhaps they only at present desist to look out for a better opportunity, " reculer pour mieux sauter," like the tiger. I dont mean to accuse them of this baseness; but, should it be the case, the less you do, the more power they will have to injure you if so inclined. Were they to prosecute you for having served the Brazilian Emperor, it would call forth no public sympathy, or but slight, in your favour. The case would be thought very hard, to be sure; but that would be all. Not so, should you triumph in the Greek cause. Transcendent glory would not only crown but protect you. No Minister would dare to wag a finger—no, nor even Crown lawyer a tongue—against you; &, if they did, the feeling of the whole English public would surround you with an impenetrable shield. Fines would be paid; imprisonment protested & petitioned against; in short, I am convinced the nation would be in a flame, & you in far less danger of any attempt to your injury than at present. This, my dear Lord Cochrane, is my firm conviction. Yours etc.

F. BURDETT.

A period of sickening delay followed. The contractors, both in England and America, either would not or could not get on with the building of the ships; delay followed upon delay, procrastination upon procrastination, roguery upon roguery. Cochrane thought of going to Greece, if he could secure even one of the ships. But for a time he was dissuaded by Burdett.

Sir F. Burdett to Lord Cochrane.

15 Jan. 1826.

DEAR LORD COCHRANE,
        I would by no means have you proceed with the first vessel, nor at all without adequate means; for, besides thinking of the Greeks, for whom I am I own greatly interested, I must think & certainly not with less interest of you, & I may add in some degree of myself too; for I am placed under much responsibility, & I dont mean to be a party to making shipwreck of you & your great naval

reputation; nor will I ever consent to your going upon a forlorn & desperate attempt—that is, without the means necessary for the fair chance of success—in other words adequate means. Although you have worked miracles, we can never be justified in expecting them, & still less in requiring them.   Yours etc.

F. BURDETT.

It was not till March 1827 that Cochrane reached Greek waters.   And even then he had only four ships, a schooner named the *Unicorn*, the *Sauveur*, a corvette purchased in France, the *Perseverance*, the only one of the steamships that were to have been built in England, and one frigate from America named the *Hellas*.

Cochrane was unable to achieve anything; the inadequate means at his disposal, the cowardice, the quarrelling, and the corruption rife among the Greeks made it impossible. The Greek question was settled by the Battle of Navarino (October 20, 1827) and the intervention of the Powers. In 1828 Cochrane returned to England.

He now resumed his interests in mechanical inventions, in improving the steam engine and adapting it to the use of ships.   He is said to have invented a " secret plan," by which powers of a nature so destructive as to be practically irresistible could be employed in war.   The " secret plan " [1] seems to have been a form of poison gas.   The Admiralty at the time of the Crimea War, while admitting its efficacy, refused to employ it, as being contrary to the usages of civilised warfare.

But Cochrane's chief efforts were directed to securing the reversal of the unjust sentence of 1814, and in these efforts he was ably seconded by Sir Francis Burdett and encouraged by the Lord High Admiral, the Duke of Clarence.   The Duke of Clarence intimated to Sir Francis

[1] See " Panmure Papers," Vol. I, p. 340, quoted in Lord Ellen-borough's " The Guilt of Lord Cochrane " (1914), p. 313.

that if Cochrane would memorialise the King, he would use his influence to procure Cochrane's restoration. Accordingly, on June 4, 1829, Cochrane addressed a memorial to the Duke of Wellington for presentation to the King. But the only answer was : " The King's Cabinet cannot comply with the prayer of the memorial."

A brighter prospect opened when the Duke of Clarence became King as William IV (1830), and the Whig administration of Lord Grey succeeded that of the Duke of Wellington. Once more it was suggested to Sir Francis Burdett that the King should be memorialised. This new memorial was presented to the King by Lord Melbourne in December 1830. But there was still some little delay. On July 1, 1831, Cochrane, by the death of his father, became Earl of Dundonald. Here is an undated letter belonging to this time.

Sir Francis Burdett to Lord Dundonald.

MY DEAR LORD DUNDONALD,

I went to the Levee on Wednesday to give your memorial to Greville, the Clerk of the Council, to present —but the King returned to Windsor immediately after the Levee, & no Council was held. Had it been, I can entertain no doubt that your memorial would have been presented & granted.

I went to see Greville about it the next day. He was so kind & so desirous of doing everything in his power to expedite it, even proposing to take it out of its usual turn, that I cannot but feel quite satisfied & assured that there will not be a moment's unnecessary delay. A little patience & all will be right. I should like to see you in a day or two, & perhaps may,

yours sincerely,

F. BURDETT.

Sir Francis also used his influence with the Prime Minister, Lord Grey, and with Lord Holland, then Chancellor of the Duchy of Lancaster.

Lord Holland to Sir Francis Burdett.

> (? May, 1831)   (The letter is undated but must have been before July 1, 1831, the day of old Lord Dundonald's death.)

I have often asked myself as well as others the same question you ask me about Lord C(ochrane), but I have never got a satisfactory answer; perhaps, if I had, I should be precluded from giving it, but I have *not*, & till I have, I will not cease asking the question, convinced as I have (been) that the restoration of rank etc. etc. would & must be advantageous to the country & creditable to the mercy at least, if not the justice of the Crown.   Yrs.

VASSALL HOLLAND.

Lord Grey to Sir F. Burdett.

Downing Street
Dec. 8, 1831.

DEAR SIR FRANCIS,

I have seen Lady Dundonald who brought me your note. You know that I feel every possible disposition to do what you wish; & I never suffered greater pain than in not being able to say at once to Lady Dundonald that I would recommend it to the King to restore Lord D. to the Service. But you know there are cases in which one cannot do what one's wishes dictate; all I can say is that I will again enter (on) a careful consideration of the subject, & that you may be assured I shall not be influenced by any fear of Croker,[1] further than to prevent

---

[1] J. W. Croker was Secretary to the Admiralty at the time of Cochrane's disgrace in 1814.

his bringing a case which he may be able to state with effect to the Public.

Ever yours,

GREY.

Lord Grey to Sir F. Burdett.

Downing Street
Jan. 28, 1832.

DEAR SIR FRANCIS,

This is a bad moment [1] for adding to the subjects of discussion which our adversaries are packing upon us, & the thing as you know is very difficult in itself. I will only say that my disposition remains unaltered, & that with respect to a pardon I think it may be obtained. The best way of proceeding for this purpose will be by an application to the King, which he will of course refer to me, when it will be regularly brought before the Cabinet, & I hope determined as we all wish. . . .

Ever yours,

GREY.

Sir F. Burdett to Lord Grey.

St. James' Place.
27 Feb. 1832.

I trust Lord Dundonald's restoration will soon take place. I almost dread his hearing about the " pardon," which I would rather have cut off my right hand than have asked, except as the necessary routine step. I am, dear Lord Grey, yours very sincerely,

F. BURDETT.

Lord Grey to Sir Francis Burdett.

Downing Street,
March 2, 1832.

MY DEAR SIR FRANCIS,

. . . I have a letter to-day from Lord Dundonald, which has relieved me from the fear of his feeling hurt

---

[1] The era of the Reform Bill.

at the application which had been made for a " Pardon." It is in *truth* a necessary preliminary to his *being reinstated* if that can ultimately be accomplished, & the only effect of it is to relieve him from the civil incapacities which attach upon his sentence. You may be assured that I have this matter much at heart; but I am very unwilling to have it brought into publick notice at a moment when the bitter & hostile spirit, which prevails in the party most opposed to the Government, would be likely to seize upon it as a good question for annoyance.

Ever yours,

GREY.

Lady Dundonald at a personal interview with the King pleaded her husband's cause.

On March 24, 1832, Lord Dundonald was granted a " free pardon "; on May 2, 1832, he was replaced on the Navy List as Rear-Admiral. In 1847 he was restored to the Order of the Bath. In 1848 he was appointed to the command of the North America Station. Burdett had by this time been dead for four years, but Sir George Sinclair, the devoted friend of Burdett's later years, wrote to Lord Dundonald :

" I cannot help contemplating with effectionate sorrow the portrait of our dearest friend, *Sir Francis Burdett*, now suspended over the chimney-piece, & thinking how happy he would have been, had he witnessed this most welcome & delightful consummation."

Lord Dundonald died in 1860, and was buried in Westminster Abbey (November 14). It was not till a few hours before his funeral that Queen Victoria ordered that his banner should be restored to Henry VII's chapel, from which it had been so ignominiously evicted in 1814.

When the eleventh Earl of Dundonald in 1869 published the " Life " of his father, the book was dedicated

To
MISS ANGELA BURDETT COUTTS
Whose honoured father
Was the firmest & most constant friend & supporter
Of my Father
During a career devoted to the welfare of his Country
And the honour of his profession.

A final step was taken in 1877, when, as the result of the Report of a Select Committee of the House of Commons, a sum of £5000 was granted to the twelfth Earl of Dundonald in recognition of the distinguished services of his grandfather.   The sum was said to be the exact equivalent to the arrears of half-pay to which Lord Cochrane would have been entitled for the years (1814–1832) that he was out of the British Navy.

PRINTED IN GREAT BRITAIN BY R. CLAY & SONS, LIMITED,
BUNGAY, SUFFOLK.